THE ISLAND SERIES

SHETLAND

OTHER SCOTTISH TITLES FROM DAVID & CHARLES

General
Orkney and Shetland : An Archaeological Guide
The Other Titanic
Scotland : A New Study
Scotland : The Shaping of a Nation
Walking Through Scotland

Islands
Island of Bute
Isle of Arran
Kintyre
Orkney
Staffa
Uists and Barra

Transport
Classic Scottish Paddle Steamers
The Clyde Puffer
Forgotten Railways : Scotland
The Golden Years of the Clyde Steamers, 1889–1914
Legends of the Glasgow & South Western Railway in LMS Days
The North British Railway, Vols 1 and 2
A Regional History of the Railways of Great Britain, Vol 6, Scotland : The Lowlands and the Borders
The Skye Railway
The West Highland Railway

SHETLAND

by JAMES R. NICOLSON

Fourth edition

DAVID & CHARLES

NEWTON ABBOT LONDON NORTH POMFRET (VT)

To my wife, Violet

British Library Cataloguing in Publication Data

Nicolson, James R.
Shetland. – 4th ed. – (The Islands series)
1. Shetland Islands – History
I. Title
941.138 DA880.S5
ISBN 0–7153–8518–6

First published 1972
Second revised edition 1975
Third revised edition 1979
Fourth revised edition 1984

Typeset and printed in Great Britain
by Redwood Burn Limited Trowbridge
for David & Charles (Publishers) Limited
Brunel House Newton Abbot Devon

Published in the United States of America
by David & Charles Inc
North Pomfret Vermont 05053 USA

CONTENTS

1	Introduction	11
2	Early History	31
3	Landlords and Crofter-Fishermen	56
4	Makings of Modern Shetland	77
5	Communications	97
6	Agriculture and Fishing	115
7	Other Industries	143
8	The Sea Around Us	162
9	The People	179
10	Lerwick and Scalloway	186
11	Shetland Today	203
12	Places to Visit	220
	Glossary	227
	Bibliography	230
	Supplementary Booklist	235
	Index	237

ILLUSTRATIONS

PLATES

South entrance Lerwick harbour 49
Weisdale Voe 49
Cliffs at Esha Ness 50
Rock scenery, St Magnus Bay 50
Bird cliffs, Noss *(Don Leslie)* 67
Rerwick, Dunrossness 68
Maywick, Dunrossness 68
Broch of Mousa 85
Jarlshof 85
An isolated croft, early twentieth century 86
Interior of croft house, early twentieth century 86
'Rooing' Shetland sheep 103
A Shetland boat 103
SS *Earl of Zetland* 104
SS *St Magnus* and SS *St Sunniva* 104
Shetland sheep 121
Shetland pony 121
Herring station, Lerwick 122
Herring fishermen at Scalloway *(Author's collection)* 122
A knitter *(Don Leslie)* 139
Loading a peat pony 140
Peat cutting *(Don Leslie)* 140
Aerial view of Scalloway *(Aerofilms)* 157
Scalloway castle *(Dennis Coutts)* 157
Aerial view of Lerwick *(Dennis Coutts)* 158
Aerial view of Sullom Voe oil terminal *(BP)* 175
Modern crofting scene, Dunrossness *(Dennis Coutts)* 176

New primary school, Dunrossness *(Dennis Coutts)* 176
On cover, the beach at Spiggie *(Don Leslie)*

Where no acknowledgement is made, photographs are from the Rattar collection now in the county museum at Lerwick.

TEXT

Weather statistics 16
The 'monks' stone' from Burra 36
Viking art from Jarlshof 39
Sketch and plan of old croft complex 65
Population trends 1755–1971 92
Stock figures 1870–1970 124
A sixern 129
A sailing drifter 135

MAPS

Shetland Islands (R. J. Anderson, based on Ordnance Survey map 1/250,000, 1962) 8 and 9
Location of oil terminal at Sullom Voe 10
Geological map (D. Flinn) 19

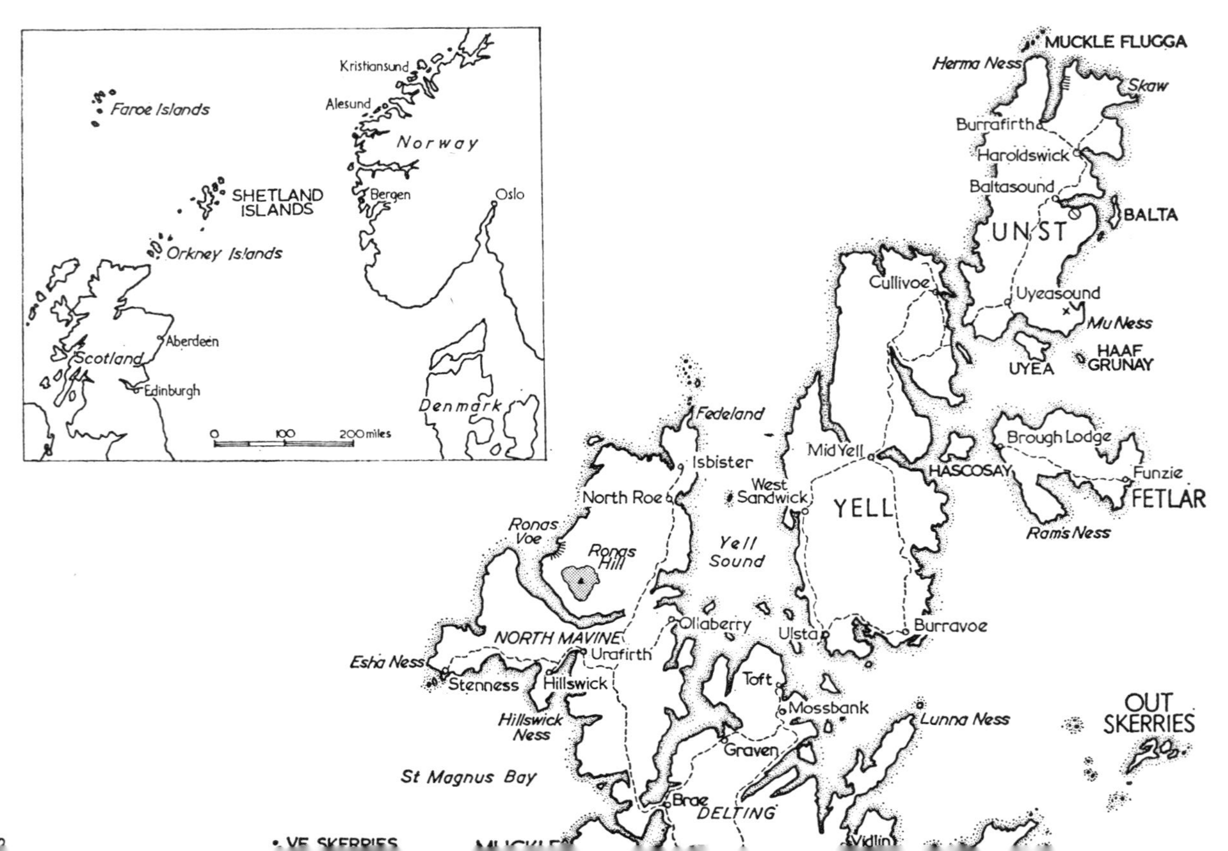
Faroe Islands
Kristiansund
Alesund
Norway
Bergen
Oslo
SHETLAND ISLANDS
Orkney Islands
Scotland
Aberdeen
Edinburgh
Denmark
0
100
200 miles
MUCKLE FLUGGA
Herma Ness
Skaw
Burrafirth
Haroldswick
Baltasound
BALTA
UNST
Cullivoe
Uyeasound
Mu Ness
UYEA
HAAF GRUNAY
Fedeland
Mid Yell
Brough Lodge
HASCOSAY
Funzie
FETLAR
Ram's Ness
Isbister
West Sandwick
North Roe
YELL
Ronas Voe
Ronas Hill
Yell Sound
Ollaberry
Ulsta
Burravoe
NORTH MAVINE
Urafirth
Esha Ness
Stenness
Hillswick
Toft
Mossbank
Lunna Ness
OUT SKERRIES
Hillswick Ness
Graven
St Magnus Bay
Brae
DELTING
Vidlin

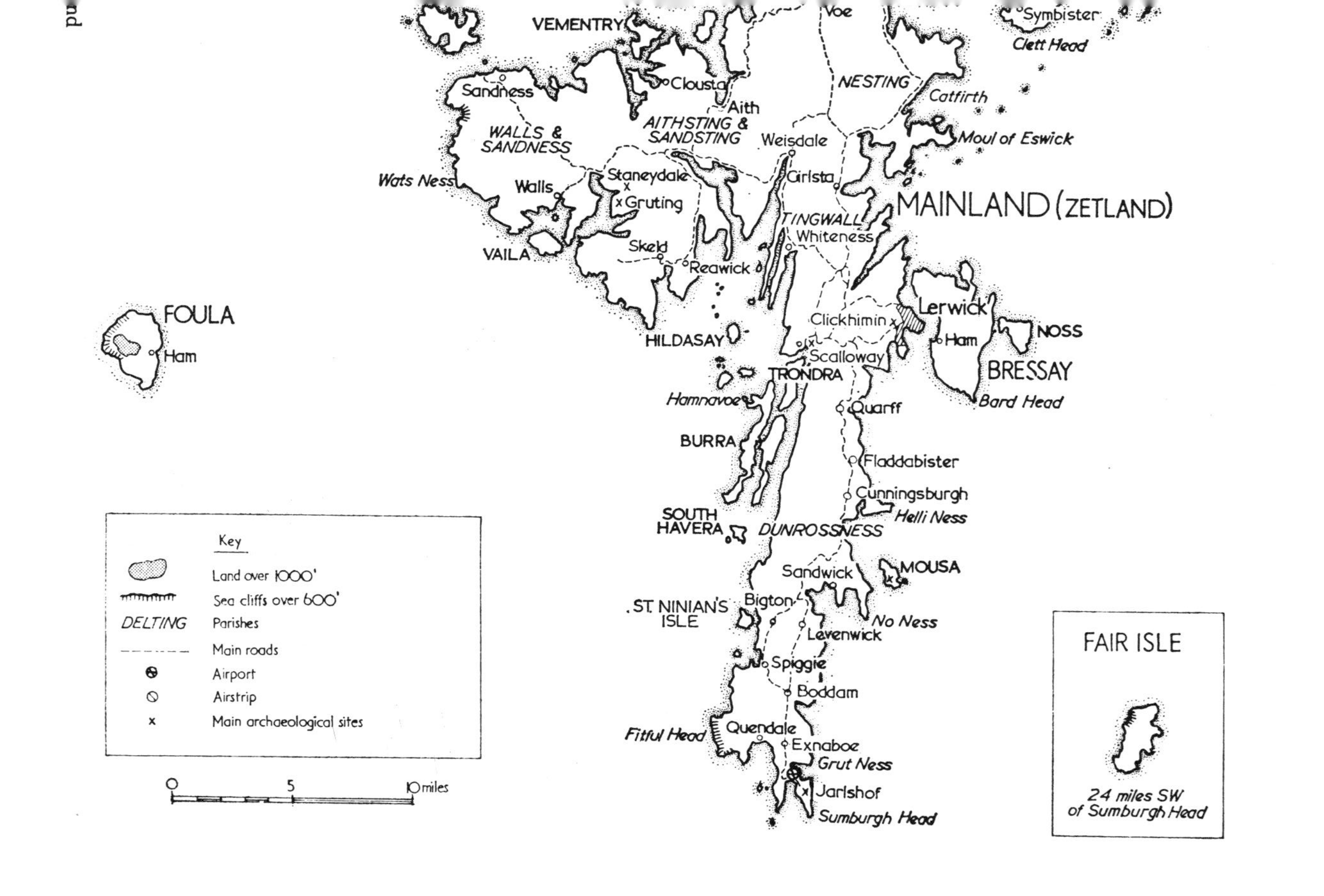
MAINLAND (ZETLAND)
Voe
Symbister
Clett Head
VEMENTRY
NESTING
Catfirth
Sandness
Clousta
Aith
AITHSTING & SANDSTING
WALLS & SANDNESS
Weisdale
Moul of Eswick
Wats Ness
Walls
Staneydale
Gruting
Girlsta
TINGWALL
Whiteness
VAILA
Skeld
Reawick
FOULA
Ham
Lerwick
Clickhimin
Ham
NOSS
HILDASAY
Scalloway
TRONDRA
BRESSAY
Hamnavoe
Quarff
Bard Head
BURRA
Fladdabister
Cunningsburgh
SOUTH HAVERA
DUNROSSNESS
Helli Ness
Sandwick
MOUSA
ST. NINIAN'S ISLE
Bigton
No Ness
Levenwick
Spiggie
Boddam
Quendale
Fitful Head
Exnaboe
Grut Ness
Jarlshof
Sumburgh Head
Key
Land over 1000'
Sea cliffs over 600'
DELTING
Parishes
Main roads
Airport
Airstrip
Main archaeological sites
0
5
10 miles
FAIR ISLE
24 miles SW of Sumburgh Head

Note to the Fourth Edition

When the third edition of this book was published in 1979 Shetland was in the throes of an oil construction boom which created full employment but brought problems in its wake. Now the construction phase is over and Shetland, having earned millions of pounds from its astute agreements with the oil companies, is again turning its attention to the development of its traditional industries determined, if possible, to avoid the slump which many people have predicted.

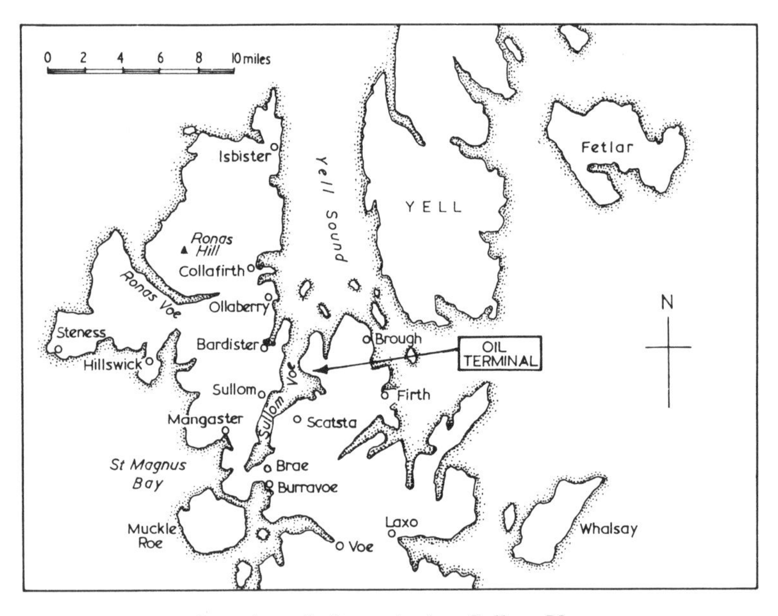

Location of oil terminal at Sullom Voe

1 INTRODUCTION

IF you travel 200 miles north of Aberdeen or 220 miles west of Bergen in Norway, you will find the Shetland Islands, an archipelago of over 100 isles of which seventeen are inhabited. Excluding isolated Fair Isle and Foula, the group stretches 70 miles from Sumburgh Head to Muckle Flugga, while the width between Out Skerries and Ve Skerries is 35 miles.

Few maps of Britain show Shetland in its true position on latitude 60° north, level with the southern tip of Greenland; it is usually placed as an inset with Orkney in the corner of the map. The scale is often reduced, giving an entirely wrong impression of size, for with a total area of 550sq mi, Shetland is more than twice as large as the Isle of Man.

Like other Scottish islands, Shetland has suffered from depopulation during the last 100 years, but, contrary to the trend in other islands, the decline has been halted and the census of 1981 showed a rise in population over that of 1971 to 23,100.

Shetland has little in common with the Highlands and Western Islands of Scotland. Here there is neither clan system nor Gaelic language; the culture is basically Scandinavian and, though English is the language of the schoolroom, when conversing among themselves the islanders use a dialect whose words come from Lowland Scots and ancient Norse. The Scandinavian influence is everywhere: the place-names on the map, the crofting townships, the boats resting on the beaches are almost identical to those in Faeroe and parts of Norway. Shetland has little in common with Orkney apart from early history. The two groups are separated by a 50-mile sea barrier containing Sumburgh Röst, a tidal stream treated with respect even by steel-hulled motor vessels today.

Shetland has had to develop its own culture and its own economy, sometimes frustrated by well-meaning legislation enacted 600 miles away in London. Political and economic trends in the rest of Britain are not always reflected here. The postwar boom did not spread to Shetland, but neither did the recession of 1970–71. Unprecedented expansion of the basic industries of fishing, agriculture and knitwear brought full employment even before the discovery of North Sea oil in 1971.

The growing number of visitors is a heartening trend, for the islands deserve to be better known. To archaeologists, botanists, bird watchers and anglers they are already famous. Facilities are improving for the ordinary tourist, but the scenery, the bracing air and the long summer days are the main attractions. Though remote, the islands are served by daily air services (Sunday excepted) from Glasgow and Aberdeen, and by a twice-weekly steamer service from Aberdeen, the trip lasting 12–13hr in normal conditions.

There is considerable confusion regarding the origin of the name. The Norsemen called the islands Hjaltland, a name liable to such variations in pronunciation and spelling as Shetland, Hetland and Yetland, all of which can be seen on early maps. The form Yetland, it is believed, gave rise to yet another name: in medieval Scots the letter Y was invariably written as Z, and to some unknown Scottish clerk must go the credit for what was until recently the official name of the county—Zetland.

ISLAND GROUPS

The Mainland and Adjacent Islands

The largest island, 378sq mi in area, is called simply the Mainland. From Sumburgh Head to Fedeland, the length is almost 55 miles, but the greatest width, however, is only 20 miles. The coastline is deeply indented with bays and long narrow voes that once provided havens for fleets of small fishing vessels. A few remain important as fishing centres today.

The district divisions are the church parishes, which in turn follow an older Norse division of the island. The names Delting, Nesting & Lunnasting, and Sandsting & Aithsting commemorate the ancient ting or law court held in each district, while Tingwall was the site of the supreme court or Alting. The most northerly parish is Northmavine, which in Old Norse means simply 'North of the narrow isthmus'. At the other end of the island is Dunrossness, a long peninsula projecting into Sumburgh Röst, which can be heard breaking even on a calm day—hence the name *dyn rastr nes*, 'the headland of the dinning röst'.

The western bulge of the Mainland is composed of the parish of Walls & Sandness. The former section is named after the many sea inlets or voes of the region, while Sandness means literally 'Sandy headland'. Newest of the districts is the parish of Lerwick, which was disjoined from Tingwall in the eighteenth century. The name is derived from the nature of the sea-bed in the bay around which the town grew: *ler* means mud or clay.

The population of the Mainland is about 18,000, of whom over one third live in Lerwick. This illustrates the importance of the capital and emphasises how sparsely populated is the remainder of the island. Scalloway with a population of 1,160 is Shetland's second largest settlement.

Opposite Lerwick lies the island of Bressay, 6 miles long and curved parallel to the Mainland shore, to provide the natural barrier that makes Lerwick harbour one of the best in northern Europe. Bressay derives some benefit from this chance situation: its fish meal and oil factory handles Lerwick's surplus herring catch and the offal from most of Shetland's white-fish processing plants. Bressay's population has risen considerably after a long period of decline to reach 335 in 1981.

Off the west coast of the Mainland, Trondra, with a population of around 100, provides shelter for Scalloway harbour; and the small island of Vaila, occupied by one family, shelters the entrance to the harbour of Walls.

In St Magnus Bay lie the islands of Muckle Roe and Papa Stour. The former, inhabited by about 100 people, is connected to the Mainland by a bridge; but the thirty inhabitants of the latter are separated from Sandness by a mile-wide sound through which a strong tide runs over submerged rocks.

Proximity to the Mainland is no compensation for lack of amenities and these islands share the problem of depopulation. In some cases the provision of electricity and a piped water supply has halted slightly the downward trend. By way of contrast, there are two fairly large islands that maintain vigorous communities, their numbers not much less than the peak figures of sixty years ago. East of the Mainland lies Whalsay, with a population of 1,026; and south-west of Scalloway lie the two islands of Burra, linked by a bridge, which support a population of over

850. It is no coincidence that these islands have maintained and even expanded their fishing fleets, which have grown since World War II to 35 large vessels 50–90ft long. Knitwear units provide part-time employment for the islands' women. In 1970 a fish-processing plant started in Whalsay and in 1971 a similar venture in Burra.

Half Shetland's full-time fishermen live in Burra and Whalsay—230 of them. Their modern well kept houses, and their astonishing number of motor cars, prove that fishing can be a well paid occupation and decline is not the inevitable fate of Britain's offshore islands.

The North Isles

North-east of the Mainland are three large islands known collectively as the North Isles. Largest is Yell, 83 sq mi in extent, 17 miles long and 7 miles wide at its broadest part. This is the least fertile of all the inhabited islands of Shetland, being covered largely with peat, but it supports large numbers of small Shetland sheep. The population, numbering 1,191 in 1981, is mostly confined to the east coast, which has sheltered harbours at Burravoe, Mid Yell, Basta Voe and Cullivoe. The island retains a fishing tradition, but with a much reduced fleet. Between Yell and the Mainland runs Yell Sound, a treacherous stretch of sea in bad weather but containing large sheltered harbours on the Mainland coast. One of them, Sullom Voe, is now playing an important role as a terminal for North Sea oil.

Next in size is Unst, 47sq mi in area. It has two good harbours at Baltasound and Uyeasound, each sheltered by a smaller island. At the beginning of this century both these centres participated in the great herring boom, but in 1971 Unst fishermen owned only one large fishing vessel. The population is around 1,140; the Royal Air Force establishment is the largest employer, but crofting and mining are also important.

North of Unst lie the rocks of Muckle Flugga, crowned by an important lighthouse manned by three keepers. Still further north lies the rugged Out Stack, the most northerly point of the United Kingdom.

The third island in the group, Fetlar, 15sq mi in extent, is often called the garden of Shetland. It is a problem island, however, with a surprisingly small population: only 102 in 1981. It lacks a harbour that is safe in all conditions, though large numbers of fishing vessels at times anchor south of the island during westerly and northerly gales.

Isolated Islands

Fair Isle lies 25 miles south of Sumburgh Head, across a tideway that forms the most treacherous part of the journey for vessels on passage between Shetland and Aberdeen. Fair Isle is world famous for its knitwear and for the legend attributing the origins of the unique patterns to Spanish seamen shipwrecked after the defeat of the Armada in 1588. There are two lighthouses and an important bird observatory. The population is stable at around seventy.

Foula, lying 27 miles west of Scalloway, is often called the loneliest inhabited island in Britain, for winter gales can disrupt communications for a month at a time. It has no proper harbour and the tiny mailboat has to be lifted clear of the sea after each crossing from Walls. The population is now under forty.

The isolated islands can also show an example of industry and tenacity. What has been said in praise of Whalsay and Burra can be said also of Out Skerries, which lies north-east of Whalsay. Here on less than 1sq mi of rock with thin patches of soil live 100 people. Part of the reason for the island's success is a good sheltered harbour and a fishing fleet consisting of three large fishing vessels and a number of smaller lobster boats. In 1970 a highly mechanised fish-processing factory was established by private enterprise.

CLIMATE

Shetland's climate is much maligned for rainy days and strong winds. The summers are cool but the winters are remarkably mild; winter temperatures compare favourably with those of places on the same latitude, like Uppsala, Helsinki and Leningrad, which each have four months when the mean temperature falls below freezing point, and also with temperatures in other parts of Britain. Lerwick's January mean of 4° C is almost the same as that of Edinburgh or London, but the July figure for Lerwick of 12° C compares with 15° C at Edinburgh and 18° C at London. It should be pointed out that Lerwick Observatory is situated 269ft above mean sea level; temperatures on lower ground are marginally higher. There are two reasons for the relatively high winter temperatures and low annual variation: (1) the Gulf Stream continues past Shetland as the North Atlantic Drift, bringing warm water to a group of small islands, and (2) the winds off the sea carry a considerable amount of warmth in winter.

Because of the low relief of the group, rainfall is not excessive. It is highest round Ronas Hill at about 50in a year, but at Lerwick Observatory the average is 45in per year. Rainfall is well spread over the year, with an average of 248 rainy days at Lerwick. The prevalence of moisture with light rain and summer fog is one of the drawbacks of the climate. Relative humidity is high, the average monthly figures being 80–85 per cent, the

	JAN	FEB	MAR	APR	MAY	JUN	JUL	AUG	SEP	OCT	NOV	DEC
HOURS OF SUNSHINE 1931-60	25	51	90	132	165	158	125	117	105	67	33	14
TEMPERATURE, °C 1921-50	3·4	3·3	3·9	5·3	7·6	9·2	12·0	12·0	10·3	7·7	5·5	4·3
RAINFALL, INS 1931-60	4·8	3·8	3·1	3·0	2·3	2·5	3·1	3·1	3·9	4·6	5·0	5·2
WIND SPEED, MPH 1923-60	20·9	20·1	18·2	17·0	14·5	14·3	12·5	12·8	15·2	17·8	18·6	20·1

Weather statistics

highest in Britain. Thunderstorms are rare, averaging three days per year.

The slow rise of temperatures in the early part of the year and the waterlogged state of the ground result in late sowing of crops. This, with the high incidence of cloud cover during summer, allows the crops to ripen only slowly and harvests are late.

Shetland does not suffer as much as the Mainland of Scotland from frost and snow; although it snows on average around forty days a year, the snow, on account of the maritime situation, seldom lies for more than twenty days a year. There are exceptions, of course, like the exceptionally hard winter and spring of 1946–47, when the snow lay for fifty-five days, causing heavy losses of sheep. On the other hand there are mild winters, such as that of 1970–71, with snow lying on only nine days.

Shetland is situated in the path of the North Atlantic depressions, which sweep in from the west, especially in winter. The average wind speed is high at 15–17mph, with gales occurring on an average of fifty-eight days a year. Some of the highest wind speeds ever recorded in Britain have been measured at the top of Saxavord in Unst : on 16 February 1962 a gust of 177mph was claimed there. The record for Lerwick Observatory was set on 27 January 1961, with a gust of 109mph and an hourly mean of 74mph. Shetland, with 236hr of gales per year, is still not as windy as the Butt of Lewis (378hr) or the Bell Rock (255hr).

Fortunately the islands do enjoy long spells of fine weather and not only in summer, when anticyclones develop nearby. High pressure over Scandinavia generally brings dry bright weather with winds from east or south-east. The long hours of daylight in summer more than compensate for the short days of winter. On 21 June the sun is above the horizon for 18hr 52min and it is possible to read a newspaper at midnight by natural light. On the shortest day the sun appears for only 5hr 52min. In winter displays of the aurora borealis are frequent.

GEOLOGY

The geology of Shetland shows strong affinities with that both of the Scottish Highlands and Norway. The structure is extremely complex and few counties have such a variety of rocks so well exposed.

Shetland is divided into blocks by several faults, one of which, the Walls boundary fault, is probably the northern extension of the Scottish Great Glen fault. The central block, the 'backbone' of Shetland, consists of schist, gneiss and blue-grey limestone, originally sediments laid down on an ancient sea-floor, then folded, uplifted and recrystallised under intense pressure during the Caledonian orogeny or mountain-building period more than 420 million years ago. These rocks appear today as parallel bands of varying hardness, giving a pronounced north-south grain to the hills, valleys and voes of the larger islands.

Unst and Fetlar are perhaps the most interesting geologically. Here a major thrust has brought gneisses into contact with a complex mass of serpentine, gabbro, and metamorphosed sediments. Hillswick Ness is famous for the greatest variety of metamorphic minerals within a small area in Shetand; here can be found precious serpentine, crystals of kyanite, garnet, actinolite, anthophyllite, talc and many other minerals.

SHETLAND

Shetland is often called 'the old rock', a term of endearment used nostalgically by exiles. Few, however, realise the aptness of the title, for in the extreme north-west of the Mainland are some of the oldest rocks in the world. They are so old, so complex, so difficult to subdivide into ages, that they are grouped together simply as Pre-Cambrian. They are at least 2,000 million years old. They are part of the basement on which the younger Caledonian mountain chain was built up.

For millions of years the Caledonian mountains gradually weathered until they became not much higher than the hills today, and almost covered by the products of their own erosion. These covering sediments are known to geologists as the Old Red Sandstone, which is represented by a strip of sandstones and flags running down the east coast of the Mainland and forming the islands of Bressay, Noss, Mousa and Fair Isle. In the west of the Mainland, sandstone considerably folded and interbanded in places with volcanic rocks composes most of the Walls-Sandness peninsula and a large part of the island of Foula. Fossils are not commonly found. Primitive plants have been found in the sandstones of Walls and of Fair Isle; and at Exnaboe, Dunrossness, a band of calcareous shale has been discovered to be packed with the traces of early fishes.

Volcanic activity was widespread in the late stages of this period. The lavas and ashes of Papa Stour and Esha Ness were poured on to the ancient land surface or forced their way along joints to form sheets in the older rock. The red granite of Ronas Hill and Muckle Roe is about 350 million years old, and may be the solidified roots of an ancient volcano.

Within the last million years the northern climate deteriorated, causing the formation of an ice sheet over northern Europe. At one time ice moving westwards from Scandinavia flowed right across Shetland: in Dunrossness there is a large boulder of laurvikite from a parent rock near Oslo that can only have been carried by the ice. Rough hilltops were smoothed, valleys and voes were deepened. How often the glaciers formed and retreated we cannot know, for at the end of the Ice Age Shetland had its own local ice cap, which has erased most of the signs of earlier events.

Since the last Ice Age the sea has been rising and the land sinking slightly. Peat and occasionally tree roots can be found

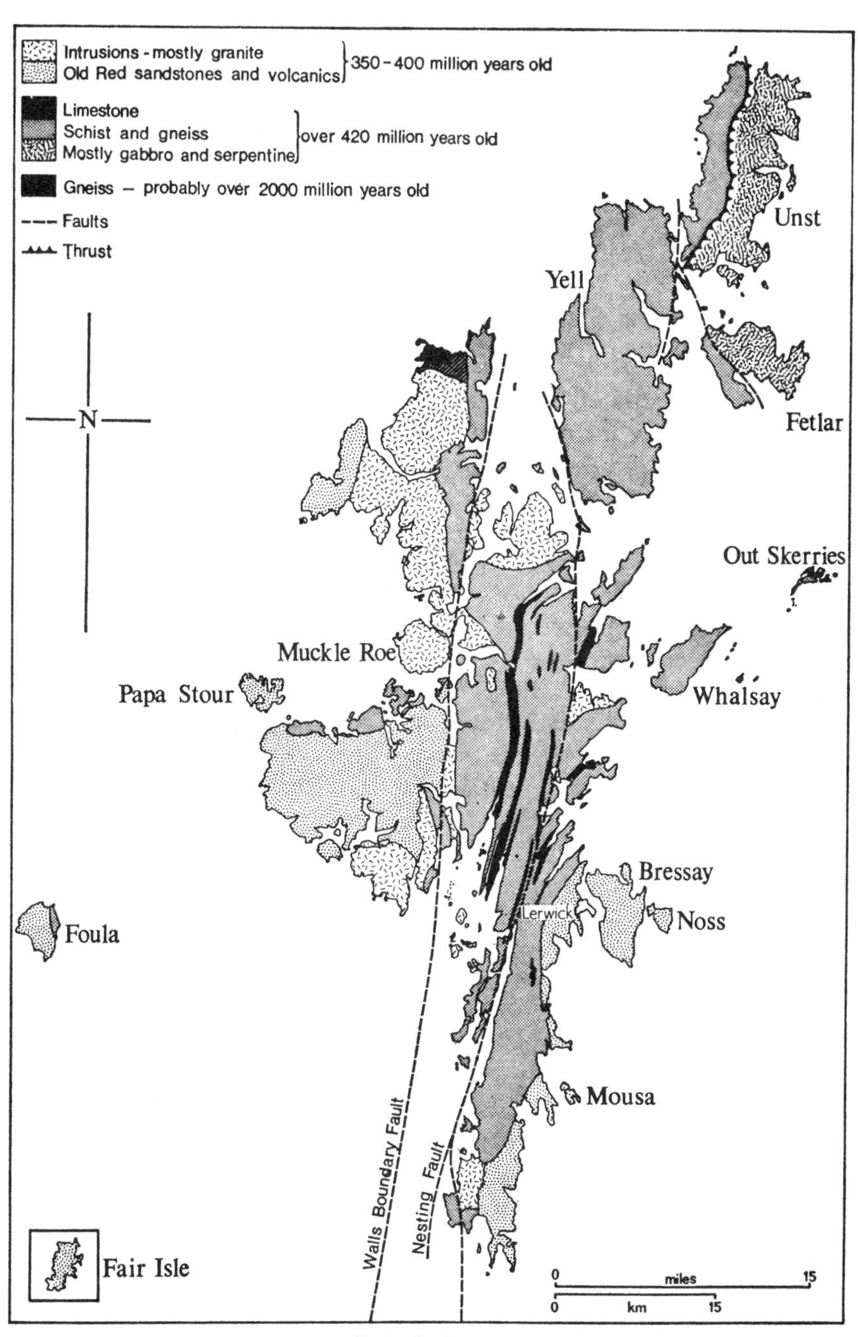

Geological map

below high water at many places and have been recovered from the sea-bed during harbour work at Lerwick, Scalloway and Whalsay. One explanation of this phenomenon is that, while Scandinavia and Britain were each depressed by an enormous weight of ice, Shetland in between was forced upwards and only comparatively recently, with the removal of the weight, is this balance being restored.

SCENERY

The close relationship between topography and geology is clearly seen in Shetland. The pronounced grain of the Caledonian rocks accounts for the chains of hills running north and south through the Mainland and the North Isles; the wide bands of limestone and shattered rocks of the fault planes, being more easily eroded, form the floors of the long through valleys.

The Mainland widens to a maximum of 20 miles but it is so deeply invaded by the Atlantic that no part of Shetland is more than 3 miles from the sea. At Mavis Grind the North Sea and Atlantic are little more than 100yd apart. In Northmavine, the highest point of Shetland, Ronas Hill, reaches a height of 1,486ft; since it rises from sea level, this mass of red granite is quite impressive, with cliffs 600ft high at Stonga Banks. Of the North Isles, Unst is the most spectacular, with the largest fresh-water loch in Shetland occupying a glacial valley that continues northwards as Burra Firth, a long fjord between the steep hill of Saxavord and the headland of Herma Ness.

Under a sparse cover of heather and grass the hills of Shetland retain evidence of intense ice action : the streamlined appearance of the hills, and the occasional areas of boulder clay with moraines, point to prolonged glaciation. Accumulations of peat further smooth but do not level the landscape, the uneven surface being a feature of Shetland's scenery. There are hundreds of small lochs of brown peaty water scattered over the poorly drained moorland. Small streams are abundant but nowhere have room to attain the status of rivers.

Far more spectacular than the work of the ice is the work of the sea, for the broken coastline is due to submergence since the Ice Age. Shetland is, in fact, a partially drowned range of hills; the islands are hilltops, the voes and firths are flooded valleys.

The recent and continuing nature of the submergence is shown by the frequent occurrence of peat below sea level. Radio-carbon dating of a specimen of peat taken in 1964 when the new harbour was being built at Whalsay indicates that 5,500 years ago the sea level was almost 30ft lower.

Other prominent results of submergence are the spits and bars known locally as ayres. They can be seen jutting out into many voes and in places cut them off from the open sea; very often they join a small island to a larger one, and are then known to geographers as tombolos. The ayre joining St Ninian's Isle and the Mainland is one of the most beautiful tombolos in the world.

Beach deposits everywhere reflect the particular local rocks: there are red granite sands at Reawick and Northmavine, and silver sands mixed with magnetite grains at Fetlar, while Yell and Unst have red garnet sands and silvery sands flecked with muscovite. One of the most magnificent is the beach at Hamnavoe, Burra, which is composed almost entirely of dazzling white shell sand.

While the sea is quietly invading the centre of Shetland, it is also vigorously attacking the outer coastline—battering exposed headlands and undermining the cliffs—to create a wealth of coastal features unrivalled in Britain. Where the rocks are well jointed the results are the more impressive: fissures are widened to become steep-sided clefts or geos; and caves are tunnelled along joints, sometimes part of the roof falling at the inner end to produce a blow-hole or gloup.The gently dipping strata of the Old Red Sandstone produce the highest cliffs in Shetland. Outstanding are those of Bard Head and Ord Head in Bressay and the Noup of Noss, while the Kame of Foula rises sheer to a height of 1,220ft, exceeded in Britain only by the cliffs of St Kilda.

The wildest and most varied scenery is found on the north-west coast where the red, grey and purple volcanic rocks of Northmavine are carved into cliffs, arches and stacks, and the lavas and ashes of Papa Stour are tunnelled to produce the most outstanding, though not the best known, set of caves in Britain. The finest individual cave, Kirstan Hole, is surpassed only by Fingal's Cave in Staffa.

Erosion is more pronounced on the Atlantic than the North Sea coast of Shetland, for storms are more frequent from the west and the waves of the North Sea never attain the breaking force of those of the wider Atlantic. It has been estimated that the sea has advanced a mile to form the cliffs at Fitful Head. The northern extremities of the Mainland, Yell and Unst also show the sea's advance, the reefs, stacks and skerries being mere remnants of land now lost.

SOILS AND VEGETATION

Good soils are scarce in Shetland, most of the land being covered in a great expanse of peat. All the requirements for peat formation are present—large stretches of non-porous rock and closely compacted boulder clay, and a generally cold damp climate for most of the year creating those waterlogged conditions that prevent bacteria converting the dead vegetation into humus.

There is little doubt that the peat originally comprised a series of isolated basin bogs, which gradually coalesced to form large areas of blanket bog. In the Kames between Girlsta and Voe the average depth is 9ft over 563 acres. Two-thirds of the island of Yell is covered in peat of an average thickness of 5ft. The peat is composed of the remains of bog moss (*Sphagnum spp*), cotton grass (*Eriophorum spp*), deer grass (*Trichophorum cespitosum*), heather (*Calluna vulgaris*) and sedge (*Carex spp*). Fragments of wood such as *Pinus sylvestris* suggest a warmer climate in former times.

A particular suite of acid-loving plants grows on peat—bog moss, heather, cross-leaved heath (*Erica tetralix*) and lichens. The heather is short and stunted owing to the high winds. It is only in recent years, through the advent of tractors and mechanical drainage equipment, that the areas covered by peat are being made fertile, with lime added to sweeten the soil and reseeding carried out with grass and clover.

The best soil and best pasture are found in the limestone areas and in the strips of porous sandstone. There are green patches everywhere round the coast and on offshore islands made fertile to some extent by the droppings of seabirds, but there are none of the sandy stretches of machair so characteristic of the Hebrides. In a few places sand blowing inland from the beaches has lightened the soil to create fertility; in one locality at least the process was too drastic, for in the seventeenth century the fertile estate of Brow, Dunrossness, was obliterated by a blanket of sand.

One of the biggest surprises to the stranger is the absence of trees from the hillsides. Trees are confined to gardens protected by high walls, except for the 9 acre plantation at Kergord, planted between 1909 and 1921, which consists chiefly of sycamore, Japanese larch and sitka spruce. Even in this relatively sheltered valley they are affected by high winds and salt spray carried from the ocean on all sides. B. C. V. Oddie has shown that no recording station in Europe collects a higher concentration of salt than Shetland, and that the most exposed station on the coast of Norway hardly collects as much salt in a year as was collected at Lerwick in the month of January 1958.

In 1953 the Forestry Commission established six trial plantations and proved that, after considerable replanting in the early years, shelter belts of sitka spruce, mountain pine and lodgepole pine from Alaska could be established.

NATURAL HISTORY

One of the unsolved problems of the northern isles is how plants and animals spread outwards from the North of Scotland after the retreat of the glaciers. Was there a land bridge via Orkney, breached only recently, or were the chance agencies of wind, sea and man entirely responsible?

Whatever the means, the isolation of Shetland has led to several peculiarities in fauna and flora through adaptation to the prevailing conditions. Best known is the effect on domestic animals: sheep, cattle, ponies and dogs have all developed special features in combating the relatively harsh conditions of winter. A study of natural history reveals many more examples, for there are species of plants and subspecies of animals found nowhere else in Britain.

Botany

First to attempt a systematic survey of the vegetation was Thomas Edmondston of Unst, who produced a slim volume called *A Flora of Shetland* in 1845. Though far from complete, this was the basis from which later botanists progressed. The most thorough work in the nineteenth century was carried out by W. H. Beeby from Surrey. In 1922 Dr G. C. Druce wrote *Flora Zetlandica*, mainly a compilation of what others had done and containing little that was new. In 1955 R. C. Palmer of Oxford and Walter Scott of Scalloway began a survey of Shetland's vegetation that is still continuing. Their results will appear eventually in book form.

In 1969 Palmer and Scott published a check list of flowering plants and ferns that includes some 680 varieties (or more correctly taxa), which indicates the richness of Shetland's flora. Many of these taxa are non-native, having been brought to the islands by man, sometimes unintentionally. The number of native varieties can be put at around 500 including fifteen taxa not found anywhere else in the world. Thirteen of these are microspecies of the genus *Hieracium*. The other two were discovered by Shetlanders—mouse-ear chickweed by Thomas Edmondston, and the Shetland mouse-ear hawkweed by Walter Scott in 1962.

There is no natural woodland, but the few surviving birches (*Betula pubescens*), aspens (*Populus tremula*) and hazel (*Corylus avellana*) point to a former wooded condition. They are confined to holms in lochs, and cliffs in Northmavine, where the sheep cannot gain access to them, for sheep are second only to man in their ability to destroy natural vegetation.

Fortunately the sheep leave most flowers alone. Outstanding are the masses of heavily scented sea pinks on every skerry and cliffside in June, the profusion of pale yellow primroses, especially at Fladdabister and the Cliffs of Cunningsburgh, and the purple of the heather on the hills in autumn.

Every type of habitat—seashore, roadside, meadow, peat moor and rugged hilltop—has its own suite of plants, while the white waterlilies in lochs in Walls & Sandness have delighted generations of visitors since they were first mentioned by George Low in 1774. Some localities have special interest for botanists, such as the infertile serpentine belt of Unst, where the Keen of Hamar is designated a Site of Special Scientific Interest. Generally, species confined to high land in England appear at progressively lower altitudes in Scotland and at sea level in Shetland; on Ronas Hill, for instance, at a level under 1,486ft an arctic-alpine flora can be found.

Zoology

As with botany, it was the remarkable Edmondston family of

Unst that laid the foundations for a scientific study of the mammals and birds of Shetland. Thomas Edmondston compiled a *Fauna of Shetland* but it is less accurate than his book on botany. His brother-in-law, Henry L. Saxby, was a keen ornithologist whose book, *The Birds of Shetland*, was published posthumously in 1874.

With improved communications, more naturalists began to visit Shetland. After 1878 came such famous workers as Howard Saunders, A. H. Evans, J. A. Harvie-Brown, Eagle Clarke and T. E. Buckley. The result was *Vertebrate Fauna of Shetland*, produced jointly in 1899 by Evans and Buckley. The most comprehensive work this century is *The Natural History of Shetland* by R. J. Berry and J. L. Johnston, published in 1980. In 1970 two local ornithologists, Bobby Tulloch, representative in Shetland of the Royal Society for the Protection of Birds, and Fred Hunter produced a very useful booklet, *A Guide to Shetland Birds,* intended primarily for the visitor.

Compared to the wealth of marine life round the islands, and on sandy beach and rocky foreshore, land life is remarkably sparse. The area, of course, is relatively small and lacks thick cover, and high winds limit the number of insects. There are few butterflies but small moths are abundant.

Another surprise to the visitor is the absence of species found in most parts of Britain, such as snakes, moles, voles and toads. Frogs were introduced this century. Shetland's list of land mammals is confined to rabbits, hares, hedgehogs, stoats, rats and mice, all introduced by man with the possible exception of the Shetland fieldmouse (*Apodemus fridariensis*), which some naturalists believe is the only indigenous land mammal in the islands. To confuse the issue there are three subspecies, for the fieldmice of Fair Isle and Foula both have distinctive characteristics not seen in those of the other islands. L. S. V. & U. M. Venables believe that the Shetland fieldmouse was the first land mammal to follow the retreating ice-fronts and to have been cut off by the separation of the land mass, 'which shut the door on all other land animals, reptiles and amphibians'.

The sea supports whales, and two species of seal—the common seal and the rarer grey seal, whose breeding colonies are a feature of Ve Skerries, Muckle Flugga and the north end of the Mainland. Equally at home on land or in the sea is the otter.

Whales still frequent these northern waters: caaing whales (*Globiocephala melaena*) appear in small numbers and are not now molested; but the larger sei whale, common fin whale and giant blue whale have never recovered from the killings of the present century. The lesser rorqual (*Balaenoptera acuto-rostrata*), called in Shetland the 'herring hog', was common after World War II, but since then Norwegian whalers have reduced its numbers considerably. Porpoises and dolphins are still common here.

Brown trout flourish in most of the lochs and burns of the islands; and sea trout and salmon frequent the voes and, during the autumn spates, ascend the larger burns to spawn. The most interesting freshwater fish is the char, a creature usually found in cold arctic waters; it was driven south during the last Ice Age, returning north ahead of the warming oceans. Some char established colonies in deep lakes in Britain where conditions suited them, such as Girlsta Loch, the deepest in Shetland. They can be mistaken for a type of trout but are not often caught by rod and line. In 1955 their existence was proved by a naturalist who, with permission from the Shetland Angling Association, set an old herring net near the beach at the north end of Girlsta Loch and netted fifty-seven overnight; the largest was 10½in long, which is considered a fair size for a non-migratory char.

The great variety and abundance of birds compensate for the scarcity of other land vertebrates, and contribute greatly to the charm of Shetland. Even the Norsemen who, 1,000 years ago, named every stack and skerry round the shore were influenced by the myriads of seabirds. Foula was to them Bird Island (Fugl ey) and the name is repeated in Fugla Stack and Fugla Skerry. Some of their names are still apt: Foula has still an incredible wealth of bird life and Ramna Stacks are still the haunt of the ravens, but the liri or manx shearwater no longer nests on Liri Skerry, and Erne Stack and Erne Head just commemorate the white-tailed eagle, now locally extinct.

Birds more than any other warm-blooded animals are independent of man. They come and they go, stay only if conditions satisfy them, and nothing that man can do can compel them to settle. A recent attempt to reintroduce the white-tailed eagle was unsuccessful, but grouse introduced last century are now thriving.

Like man, birds extend their territory, colonise and sometimes drive out earlier inhabitants. The gannet only began nesting in 1914, though it was a common visitor before, but from one pair at Noss the colony had increased to over 2,000 pairs by 1949, while the colony at the north end of Unst showed a comparable increase. The collared dove first nested in 1965 after a rapid spread over the mainland of Britain. Most amazing, however, has been the spread of the fulmar petrel: first established in 1878 at Foula, it has spread all over the islands and has even displaced the gulls at some localities.

Shetland's list of breeding species is quite spectacular: Tulloch and Hunter list sixty-four, including Scandinavian species, such as whimbrel, snowy owl, red-throated diver, red-necked phalarope and fieldfare, nesting at the southern extremity of their range. There are two island subspecies—a Shetland wren (*Troglodytes troglodytes zetlandicus*) and a Shetland starling (*Sturnus vulgaris zetlandicus*). The former has a longer wing span than the normal species, but the latter is common among the northern and western islands of Scotland.

Visitors from the Far North spend the winter in Shetland: whooper swans, usually about 100, winter on Spiggie Loch, with tufted duck, goldeneye, pochard, wigeon and mallard. But the breeding species and wintering species comprise less than half the number of birds recorded in a single year, for the islands lie like stepping-stones on the great migration routes, and it is the hordes of unexpected visitors that make birdwatching so rewarding in Shetland.

Most favoured of all the islands is Fair Isle, where, in 1948, George Waterston established a bird observatory in an ex-naval station. No other locality in Britain has recorded so many species: 81,000 birds have been caught, examined and ringed, with recoveries reported from as far afield as Siberia and Brazil. The work of the observatory has been told by Kenneth Williamson in *Fair Isle and its Birds*.

An appeal was launched in 1967 to provide improved facilities for the warden and his staff; £51,000 was donated by the government, trusts and individuals and in 1969 a new observatory was opened with accommodation for twenty-four visitors in centrally heated rooms. The island is now owned by the National Trust for Scotland.

Man and Nature

Man has introduced many species of plants and animals to Shetland; unfortunately his record is not entirely without reproach. Extensive fishing of the voes for salmon and sea trout is causing concern, as is the killing of seals for their pelts.

Even unintentionally man can affect the balance of nature. It is believed that the import of large quantities of cabbages during World War II caused the introduction of the cabbage white butterfly, which spread at an astonishing rate, helped by the numerous dry stone dykes that protected the species' chrysalis during the winter. In some areas of Shetland every cabbage plot was reduced to a miniature forest of bare ribs. Then nature herself stepped in to control the pest, in the form of the tiny ichneumon fly, which lays its eggs in the living caterpillar of the cabbage white butterfly, the larvae living off their host until it dies.

Mechanised farming has spread to Shetland, though there are a few places where grass and oats are still cut by scythe. As elsewhere in Britain the call of the corncrake is now rarely heard, and the use of insecticides is blamed for the decline in the number of falcons.

Possibly the earliest attempt to preserve a species in Shetland was the rule observed in Foula in the eighteenth century that any person killing the great skua would be liable to a fine of 16s 8d (84p). This rule fell into disuse and by 1920 there was only one pair breeding in the island. They have made a remarkable recovery, however, and have spread all over Shetland and the north coasts of Scotland, to the regret of many people, for the great skua (or bonxie as it is known in Shetland) is a cruel bird, killing smaller birds such as kittiwakes by the ruthless method of sitting on their backs and forcing their heads under water until they drown.

Under the Protection of Birds Act, 1954, with later amendments, all wild birds except for a few classified as farmers' pests, which may be killed by authorised persons, are protected during the nesting season. Rare birds listed under Schedule One of the Act are protected by special penalties against wilful disturbance, including even the setting up of a photographic hide. Shetland birds on the list include corncrake, red-throated diver, merlin, snowy owl, peregrine, red-necked phalarope, common quail, whimbrel, black-tailed godwit and common scoter. Permission to photograph any of these near the nest must be obtained from the Natural Environment Research Council, 19 Belgrave Square, London W.1. Nevertheless the visitor is encouraged to study several of these species under supervision.

The Royal Society for the Protection of Birds is extremely active in Shetland. One of the ornithological events of the century occurred in 1967, when a pair of snowy owls chose a nesting site on Fetlar, the first recorded nesting in the wild in Britain. In co-operation with the owner of the land and the Secretary of State for Scotland, the RSPB had the area round the nest declared a Statutory Bird Sanctuary, and since then has managed it as the Fetlar Bird Reserve with a resident warden.

There are bird sanctuaries at Herma Ness and Noss. The latter is the better known; its gently dipping strata of Old Red Sandstone have created nesting ledges for many thousands of birds in a sheer cliff face 600ft high. Here is one of Shetland's two gannet colonies, but by far the most numerous are tier upon tier of guillemots, razorbills, kittiwakes, fulmars, puffins and shags. To see them when disturbed from their ledges is like looking down through a snowstorm.

HUMAN SETTLEMENT

While the nature of the rocks and soil linked with climate determine the nature of the initial vegetation, it is man who, within limits set by these factors, controls the secondary vegetation. Unlike Orkney, where large farms are the rule, the traditional agricultural unit in Shetland is the croft, generally 5–10 acres of arable land with rights of pasturage in the hills. Isolated crofts are rare. They are generally grouped together in townships of varying size and separated from neighbouring settlements by several miles of hill and moorland. The townships are a legacy of Norse settlement, their boundary walls of turf still standing in places, as they have done for 1,000 years, but the croft houses are new or improved, and the fields cleared and tilled so laboriously by the first settlers are now cultivated by mechanical means.

Everywhere one is struck by the great disparity between the cultivated land and the barren wastes of the hills—the scattald or common grazing—which can provide adequate pasture only in summer. A generation ago, the scattald was practically the only source of fuel.

The croft houses invariably face the sea, often standing a mere stone's throw from the shore. Above the highwater mark is the naust, or shelter for a small boat; the Shetland crofter still enjoys the change of diet that a night's fishing can provide from mackerel, haddock or young saithe. The fields surround the house, extending inland as far as the dry stone dyke that encloses the improved land of the township. Traditionally everything was utilised to make a living possible: the sea provided fish, the foreshore seaweed and shellfish, the green areas crops, and the hills pasture, fuel and roofing turf.

Until recently the only true villages were Scalloway and Hamnavoe, where the fishing industry caused the growth of compact communities. Within recent years crofting townships such as Brae and Sandwick have increased in size to become villages. Such developments generally indicate a movement from the land instigated by some small industrial concern, such as a knitwear unit or a bakery. Both of these districts are expanding considerably owing to the effects of oil-related developments.

The town of Lerwick is different. Owing its origin to trade with foreign fishermen, it became the centre of Shetland's herring fishery, and had the additional advantage of being the administrative centre for the islands.

2 EARLY HISTORY

THERE is no certain evidence that the Romans ever visited Shetland. In AD 83 an army under Agricola fought in Scotland, and his fleet reached Orkney, but whether the sailors saw Shetland is doubtful. Tacitus says '*Dispecta est Thule* (Even Thule was seen)', but he was Agricola's son-in-law, and biased. Ptolemy's map of the second century AD shows the *Orcades Insulae* (Orkney) and north of that *Thule* (Shetland).

PRE-HISTORY

The land beyond the bounds of the Roman Empire had already been inhabited for more than 3,000 years. Archaeologists believe that the first settlers of whom there are traces came here about 3,500 BC, in the Neolithic or late Stone Age. Different levels of habitation point to waves of colonisation, with progressively newer ideas and building techniques; but there are sites, such as Jarlshof, where settlement appears to have been continuous from early Bronze Age times to the Viking era.

Since 1948 over sixty Neolithic dwellings have been discovered in Shetland. The earliest settlers left no records of their voyages, their beliefs, or their battles against man and nature, but in their dwellings they left a more eloquent record of their way of life than has been found elsewhere in Britain.

They built large circular or oval detached houses with massive walls of stone and earth, differing from the communal complex of Skara Brae in Orkney and possibly of an even older type. The walls were low, but greater headroom was achieved by deepening the floor; and the roof probably consisted of driftwood covered with turf. The people were farmers, clearing the land of stones that they piled into heaps at the sides of the fields, as was still done recently in Shetland. From discoveries of bones, it is clear that horses, oxen, sheep, pigs and dogs were kept. The settlers also ate shellfish, vast amounts of cockles, mussels and limpets being available on the shore.

Their implements were stone, but show a great deal of skill and artistry in their manufacture as well as an understanding of the various types of rock. Clubs and cleavers were made of sandstone, often with decorated handles; and tough fine-grained porphyry was chipped and fashioned into adzes, then smoothed and polished so carefully as to acquire a metallic shine. Porphyry was also cut into thin oval-shaped 'knives', highly polished and finely sharpened; these implements are unique to these islands and are usually called by archaeologists 'Shetland knives'.

Pointed bars of stone, usually 1–3ft long, have also been found; smoothed by friction on one face, their purpose was for long a mystery, but since 1956 they have been regarded as primitive ploughshares, the earliest evidence of cultivation in the whole of Scotland. At the Ness of Gruting site, under a layer of reddish peat ash, was found a large quantity of bere or barley, burned black but still recognisable. This may indicate a disastrous day for a farmer when his drying kiln took fire, but it is more important now, as the most northerly discovery of Neolithic grain in Europe.

These early Shetlanders had little or no contact with Orkney; at least there is no trace of this culture there. It has been suggested that they came from Iberia via Ireland and the west of Scotland. Perhaps Orkney was already inhabited by a rival or even unfriendly race, for it is difficult to believe that colonists would pass by the more fertile southerly group.

Best known of Neolithic structures are the tombs. There are none so spectacular as Maeshowe in Orkney, but Shetland has its own type. From the external outline—a concave façade containing the entrance, and a rounded back—the Shetland variety is known as the heel-shaped cairn, a development of a type known in Mediterranean countries. In 1948 a much larger building of the same shape was excavated at Staneydale, and in 1955 another at Yoxie in Whalsay. The most interesting point about them is that they resemble Neolithic buildings in Malta and Gozo, where they are classed as temples. The temples in Shetland (they are now confidently classed as such) are the only known examples of their kind in Britain.

There is no clear break in Shetland between the Neolithic and

Bronze Ages. It is possible that owing to the remoteness of the islands Stone-Age culture continued when bronze implements were in use elsewhere. The excavations at Jarlshof show that the people continued as farmers, and this site has produced the earliest evidence in Britain of the stalling of cattle. At the rear of one of the dwellings was a channel to direct the flow of urine into a special tank in the courtyard, where Dr Curle, who excavated the ruins, could also detect a stain representing the manure heap. A whale's vertebra set into the wall of the house had been used as a tethering post.

In late Bronze Age times an Irish metal worker settled at Jarlshof, and set up shop in a room no longer used as a dwelling. There, some 2,000 years later, Dr Curle found the sand-filled casting pit in which the moulds of clay rested while the molten metal was poured in. The broken remains of the moulds tell that the smith produced socketed axes and knives, swords and 'sunflower' pins of typical Irish late Bronze Age type. Only one casting was discovered—a bronze dagger—which can be seen in the National Museum of Antiquities in Edinburgh.

The smith established himself at Jarlshof not long before newcomers who used iron tools built roundhouses there. It is possible that the smith migrated to Shetland because the discovery of iron had ruined the market for his wares farther south.

The Broch-builders

Even more spectacular than the Neolithic and Bronze Age relics are the circular fortresses known as brochs. Built entirely without mortar, they are regarded as the highest development of dry-stone building in Western Europe.

Commonly known as 'Picts houses', they have been attributed both to the Norsemen and as a defence against them, but recent excavations prove them to be of Iron Age times. It has been suggested that they were the forts of a conquering race, but the plan of a broch clearly suggests a defensive rather than an offensive role. The walls are designed to make scaling impossible and there is only one opening, a low passage that could be quickly barricaded from within. The height of the walls, rising to over 40ft, suggests the function of a watchtower, and from their position, at least in Shetland, at strategic headlands and sites along the shore, it is clear the inhabitants feared an attack from the sea.

Best preserved of all the brochs in Britain is that on the island of Mousa. The broch of Clickhimin near Lerwick is also important. A typical broch was roughly bell-shaped, wide at ground level, then narrowing upwards, and finally rising straight towards the top. At ground level the diameter was about 60ft, with walls up to 20ft thick enclosing a central courtyard. The lower part of the wall was solid, but higher up it was hollow, which space was occupied by a succession of low galleries running round the tower, the roof of each gallery forming the floor of the one above, and the galleries being reached by a spiral stairway, also within the wall.

Brochs are confined almost exclusively to the North of Scotland and the islands; over 500 are known, of which ninety-five are in Shetland. Their distribution suggests a people—a well defined political unit, rare at the time—pushed into the northern extremities of the country. Who was the enemy that caused this spate of fort-building? J. R. C. Hamilton in *The Northern Isles* suggests that it was the Celtic invaders from the North of England, builders of their own hill forts in a belt across Central Scotland and along the Great Glen about the year 100 BC.

It is known that the Iron Age was a time of deteriorating climatic conditions, with the onset of the wetter more stormy sub-Atlantic period. These conditions favoured the development of peat deposits, which spread over the arable land and the pasture of former agricultural areas, and the resulting land hunger in Northern Europe caused a stirring among the tribes and large-scale migrations. The great advance of the Roman armies across Europe probably helped to create unsettled conditions.

How long the emergency lasted we do not know. The end of broch-building can be dated from the discovery of second-century Roman coins in post-broch dwelling houses on the mainland of Scotland. Mr Hamilton suggests that the victory of the Romans over the Caledonians at Mons Graupius in AD 83 removed the threat from the southern enemy. He provides the intriguing suggestion that the broch-builders became allies of the Romans, and upon the withdrawal of the latter from northern Scotland, the broch-builders were taken to garrison the frontier. This theory would account for the existence of a few isolated brochs in the Southern Uplands and in the Midland Valley of Scotland.

With the return of settled conditions the brochs were abandoned, and at Jarlshof and Clickhimin we can actually tell what happened next. The broch at Jarlshof had an outer defensive wall, and a section of this was used to build a large roundhouse, still in the shelter of the broch. In the second or early third centuries AD a new people arrived, probably from the North of Scotland, and proceeded to build a new type of house, using the stones of the broch itself.

The new houses were circular, with a diameter of 30–40ft. They had a central hearth surrounded by seven or eight roofed bed recesses separated from each other by stone walls; this arrangement, suggesting the spokes of a wheel, has given the name 'wheel-house' to these houses. The family was the social unit involved in building a 'wheel-house', but a broch could only have been built by several families working together.

Picts and Celtic Missionaries

There is little doubt that Shetland formed part of the kingdom of the Picts, a political grouping of Celtic tribes of the East and North of Scotland that first came into being about AD 300, and which continued as a unit until about 843, when Kenneth mac Alpin united the Picts and the Scots. The Picts were descendants of the broch-builders, but these fortresses had already been abandoned by the time the name Pict was first applied, hence the modern emphasis on the distinction between Picts and broch-builders.

This period was far more settled than the turbulent era of broch-building. The inhabitants of Pictland continued to till the soil and graze their flocks and herds, but they found time to create on slabs of stone a most elaborate art of incised symbols. These symbols depict animals such as bulls, snakes and eagles, highly stylised yet marvellously natural; more common are the abstract designs whose meaning and purpose are still a complete mystery.

From the West of Scotland and Ireland came the first word of a new faith, the religion of the Cross. Quiet dignified priests, showing great skill in navigation and seamanship as well as great personal bravery, spread to Orkney and Shetland, even to Faeroe and Iceland. It is not certain whether they were of the school of St Columba or of St Ninian, for the dedication of a church to St Ninian is no proof that he or his followers ever visited Shetland. It is only safe to assume that the first missionaries of the Celtic church arrived here in the sixth century AD.

Tangible proof of the early church came to light in the nineteenth century. Monumental stones were found in the old churchyard of St Ninian's Isle, and in the parish of Lunnasting, bearing inscriptions in Ogam, a form of writing devised by the Irish and Scots but altered by the Pictish inhabitants of Orkney and Shetland into a form that still confuses the scholar. The letters are legible but so far have defied all attempts to translate them. Whatever message the Picts wished to leave to posterity remains unknown.

More famous are the beautifully sculptured stones found at Bressay and in the churchyard at Papil in Burra. From Papil also came the 'monks' stone', measuring 3ft 4in by 1ft 10½in and 2–2½in thick, and once a side slab in a composite shrine. On it are carved four cowled figures walking and one riding on horseback towards a free-standing cross. It can be seen in the County Museum at Lerwick.

Eighth-century Shetland was developing peacefully under strong Celtic influences when its whole history was changed by the coming of the Norse. They came first as rovers, then as settlers who took control of the islands, replacing the culture and way of life. They became so dominant that hardly any trace of Pictish life survives. Some scholars even suggest that they came to an

The 'monks' stone' from Papil, Burra, an example of early Celtic art

uninhabited land, a 'veritable museum' of mysterious brochs and earlier relics; others argue that the Picts were exterminated by the Norse; but neither of these theories is valid, for the Pictish name does survive in places that incorporate the name *Pettr*, the old Norse word for a Pict. Generally it is in the plural form *Petta*. There is Pettister, originally *Petta setr* (the farm of the Picts); there is Pettadale, originally *Petta dalr* (the valley of the Picts). It is perhaps significant that these names survive in remote regions of the hills, where the Norsemen could not combine their joint occupation of farming and seafaring. Elsewhere the incomers seized the land, and if the former inhabitants survived they became servants or thralls of the Norse.

The Papae, as the Norse called the Irish-Scottish priests, fared better in their monastic settlements; it is clear that they continued unmolested in several places, for their name is perpetuated especially in small islands. There are Papa Stour and Papa Little in St Magnus Bay, originally *Papa ey Storr* and *Papa ey Litla*, the big island and the small island of the priests. The name Papil is quite common, as in Burra and in Yell.

THE NORSEMEN

Between the eighth and eleventh centuries the people of Scandinavia raided and then settled in many lands. This was the Viking age when Norsemen ravaged the coasts of England and Southern Europe as far as the Mediterranean, and reached America via Greenland centuries before Columbus. Those Norsemen who settled outside Scandinavia made the more lasting impression, however.

The Norse left records of their exploits in the sagas, of which the *Orkneyinga Saga* contains most reference to Shetland. The sagas have to be interpreted with caution in so far as they glorify the spectacular deeds of the great Vikings, for they were transmitted in song and narrative for ages before being written down in the thirteenth century in Iceland. According to them, the political upheavals in Norway, culminating in Harald Fairhair's unification of the country in the year 872, caused a great flow of political refugees to the islands north and west of the Scottish mainland, where we now know there had been Norse settlers for at least 100 years. Repeated attacks from these islands brought a retaliatory expedition from Harald, who began with Shetland, landing first at Fetlar, then at the bay in Unst still known as Haroldswick. After arranging matters to his satisfaction here, he proceeded to Orkney, the Hebrides and the Isle of Man. Having subdued all opposition, he set up the earldom of Orkney and Shetland to free Norway from further attacks from the west. Thereafter Shetland was ruled by the earls of Orkney as a very subordinate part of the earldom. The earls recruited men and raised fleets in Shetland, but few honoured the islands with more than a temporary residence.

There are conflicting schools of thought regarding the nature of the colonisation. It is traditional to regard all Norsemen of this period as 'blood-thirsty Vikings', and certainly there is indisputable evidence that the Vikings sacked many monastic establishments, including Lindisfarne in 793 and Iona in 802; but this behaviour is not typical of the majority of the settlers. Some scholars, such as A. W. Brögger, maintain that they came to Orkney and Shetland as peaceful colonists, not unlike the settlers who emigrated to America in the nineteenth century.

Again a considerable amount of archaeological evidence is available in Shetland, and this suggests a compromise between the two points of view. It confirms that the settlers were mainly farmers who arrived with their families, but they certainly came armed, prepared at least to fight for their new country.

Very few Norse graves have so far been found, though many interesting mounds are in urgent need of examination. Over 100 years ago the grave of a Norse woman was found at Clibberswick in Unst, and three interesting bronze brooches were recovered—one of them trefoil-shaped, the other two shaped like the shell of a tortoise. These were standard adornments for a Norse woman of class in the ninth and tenth centuries, the tortoise-shaped brooches being worn one on each shoulder, and the trefoil making a clasp for a cloak. In the churchyard at South Whiteness the grave of a warrior was discovered, and his bronze axe, believed to date from the ninth century, can be seen in Zetland County Museum. Within recent years a warrior's grave complete with weapons was destroyed by machinery levelling the site of the control tower at Sumburgh airport, and drain-cutting in the same area destroyed another, though a bowl-shaped brooch was recovered and can also be seen in the county museum.

Between 1929 and 1967 the foundations of eleven Norse houses were found in Shetland, including seven at Jarlshof. Within the next four years ten more were discovered, eight of them by a single enthusiast, Peter Moar of Lerwick. A typical house was rectangular, measuring up to 70ft long and 20ft wide, the long walls curving slightly inwards at the ends. Some were divided internally into a living room, a sleeping room and a room for the cattle, an arrangement that prevailed in Shetland croft houses until the mid-nineteenth century.

Portrait of a Viking incised on sandstone from Jarlshof

Personal belongings found include decorated needles and combs of bone, glass beads and bronze pins (some bent into the shape of fish-hooks). Soapstone was quarried to make cooking pots, lamps that burned fish oil, weights for fishing lines and whorls for spinning woollen thread. Tiny millstones and model boats were carved as toys for the children. At Jarlshof a local artist left drawings scratched on slate of Viking ships with dragon-headed prows, and two portraits, one of an old man, another of a young bearded Viking. At Jarlshof, Norse settlement is believed to have been continuous from the ninth century to the fourteenth.

It is surprising that the sites of Norse farmhouses are not more numerous, but it must be remembered that the arable land of the Norseman has been cultivated continuously for over 1,000 years and the foundations of many of their long houses are probably under the walls of modern croft houses. Many more will no doubt be found, for the study of archaeology is attracting more local enthusiasts.

Life in Norse Times

The Norsemen pillaged and plundered the coasts of Britain, but they left in the northern islands a heritage of freedom. They were harsh in dealing with their enemies, but at home they were cultured, interested in art and poetry and obsessed with the study of law. The book of laws given to them by the wise King Olaf was their Bible, consulted as late as 1602 to find the proper penalties for the murderers of Matthew Sinclair of Ness. In each of their provinces they ruled through a court of justice, the earliest type of democratic assembly ever known in Britain. In Shetland the district where the supreme court or Alting was held is still known as Tingwall; the court is believed to have been held on a little island in Tingwall Loch, reached in those days by stepping-stones. Since Norse times the level of the loch has been lowered by drainage and the islet is now a promontory on the north shore of the loch.

Shetland was governed by a magistrate known as the great foude, who derived his authority from the King of Norway. The book of laws was entrusted to a lawman, elected to the important office of legal adviser and judge of assize. Nicol Reid of Bressay, who was elected lawman-general of all Shetland in 1532, was probably the last of these officials.

The islands were subdivided into ten or eleven districts, each governed by an inferior foude, who held periodic courts to decide minor cases. He was assisted by a group of officers known as ranselmen, usually ten in number, who had wide powers of spying upon their neighbours and the right to enter any premises in search of stolen goods. There was also in every district a law-rightman, a trustworthy person acceptable both to the foude and to the people, whose main function was the regulation of weights and measures, especially with regard to the payment of land tax, which was then paid in kind.

The great foude and lawman made an annual circuit of the islands with a large retinue to preside over the lesser tings. The final meeting of the year was the great assembly at the Alting, which all freemen were obliged to attend. There new legislation was enacted, appeals heard against decisions of inferior foudes, and causes involving the life and death of an accused were determined by the voice of the people.

Throughout the Norse period most of the land was held under

the Norwegian system of udal tenure. Unlike feudal tenure, which implied the holding of land from a superior with obligations of military or personal service, udal tenure carried no such obligation; land was the property of the first improver, and any settler could enclose as much land as he wished for improvement. The basis of land valuation was the merk, a term denoting quality rather than quantity. A merk of the best land was approximately an acre in extent, but a merk of poor land was often 4 or 5 acres. The important point was that each merk was approximately the same value for producing crops.

Beyond the turf and stone dykes of the township lay the scattald or common grazing, which belonged to no one but was vested in the king as representing the community. For the freedom to use the scattald for grazing and peat-cutting, a land tax was levied known as skat (hence the original name for the common grazing of *skathold*). As a basis of taxation skat was levied on every merk of enclosed land.

Next development was a communal distribution of the arable land. Each man had a share of the good land and of the poor, a share of the land exposed to the sea blast as well as a share of that lying open to the south and to the sun. The fields were divided into long narrow rectangles separated by strips of grass. At first each plot was cultivated by the farmers of the township in rotation and the whole system was known as rigga rendal.

Under the udal law of succession, the death of a udaller meant the division of his estate among the family under the supervision of the district foude. The sons had equal shares and the daughters received half a son's share. It was an important point in udal law that no written title was necessary to establish ownership of land, but in later years it became the practice for the district foude to issue what was known as a Shynd Bill to finalise the division of an estate.

Large flocks of sheep grazed on the scattalds, then entirely unfenced. Ownership was readily established by the ingenious method of cutting their ears: each farmer had his own mark carefully registered with the foude, a combination of half-moons and wide and narrow-angled notches that are as distinctive and as carefully registered today, under such names as rits, crooks and shears. The wool of the small native sheep was not shorn but was pulled off by hand, as is still done today. The extent of sheep-rearing can be gauged from the size of the tithe of wool payable to the Pope in 1328—22cwt.

Shetland lacked the abundance of game the settlers had been accustomed to hunt in Norway, but the cliffs had large numbers of seabirds, whose eggs and young afforded a change of diet every summer. More important were the shoals of fish round the shores, and the successive layers of Norse settlement at Jarlshof show an ever increasing interest in fishing.

The Christian Church in Norse Times

The Norsemen are imagined as worshippers of Odin, Thor and Freyja, believing in a future life in Valhalla of eternal fighting and feasting for those who fell in battle. As has been pointed out, however, the Norsemen in Shetland accepted the Christian faith, or at least tolerated the Celtic priests. Few pagan graves have been located and more may be found, but it is significant that a ninth-century warrior's grave at South Whiteness was within the walls of a Christian churchyard.

There were certainly exceptions, such as the Vikings who destroyed the churches on Lindisfarne and Iona. In Shetland a vivid example of the hand of the raider came to light in 1958 at St Ninian's Isle. A party of students from Aberdeen University, excavating the ruins of the old chapel, prised up a stone slab faintly marked with a cross and found underneath a priceless treasure in silverware; it included seven small shallow bowls, a spoon, a 'fork-like' implement with one prong and a cutting edge, three heavily decorated hollow cones of uncertain use and twelve brooches. It is not known whether the silver belonged to the church or to a wealthy person who regarded the church as the safest place to hide his valuables. Whoever the owner, he had placed his hoard in a wooden box and buried it in haste upside down. The church was destroyed, and the faithful killed or dispersed, for no one returned to claim the treasure, until it was recovered by the spade of a Lerwick schoolboy helping at the 'dig'.

The *Orkneyinga Saga* suggests that the light of Christianity was extinguished during the Norse era, and that it was Olaf Tryggvesson, future king of Norway, who reintroduced the faith into Orkney and Shetland in 995. After his own conversion, while on a visit to Ireland, he called at Orkney on his way home and there seized upon Earl Sigurd, ordering him and all his vassals to undergo baptism on pain of death. Such a forced conversion could have made little impact on the islands, but perhaps the official recognition shown to the Church brought into the open secret groups of believers. The faith certainly flourished in the later Norse period, as is shown by the large number of chapels whose foundations have been found—no fewer than twenty in Yell alone. Many of these must have been the private chapels of wealthy udal farmers.

It is believed that the first territorial arrangement of parishes was organised in the twelfth century after the establishment of the bishopric of Orkney and Shetland under ecclesiastical administration from Norway. Central parish churches replaced the old private chapels, and each parish or group of parishes was administered by a priest under the authority of the Archdeacon, who resided at Tingwall, which thus became the seat of civil and religious authority for the whole islands. St Magnus Church was built in 1150, the first of three towered churches in Shetland, the others being built at the long hallowed sites of Papil, Burra, and Ireland, Dunrossness.

St Magnus Church was a magnificent building with a nave, a chancel and a tower 60 or 70ft high. Its nave measured 49ft by 18ft internally, slightly larger than that of the famous towered church still standing on the island of Egilsay in Orkney. The church of St Magnus, Tingwall, and the church of St Laurence at Papil both survived until about 1790, when, as Dr Edmondston stated in 1809, they were demolished 'from a principle of barbarous economy to supply stones at a cheap rate for building the plain presbyterian churches which now occupy their places'.

Norway's Waning Influence

In 1194 the earldom became the centre of a plot to depose King Sverre of Norway. A large force of islanders was taken to Norway and, after initial successes, was crushed at the battle of Florevag near Bergen. Next year Earl Harald made his submission to Sverre, who separated Shetland from the earldom as a punishment, and for almost 200 years Shetland was ruled directly from Norway, which developed even stronger ties between the two countries.

While Norway's hold on Shetland was stronger than ever, her

hold on the southern dominions gradually weakened. In July 1263, Bressay Sound was filled with King Haakon's war galleys on their way to regain control. The battle of Largs, fought against the army of King Alexander III of Scotland, is described in the sagas as a minor and inconclusive skirmish, but the strain was too much for Haakon. He returned to Orkney and died at Kirkwall on 15 December 1263.

By the treaty of 1266 Norway retained Orkney and Shetland but renounced all claims to the Western Isles and the Isle of Man on condition that Alexander should pay the sum of 4,000 marks compensation and an annual tribute of 100 marks each year in St Magnus Cathedral, Kirkwall. This 'annual of Norway', or rather the subsequent failure to pay it, was an important step in the mortgaging of the isles to Scotland in 1468 and 1469.

In Orkney, Scottish influence became more and more pronounced. In 1231 the Norse line of earls came to an end with the murder of John in Caithness; then began the Scottish line of Angus, succeeded in 1321 by the line of Strathearne and in 1379 by the line of St Clair. In 1379 Shetland was rejoined with Orkney under continuing Scottish influence, while Norway became a mere shadow of her former self. In 1319 Norway had united with Sweden and in 1397 came the union of Denmark, Sweden and Norway under a Danish king.

The Transfer

It is unimaginable that a king of Norway would ever have abandoned Shetland, with its Norse laws, language and culture. Indeed trading and cultural links between Norway and Shetland remained strong until the nineteenth century. In distant Denmark, however, there was no appreciation of this special relationship and the islands became mere pawns in international politics.

The Danish exchequer was severely strained after the previous war against Sweden. King Christian realised that the 'annual of Norway' had been long neglected and an enormous sum had accrued. He demanded payment in full. It was King Charles VII of France who acted as peacemaker and helped to arrange the marriage between Princess Margaret of Denmark and Prince James, soon to be King James III of Scotland.

By the marriage treaty of 1468 the arrears of the 'annual' were cancelled, and the princess's dowry was fixed at 60,000 florins, of which 10,000 were to be paid within the year, the crown lands of Orkney to be pledged for the remainder. Only 2,000 florins were paid within the stipulated time, and on 20 May 1469 the crown lands of Shetland were pledged for the remaining 8,000 florins. The conditions were that Shetland should revert to the kings of Norway as soon as the debt was discharged, and that the islanders should enjoy their own customs and laws while temporarily under Scottish rule. In 1470 Earl William St Clair resigned to King James III his entire rights to the earldom, and in 1471 the northern isles were annexed to the Scottish crown; but as late as 1567 an act of the Scottish parliament confirmed the ancient Norse laws in Orkney and Shetland. Denmark tried on numerous occasions to redeem her mortgaged territories and in theory can still do so.

The Legacy of the Norse

The Norsemen left an imprint on every aspect of life in Shetland still visible today, 500 years after the islands became officially Scottish. Most conspicuous is the overwhelming abundance of Norse place names. The Norn word *vik* or bay is incorporated in Lerwick, Sandwick, Levenwick, Gulberwick, and *nes* or headland in Sandness, Eshaness, Whiteness and many more. Inland, the word *bolstadr* or farm, corrupted to a suffix—bister—is particularly common, as in Fladdabister, Isbister, and Wadbister. *Saetr* or summer pasture is incorporated in Aithsetter, Dalsetter or plain Setter.

Practically every feature down to streams and hillocks was named by the Norse, and only a few are definitely recent additions. Some names look English or Scots but are meaningless corruptions of Norse words. Mavis Grind does not take its name from the mavis or song thrush but was originally *maev eiths grind* (the gate of the narrow isthmus), and how apt a description for this locality where there is space for little more than a road between North Sea and Atlantic. Between 1893 and 1895 Dr Jakobsen, a Faeroese philologist, made a scientific study of the language and place names of Shetland. He collected over 50,000 names that are definitely Norse.

We can learn much from a cautious study of place-names. Dr Jakobsen was able to show from the districts in Norway where the words *bolstadr* and *saetr* were most common that the bulk of

Shetland's Norse settlers came from the regions south and north of Bergen, especially Hordaland and Rogaland. He found the element *vin* of special interest. He pointed out that names compounded with *vin* had ceased to be formed in Norway before the Viking age, and so deduced a settlement in Shetland about the year 700, which is believed by modern experts to be slightly too early. All agree on one point, that the abundance of Norse place names points to a mass migration over a relatively short period.

Personal surnames, too, are largely Norse: some are territorial in origin, such as Isbister, Inkster and Rendall, but most common are the names ending in -son. This is due to the old Norse system of patronymics whereby a person took as his surname the Christian name of his father with the suffix -son or -dochter. This system was superseded by the adoption of regular surnames late in the nineteenth century, though it is still in use today in Iceland.

The old Norn language survived a surprisingly long time, especially in remote places. In 1774 when George Low visited Foula, he found the language almost extinct, but he managed to record the Lord's Prayer in Norn and three remnants of song, one consisting of thirty-four verses. Norn degenerated into a dialect with the incorporation of Scots and English words, but between 1893 and 1895 Dr Jakobsen collected 10,000 Scandinavian words in use in Shetland, though more than half were obsolescent. Today the Shetland dialect is richly sprinkled with Norse words and phrases, especially when related to subjects such as the sea and weather.

Norse domestic and farm implements continued long in use, some until the beginning of the twentieth century. Articles of great importance were contrived from simple materials: a sheepskin with wool removed could be made into a sieve or a buoy for fishing lines; and shoes of cowhide or sealskin and known as rivlins were in common use a generation ago. The quern, a small domestic mill, was still in use at the beginning of this century. The old type of scythe and the single-stilted plough were not replaced until the middle of the nineteenth century by more efficient Scottish implements.

The Shetland versions of these and other articles did not develop independently of their Norwegian originals. Improvements were introduced through continued contact with Norway. In 1969 an exhibition was held in the county museum of traditional Shetland articles, and placed alongside each was the equivalent in use a generation ago in Norway. Only after studying the accompanying descriptions could the two sets be distinguished. Two Norse implements survive—the small-bladed Shetland spade, designed for use in shallow soil, and the tushkar (from Old Norse *torfskeri*), a type of peat-cutting implement unique to Shetland.

The design of the Norse farmhouse survived until the late nineteeenth century with such innovations as glass skylights and roofing slates. Even in 1934 the Danish scholar Aage Roussel found several examples of old Norse-type farmhouses; some, long-abandoned, had only a partition between living-room and byre.

Of greater interest to generations of visitors were the Shetland watermills, small and inefficient, with a horizontal wheel that was unique in Britain. They stood on every stream that had sufficient force in winter to turn the axle. Sometimes they stood alone, sometimes in a series of three or more. In 1886 they were described by Gilbert Goudie, the Shetland historian, as 'an indispensable feature in every scene of Shetland life', but in 1903, he wrote, 'the old native mill is now entirely obsolete'. In 1934 Roussel could still study the machinery of some in a reasonable state of repair, and he commented: 'In the Shetland water-mill we are justified in recognising a relic of Norse times, a design that has been repeated for at least seven hundred years'.

SCOTTISH RULE

The change to Scottish rule did not at first affect the people of Shetland; they remained Norse in character, and legal documents show that the Norse legal system was still being honoured at the end of the sixteenth century. The islands were let out to tacksmen who paid an annual sum to the Crown for the right to collect taxes, but apart from this they did not interfere in the life of the people. The number of Scottish immigrants increased slowly but never in sufficient proportions to swamp the basically Norse inhabitants. This process has continued right down to the present day: with very few exceptions all incomers have been assimilated into what can only be called a Shetland way of life.

Most obvious of the early changes brought about by the Scots was in the language, for by the end of the sixteenth century the people were bi-lingual, understanding Scots, the language of church and law court, but speaking a despised Norn language which was to absorb more and more Scots and English words until it became the Shetland dialect of today.

The Stewarts

Most eventful period in the early Scottish era was the half century when a father and son held the earldom of Orkney and Shetland. Robert Stewart was an illegitimate son of King James V, and in 1564 his half-sister Mary Queen of Scots made him a heritable grant of the islands and the office of Sheriff for a feu duty of £2,000. His son Patrick succeeded him in 1593.

Unlike the Norse earls who seldom visited Shetland, Robert Stewart built a mansion at Sumburgh and had a house at Wethersta in the parish of Delting, while Patrick Stewart built Scalloway Castle in 1600. Under the Stewarts also came a gradual change from Norse law to Scottish. In 1576 the last foude was appointed and in 1580 Robert Stewart was administering Norse law through four sheriff deputies. The offices of lawman and lawrightman were dropped, though underfoudes continued to play their part in local government under the Scottish name of bailie well into the eighteenth century, and ranselmen continued to be appointed until the late nineteenth century.

Under Earl Patrick's rule the book of laws disappeared and he moved the Alting from Tingwall to Scalloway Castle, where, by entering the large hall, the udallers had to acknowledge the supremacy of the Earl. But he did not interfere with udal law, apart from acquiring a large estate, nor did he fill the court with Scottish favourites, for the names of the underfoudes of this period are definitely Norse.

The events leading to the downfall of the régime took place outside Shetland. Patrick was arrested in 1609 and taken to Edinburgh, and, in an attempt to regain his lost estates, his young son Robert led an insurrection in Orkney that resulted in both their executions in 1615.

It is difficult to get a clear unbiased picture of the role played by the Stewarts in the islands. A list of Earl Robert's mis-

Page 49 (above) South entrance to Lerwick harbour, looking towards Bressay lighthouse; *(below)* Weisdale Voe with its islands; coastal scenery is the result of submergence since the Ice Age

Page 50 (above) Cliffs at Esha Ness, attacked by waves of the Atlantic; *(below)* arches and stacks on the north side of St Magnus Bay

demeanours was presented by the leading men of Orkney as a Complaint to the Crown in 1575; and a list of Earl Patrick's crimes was compiled by James Law, Bishop of Orkney, who was instrumental in having him arrested. These show the Stewart earls to be cruel ruthless tyrants, confiscating land, even punishing those who tried to help shipwrecked seamen. We are fortunate, however, in the preservation of the Court book of 1602–4, from which Professor Gordon Donaldson has produced a fascinating account called *Shetland Life under Earl Patrick*. He points out that there were remarkably few paupers at this time, and even some of the ordinary people possessed articles of value. What is more important, the people were not cowed; they were eager to assert their rights in the court of law and there is a case of a complainant declaring that he would seek justice from the Earl himself. This is so untypical of the poor underdog of a crofter-fisherman who was to appear later.

More lasting and more damaging to the ordinary people was the effect of the clergy and other court favourites who arrived with the Stewarts and even after Patrick's death and proceeded to build up estates and personal fortunes. Laurence Bruce, half-brother to Robert Stewart, accumulated lands in Unst, where in 1598 he completed the castle of Muness. He died in 1617 leaving an estate worth £4,000, a fortune in those days. James Pitcairn, minister of Northmavine, somehow found time from preaching the gospel to amass an estate worth £3,000.

The period of Scottish consolidation in Shetland is still poorly understood. Some authorities infer that the udal farmer was so inefficient, so extravagant, that he willingly sold his lands to the Scottish incomers. Others, such as Thomas Gifford, himself a member of a landed family, who wrote in 1733 a *Historical Description of the Zetland Islands*, hint at more shady dealings:

> When gentlemen from Scotland came to settle in Zetland, . . . these incomers found no great difficulty in purchasing of land from the poor simple inhabitants. . . . They began to lay aside the Shynd Bill and to use dispositions and sasines, and thereupon followed that long train of conveyances filled with all the clauses and quirks that the lawyer and noter could invent for lengthening the writing and making it so intricate that its true sense and meaning thereof might only be known to themselves.

Whether by fair means or foul, the result was that in a very short time the bulk of Shetland's inhabitants had changed from being small landowners supporting themselves on their own farms to mere tenants paying rent to landlords. Perhaps the real oppressors were the very people who condemned the Stewarts, and who perpetuated the legend of a castle built of blood and maidens' hair.

The Reformed Church

At the time of the Reformation Robert Stewart found it to his advantage to establish Episcopacy, and there was no reformer more zealous than he. Adam Bothwell, first Protestant bishop of Orkney and Shetland visited his diocese several times in the 1560s, but he was bishop in name only, for in 1568 he was compelled to relinquish to Earl Robert the rights and revenues of the islands. The weakness of church discipline is shown by the extent of the earls' jurisdiction, for slander was a criminal offence in Earl Patrick's day. Again in 1604 a man was charged in the earl's court with 'fishing on the Sabbath day and laying his lines'.

By 1567 there were two ministers and nine readers for the eleven ministries, but neither they nor their successors can be praised for the example they set. In the court book of 1602–4 the names of two clergymen appear, both charged with assault; and it has been shown already that the clergy were concerned more with their parishioners' land than with their souls.

On the death of his father, Earl Patrick continued to collect the church revenues, but some years after Bothwell's death a new bishop, James Law, came north to collect his tithes and offerings. In spite of Law's insistence that the former agreement was invalidated by the death of the contracting parties, Earl Patrick refused to relinquish what was now an important part of the revenues of the earldom. This led to a bitter conflict between the two men, a struggle in which the bishop emerged victor.

This was an age when the turmoil outside and within the church was mirrored by fear and superstition within the minds of the people, when men and women accused of being wizards and witches were tried on absurd charges and, in the name of God, burned to death on a hill overlooking the village of Scalloway. One of the charges brought against Marion Pardoun of Hillswick, burned as a witch in 1644, was that she had appeared in the form of a 'pellack' whale and upset a fishing boat, whereby four men were drowned.

The seventeenth century was marked by a struggle for power in Britain, and a constant seesawing between Episcopal and Presbyterian forms of church government. The Church of Scotland became officially Presbyterian in 1690 but the ministers of Shetland were left unmolested under Episcopalian ordination for a full decade longer. In 1700 the General Assembly of the Church of Scotland sent a commission of seven ministers to examine the state of the church in the north, and one of them, the Rev John Brand, found time to write a very inaccurate account of the islands. They had little difficulty in establishing Presbyterianism, however, and only a few of the landed gentry remained Episcopalian, with a single minister to serve them. The last of these was Mr Hunter (1734–45), and after his death there was no Episcopalian church in Shetland until 1864, when St Magnus Church was erected in Lerwick.

The people adopted the reformed faith only slowly. They remained two steps behind their leaders, for Roman Catholic festivals continued to be observed until the beginning of the eighteenth century, with traces surviving even longer. Rev John Brand discovered that the pre-Reformation chapels had become centres for superstitious rites (in his view) on Easter Sunday and during Lent, and that candles were burned on the altar of the ruined church at St Ninian's Isle. Brand recommended that all old chapels should be removed, in which he was following the example of Hercules Sinclair, zealous minister of Northmavine, who had the old Cross Kirk rased to the ground. Brand felt that Sinclair's action had made the people of Northmavine more civilised than those of the rest of Shetland.

The Beginnings of Trade

The fourteenth century, or possibly even earlier, saw the foundation of an export trade in fish that was to dominate the life of the islands for over 400 years. The impetus came from the far-sighted merchants of the Hanseatic league. In theory the Danish king held a monopoly of trade with Shetland, but the penalties imposed had little effect on the merchants, so great were the returns. After 1469, though free from Danish royal restrictions, they had to compete with Scottish merchants, who, it was pointed out, had the unfair advantage of wintering in Shetland and perhaps arranging for the disposal of the following season's catch.

Between early May and early August each year the vessels arrived from Hamburg, Lübeck and Bremen. The merchants rented booths or the ground on which to build them from the landowners, then displayed, for sale or barter, a variety of goods —hooks, lines, and herring nets, corn and flour, a kind of bread called 'cringel bread', salt, fruit, mead, spirits, hempen cloth, linen and muslin.

To obtain these necessities (and luxuries) the men of Shetland had merely to launch their small boats and catch ling and cod from the shoals that then frequented the voes of the islands. The fish were landed at the merchants' booths, and they organised the splitting, salting and drying of the catch for shipment to Germany. The Germans also bought wool, woollen cloth, knitted stockings, seal and otter skins, beef for salting; also the butter and fish liver oil in which the taxes were paid.

The Stewart earls regulated this trade, issuing monopolies to the merchants to operate within a certain island or district. Some merchants appear to have taken up residence in Shetland, like Segebad Detken, burgess and merchant of Bremen, who carried on his business in Unst for fifty-two years and who was buried in the churchyard of Lund in 1573.

More numerous by far than the Germans were Dutch herring fishermen, who, in the sixteenth century, discovered a veritable silver mine to the east of Shetland. They used the wide empty sound between Bressay and the Mainland for the annual assembly of their fleet of busses, waiting until 24 June, the agreed date for the start of the herring season. Like the Germans, they traded with the country people, buying fresh meat and vegetables and large quantities of woollen stockings. The site of the early market place, midway between Scalloway, then the islands' capital, and Bressay Sound, is still known as the Hollanders' Knowe. Early in the seventeenth century a settlement of booths established itself on the shores of Bressay Sound round the little bay known as Ler wick, and so great was its trade that by the end of the century the new town of Lerwick had 2–300 families.

Shetland's growing prosperity attracted small cargo vessels from the more fertile islands of Orkney, laden with corn, meal and malt. In 1700 Rev John Brand observed: 'so great is the

Advantage that these Isles do reap by their Neighbourly Commerce with one another, for as Zetland could not well live without Orkney's Corns, so neither could Orkney be so well without Zetland's Money'.

Dutch stivers and half stivers were for many years the most common coins in circulation in Shetland. The Dutch also found the islands a valuable dumping ground for their old and devalued coins, which made their difficult passage from hand to hand until they ended, as a last resort, in the collection plate in church. The quandaries of the kirk sessions can be seen from the surviving minutes: nobody wanted these debased coins, so they just accumulated. Some were disposed of only in recent years, but they are of little value to collectors.

3 LANDLORDS AND CROFTER-FISHERMEN

AFTER the removal of Patrick Stewart, Orkney and Shetland were annexed to the Crown and the rents were again leased to a succession of tacksmen until 1643, when Charles I granted the islands as a personal favour to Douglas, Earl of Morton. Oliver Cromwell came to power soon afterwards and his influence was extended even to Shetland, where he stripped the Earl of Morton of his lands, and, suspicious of the activities of Dutch herring fishermen, sent troops to garrison Scalloway Castle and start the building of a fort at Lerwick.

On the restoration of Charles II the islands were returned to the Earl of Morton, but in 1669 the grant was rescinded again, for the King was displeased at the Earl's appropriation of treasure from a ship wrecked at Out Skerries. A fresh grant was made in 1707 to the Morton family, which sold its rights in 1766 to Sir Laurence Dundas, ancestor of the Earls of Zetland.

Local courts continued to be held after the Stewart era, the Earl of Morton being represented by a 'steward and justiciar-depute'—usually one of the new class of landed proprietors. Legislation enacted for the government of the islands became codified as the Country Acts, which regulated crofting and fishing, standardised weights and measures, enforced Sunday observance, and even took cognisance of peculiarities of island life down to such details as 'that none repair to feasts uncalled'.

The abolition of heritable jurisdiction in 1747 limited the power of the earls and left the landowners or lairds the dominant force in the islands. They had already assumed extraordinary powers, for in 1725 they accused the people of all sorts of vices and formed the ranselmen and kirk elders into a Society for the Regulation and Reformation of Manners. Of far greater importance was their handling of the economy of the islands.

The Salt Tax, introduced in 1712 to encourage British shipping, had unforeseen and far-reaching effects on Shetland. Since imports of salt carried in foreign vessels were subject to a heavy duty, the act killed the activities of the Hanseatic merchants. The earnings from the fishing industry, however, had become the sole means of paying the rent of the croft, and so, partly in their own interests, the lairds were forced to become fish merchants and general traders. They were encouraged by the government in the form of a bounty of 3s (15p) per cwt on all cured fish exported.

The industry developed from sporadic fishing in small boats near the shore to a fishery for ling and cod prosecuted at ever greater distances from land and ever more vigorously until it became the summer pursuit of the entire male population of the islands. Larger boats were required, and longer fleets of lines, but few crofter-fishermen could afford these, and the laird became boatowner as well as owner of the crofter's house and land, and merchant and banker for the whole district. Such a monopoly of power gave the lairds a tremendous control over the lives of their tenants which unscrupulous landowners could easily turn to their own advantage.

The system of barter continued, and, through the poverty of the crofter-fishermen, the truck system developed and little money changed hands. A running account was kept, usually settled once a year : the tenant was credited with the value of goods delivered, debited with rent and the cost of articles bought at the shop. The whole system of land tenure changed : leases became short, the tenant commonly holding his land under a verbal agreement for one year at a time, after which both parties were free to renegotiate terms. The rent was supposedly reduced on condition that the tenant agreed to serve as a hand on a fishing boat and deliver all his fish, surplus butter and eggs, and the knitwear produced by his wife and daughter, at prices below those of the open market.

The fishing industry was a great stimulus to the population. The marriage rate increased : youths after a season at the fishing considered themselves men and the minister of Yell commented that in his parish there were few bachelors. Between 1755 and 1793 Dr Edmondston estimated that the population of Shetland increased by almost 5,000, compared to an increase of only

100 in Orkney, where fishing was less important. But it was an unhappy time for the people, a time of snobbery and class-consciousness, when land was the symbol of a man's importance. Some landlords were enlightened and sought to remedy the situation on their estates by removing fishing as a condition of tenancy, but they were at the mercy of the system, for credit was essential, and the crofter could not pay his way unless he fished also.

The upshot of the system was obvious, but the actual cause of the distress is more difficult to pinpoint. Contemporary writers maintained that the landlords embarked on a deliberate policy of encouraging early marriages and dividing the crofts into even smaller units to increase the number of fishermen. Recent opinion suggests that fragmentation of the crofts was merely necessary to accommodate the increase in population caused by the eradication of smallpox. There can be no doubt, however, that the landlords regarded fishermen as fundamental to their own prosperity and to the economy of the islands. When a young man, attracted by wages of up to £2 a month, engaged on a whaling ship bound for the Arctic, thus escaping from the islands, his family were fined a guinea by the laird as compensation.

The main cause of the poverty of the islanders was the total dependence of the lairds on a single industry—a fishery run on a shoestring by craft far too small for the waters in which they operated. Even the method of fishing was incapable of giving fishermen adequate returns for the amount of work and dangers involved.

THE OLD STATISTICAL ACCOUNT

In the 1790s the distinguished Caithness baronet Sir John Sinclair undertook the enormous and novel task of compiling a Statistical Account of Scotland. For his information he sent to every parish minister a questionnaire of 166 items touching on every aspect of social and economic life. The results were published between 1791 and 1799 in twenty-one volumes, the accounts for Shetland being spread over twelve volumes. They were later assembled in one volume as *The Statistical Account of Shetland, 1791–1799*; it is common to refer to this work as the Old Statistical Account to distinguish it from the 'new' account published in 1841.

The Ministers

At this time the minister was the most respected, best educated and, next to the laird, the most influential man in the parish. Patronage was in the hands of Sir Thomas Dundas and a young minister had a better chance of securing a position if he had an influential friend who could apply to the patron on his behalf.

His stipend was provided by the laird and by the casual teinds (tithes) of the crofter-fishermen in butter, oil and fish. Each adult had to give three days' unpaid labour each year working at the minister's peats or on his glebe, the area of farmland attached to the manse. By placing a value on all these items, the minister of Unst calculated his stipend at £108 a year, with which he was well satisfied. The manses were cold and cheerless stone buildings, but not one grumble was made in the Old Statistical Account, though the minister of Unst remarked that his manse was 'rather in a ruinous condition'.

At the end of the eighteenth century the church was again supreme as the corrector of morals, levying fines which it gave to the poor, and punishing moral lapses by having the offenders appear in church for public condemnation. The ordeal of a young woman in being subjected to the sneers of the whole parish for up to fifty-two successive Sundays must have left a deep scar on her personality, and must have created in her a hidden contempt for the established church and those who represented it. Yet the ministers were only doing what they believed was their duty in safeguarding the moral life of the parish.

Most outstanding of the ministers was the Rev John Mill of Dunrossness, who, when he wrote his account in 1793, was eighty-two. In addition to this account, his diary carefully kept between 1740 and 1803 gives a detailed record of life at this time. He feared neither man nor devil, though attacked constantly by both. He was persecuted by the laird of Quendale, one of the few in Shetland who supported the Jacobite cause during the rebellion of 1745, and forced to preach in the open for a time. He was harassed by the laird of Sumburgh, who encroached upon the lands of the glebe.

John Mill even criticised his fellow ministers, claiming that they were 'lax in principle and practice'. Like other ministers of this period he believed in and actually encountered a personal Satan who spent a great deal of time and effort in opposing him.

Unlike other ministers he approved of the 'independent' preachers who arrived in 1799. He offered his pulpit to James Haldane and the Rev William Innes in spite of the pastoral admonition, issued by the General Assembly of the Church of Scotland, warning the nation against the missionaries of the Society for Propagating the Gospel at Home.

The rival claims of Calvinism and Arminianism did not make much impression on the people of Shetland, but there were many who believed sincerely that the teaching of the Independents was more in accordance with New Testament doctrine than was that of the Church of Scotland, and an outburst of religious fervour swept the islands. The Independents became known as the Congregationalists; Methodist preachers came in 1822 and the first Baptist church was established at Dunrossness in 1815 by a local fisherman, Sinclair Thomson.

None of the ministers of the 1790s could foresee these developments of the next two decades and the minister of Yell could write of his parishioners with some satisfaction. 'In religious matters they enjoy a happy moderation and uniformity of sentiment, their faith not being distracted by controversy nor sectarianism infesting their abodes.'

The Islands

At the end of the eighteenth century Shetland was as backward as it was remote from the Mainland of Britain. Its only road was a stretch between Lerwick and the centre of Tingwall, constructed through the efforts of two leading landowners. It had a thriving export trade with Europe but communications with Scotland were limited to small vessels sailing ten times a year. Shetland was, however, known to the British government as a 'nursery' for good seamen, and the activities of the 'press gang' helped to increase the uncertainty of the period.

There was at least one school in every parish, where pupils received a very elementary education. Tingwall, however, lacked a schoolmaster, for, as the minister commented, no 'decent man' would take charge of the school unless the salary were increased.

The People

Most ministers spoke highly of their parishioners. The minister at Mid & South Yell could say:

> The people, in general, are sober and inoffensive. Crimes of an atrocious nature are little known amongst them. They are judicious, of a ready and acute understanding, capable of enduring great toil, cold and hunger. . . . They prove excellent seamen, when they go abroad, are much esteemed in the British Navy, and considered in this point of view, well merit the attention and favour of government. This observation may be applied with equal justice to Shetland in general.

Already some ministers were complaining of changes in the lives of the people. The minister of Sandsting & Aithsting spoke of a 'great alteration in the mode of living': he complained that tea, though only recently introduced, was drunk in excess by even the poorest families, who would sell their clothes to purchase it; and that a large amount of gin was smuggled into Shetland by Dutch fishermen, Sandsting & Aithsting having thirty or forty 'gin and tea' shops. Both types of beverage were equally hateful to the Rev Patrick Barclay.

Almost all the clothing worn by the family was home-produced. Underwear, socks, pullovers, shawls, scarves and gloves were knitted; woollen 'claith' was woven for making working clothes; and a kind of flannel was woven for women's dresses and underclothes. Most distinctive was the headdress worn by the father of a household—a red knitted cap tapering to a point. Instead of shoes, rivlins of untanned hide or sealskin were worn. At sea, fishermen wore coats made from sheepskin and wide leather boots. These fashions continued for many years longer, but several ministers were critical of the desire of the people to appear better dressed at church and social gatherings, and they complained of a too great extravagance.

It is difficult to see how the people could have been extravagant considering their wages: a labourer received 6d (2½p) a day; a woman servant £1 a year, with a shirt worth 3s (15p) and a pair of shoes worth about the same; a female outdoors servant 10s (50p) a year, with a pair of shoes; and a manservant 15s (75p) and a pair of shoes for nine months' work. No manservant could be obtained during the summer, for at the fishing he could earn the princely sum of £1–£2 for three months' work!

On one point the ministers were all agreed—the deplorable conditions of the crofter-fishermen. Most critical was the Rev John Menzies:

> Many services, the sad marks of slavery are demanded. They must fish for their masters, who either give them a fee entirely inadequate to their labour and their dangers, or take their fish at a lower price than others would give.

The crofter-fisherman was burdened with taxes, more degrading than heavy. He paid his share of the Scottish land tax, generally 3d for each merk of land, but he still paid to Lord Dundas the ancient Norse land tax of skat, in spite of repeated protests that this was a double imposition. To his landlord he paid each year rent, three days' unpaid labour, and a fowl for each merk. To the minister he also paid three days' unpaid labour, plus corn teinds and casual teinds. Corn teinds were paid in cash at the rate of 8d or 10d for each merk. The casual teinds were paid in 2–4 marks (approximately $2\frac{1}{2}$–5lb) butter for each cow; 1d for each sheep, payable in lambs and wool; and twelve ling for each six-oared fishing boat, paid by the crew. Sir Thomas Dundas exacted skat, wattle and sheep and oxpenny, which together varied from 4d to over 1s for each merk. Finally, towards the salary of the parish schoolmaster, the tenant paid 2d for each merk of land.

THE NEW STATISTICAL ACCOUNT

In 1841 the ministers were again asked to contribute information to a survey of the parishes, also combined into a single volume usually referred to as the New Statistical Account.

A few improvements had come by this time. Shetland had a weekly mail service by steamer during half the year, and following the introduction of the penny post the first rural post offices were starting; but the only road was still the few miles between Lerwick and Tingwall.

Education had made rapid progress: in the island of Fetlar, for instance, only seventeen people over the age of fifteen could not read out of a population of 859, though 275 in this age group could not write. Smuggling had been greatly reduced, and in the parish of Sandsting & Aithsting there were only two alehouses, the minister commenting, 'There is no propensity in the people, generally, to indulge to excess in spirituous liquors'. The minister of Fetlar & North Yell also remarked that smuggling had been almost entirely suppressed, but his parishioners had 'fallen into an abominable habit of smoking tobacco'.

Wages had doubled since the 1790s. A labourer received 10d (4p) to 1s 6d (7½p) a day, a housemaid £2 a year and a female farm servant £1 a year, but fishing was still a condition of land tenure and the ministers were still as critical of the conditions of the crofter-fisherman.

Greatest change was in the state of the established church: some ministers could boast that they had no dissenting families in their parishes, but in Lerwick one in three belonged to one of the new denominations, and in Walls & Sandness the ratio was one in seven. There were still some outstanding ministers, such as the Rev John Turnbull of Tingwall, the Rev James Ingram of Unst, and the Rev John Bryden of Sandsting & Aithsting, whose contribution is the most detailed of any in the New Statistical Account.

LIVING CONDITIONS

Until the late nineteenth century a typical Shetland croft house was built of rough stones cemented together with dry mortar; dimensions were usually 28–30ft long and 8–10ft wide. The roof was raised on couples sawn from driftwood overlain by purlings of varying width and thickness, spaced several inches apart. The covering consisted of overlapping slabs of turf, known as pones, overspread in turn with a thick layer of straw, the whole held in place against winter storms with ropes of twisted heather or straw weighted down with large stones.

One had to grope one's way through the byre past the cows to reach the door of the dwelling house. Although insanitary, this arrangement had the advantage of sheltering the house, and the crofter could tend his cattle during severe weather without being exposed to the elements.

The interior of the house was divided by a wooden partition into two rooms—the but end and the ben end. The but end was the kitchen and living-room, whose central peat fire was never allowed to go out. There was no chimney; smoke filled this room, the excess escaping through two or more holes or lums in the roof, and eyes unaccustomed to these conditions smarted and watered continuously from the all-pervading peat smoke.

Dogs enjoyed the right to lodge in the but end, and young

calves, piglets and motherless lambs were reared beside the fire for humanitarian reasons. Hens and chickens sought a change of scenery from their quarters in the byre and kept the floor free of bread crumbs.

The ben end was the bedroom, its large box beds placed along one wall in some cases forming the partition separating the rooms. Usually one box bed was reserved for the sons of the family, one for the daughters and unattached females, and a third for the parents. The box beds had doors that could be drawn during cold weather.

The floors of both rooms were usually of trodden earth, and the walls were left rough but plastered with lime; overhead could be seen the bare rafters and slabs of turf all tanned brown by the perpetual smoke. There were no windows but some light fought its way in, against the smoke, through the roof apertures.

Minor improvements were added throughout the nineteenth century. Glass roof lights appeared, then windows; sometimes the family could not afford to purchase glass and the window space was filled with a fleeceless untanned sheepskin. Towards the end of the century the fireplace began to be set into the gable wall and a proper chimney removed the nuisance of the smoke.

However primitive the old Shetland house may appear from the above description, it was superior to those of many parts of Scotland, such as the 'black houses' of the Hebrides. Two things the Shetlander did have in abundance were peat for fuel, and fish-liver oil for lighting his little iron lamps, known as kollies.

Food

Food was plentiful for eight months of the year. Cabbages were introduced in the seventeenth century, potatoes about 1730. The latter, being a more reliable crop than grain in this climate, soon became the main item in the diet. The grain crop consisted of bere and oats, the former being the more important; it was baked into bread or boiled into porridge.

To prepare bere for milling was a difficult and time-consuming task. It was first threshed to separate the grain from the straw; then the grain was itself heavily threshed to remove loose husks and 'beards' or anns, a process known as hummeling. Winnowing followed, on a special mat called a flaakie, and a final beating in a tub with a shovel was required to remove the last of the troublesome anns.

In such a damp climate it was essential to dry the grain by artificial means before milling. Each croft had a kiln, an oblong stone-walled box situated in the barn. Across the top of the kiln were ribs of wood that were covered with straw before the grain was spread on top. A fire was lit in the free end of the kiln, the smoke escaping into the barn through a flue in the back wall. This rectangular kiln was similar to that used in the Hebrides but different from that used in Orkney and in the parish of Dunrossness in Shetland, where the availability of good building stone enabled the crofter to build a more elaborate circular kiln as an addition to the barn. The old croft house recently restored at Dunrossness provides a good example of a circular kiln.

After milling, two sieves constructed from sheepskin, one coarse and one fine, were used to separate the sids from the meal. The coarse portion removed by the large-holed sieve was fed to the cattle, while the other was again divided into two by the fine sieve to separate the bere meal. Small amounts of grain could be

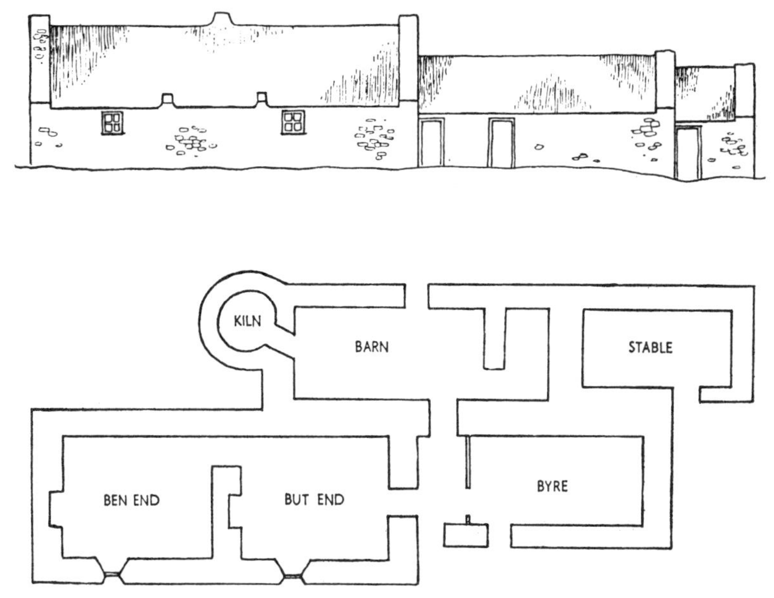

Sketch and plan of old croft complex recently restored at South Voe, Dunrossness

bruised and husked in a 'knocking stane' to produce 'bruised' oats, and small amounts of meal could be produced in a quern or hand-operated mill.

In the early summer seabirds' eggs and their young helped to relieve the food situation. Young kittiwakes were regarded as a great delicacy and in Foula the young of several species were eaten.

Most reliable of all was the constant supply of fish, for nowhere in the world is there such a variety—halibut, skate, haddock, cod, ling, herring, mackerel—and many more, which could be eaten fresh or salted as a standby for the winter. Shellfish were abundant, but, surprisingly, crabs and lobsters were not appreciated. No edible part of the fish was wasted, livers and heads both being used. Several recipes still survive, such as 'liver heads' and 'liver muggies', where the liver is packed either into the heads or the stomach of the fish and boiled.

The most important single species as food was the saithe, especially the young fish, called up to two years old sillocks, and between two and four years old piltocks. The flesh was dark and less inviting than that of other species, but it was the abundance of the shoals and the ease with which they could be caught that made them so important. They provided food for the islanders at seasons of the year when there was nothing else.

Meat was plentiful at hairst (harvest) when the lambs were ready for slaughter, and about Martinmas the people had to decide which cattle they would try and maintain during the winter. The rest were slaughtered and salted in tubs; some joints were hung up and dried after only a few days in pickle. Even in the more sophisticated environment of Lerwick the killing of 'merts' was an annual rite in many households until the end of the nineteenth century.

Nothing of food value was wasted: a sheep's head became the basis of a tasty broth, puddings were made from entrails, and the practice of filling the intestines with chopped meat to be hung up and dried continues in a few localities even today. One practice not appreciated by early visitors was the drying of meat unsalted in larders, or skeos loosely built of stones to allow the wind to penetrate freely, for the smell was abominable. The hard dried meat resulting was called vivda and highly esteemed. Fish preserved by this method was termed 'blawn fish'. In 1817 Dr

Page 67 Bird cliffs at Noss, with gannets on their nesting ledges

Page 68 (above) Rerwick, Dunrossness, c 1930. A typical crofting township with fields of grass, oats and potatoes; *(below)* Maywick, Dunrossness, c 1930, another compact crofting township

Hibbert reported that the skeos were roofless and fallen into decay; but the practice of drying salted fish in strings at the gables of houses still continues.

On the croft, milk was abundant and churning took place up to three times a week. When the butter was on the point of solidifying, it was the custom to throw red-hot stones into the churn to make separation more complete. The attention paid to the purity of the butter depended on whether it was destined for use in the home or for payment of teinds, the latter acquiring a reputation of being fit for little better than greasing cartwheels.

When the butter was removed from the churn, boiling water was poured into the buttermilk. The remaining solids separated to form kirn-milk, a kind of soft cheese, while the remaining acid but pleasant-tasting liquid, known as blaand, was the most common beverage in Shetland until the end of the nineteenth century. Ale was seldom made on account of the scarcity of grain.

Generally speaking the people of Shetland had better food and a more varied diet than did the common people elsewhere in Britain; but on several occasions near famine conditions prevailed. Between 1782 and 1786 the summers were wet and snow came early each year. There was severe loss of livestock with a failure of the crops, and the people could not afford to buy imported meal at £2 5s a boll. Money was raised by subscription by friends in England and Scotland, and government aid bought potatoes and meal to send to the starving islanders. Famine became more serious with increasing population and the neglect of farming caused by the disruptions of the wars with France. In 1803 the grain, meal and bread imported into Shetland was valued at £30,000, a sum greatly exceeding the price of all the fish caught that year, and nearly equal to the amount of all the exports.

Even more distressing was the series of disastrous harvests between 1835 and 1841; in 1836 and 1837 the grain crop was sufficient for four months only each year. Again sums of money were collected by friends in England and Scotland and the Society of Friends assisted generously. Between 1846 and 1849 the potato crop was affected by blight, but famine was averted by organising the construction of a network of roads covering the Mainland and Yell and paying the workers in meal.

THE PRACTICE OF MEDICINE

Many of the early visitors to Shetland commented that although the climate was damp the islands were surprisingly healthy, judging by the number of vigorous old people. The Rev John Brand in 1700 proposed as possible reasons the quality of their diet, the freeness and purity of the air and the sobriety of their living.

Scurvy was the most disturbing disease of the seventeenth and eighteenth centuries, a disease formerly common all over Scotland that lingered longest in Shetland. Sometimes it degenerated into a form of leprosy, when the hair fell from the eyebrows and the nose wasted away. In the Shetland dialect the disease was known as spilt; the victims were set apart from the community in little stone huts among the hills, where they were provided with food and clothing, but exposure to the cold probably hastened death.

Several theories were put forward as to the cause of this disease. Some claimed it was more common in districts such as Dunrossness and Nesting where the greatest amounts of 'grey fish' (saithe) were consumed. In the eighteenth century it was most common in the parish of Walls & Sandness, where the 'lepers' were isolated in a colony outside the township dykes of Papa Stour.

In 1798 a 'leper' from Shetland (probably the last victim of the disease) was treated unsuccessfully in the Edinburgh Infirmary. His doctor diagnosed the disease as Greek elephantiasis and came to the conclusion that it was not contagious but hereditary. It is sad to think that all the men and women who died alone in little stone huts could at least have enjoyed the comfort and companionship of their homes during their last years.

Owing to the remoteness of the islands the people had no immunity to disease transmitted by travellers. In the eighteenth century outbreaks of smallpox occurred regularly in one island or another at twenty-year intervals, at times killing a quarter or a third of the population. In 1720, when the disease reached Foula, the death rate was so great that there were scarcely people left to bury the dead. Fetlar was especially unfortunate : ninety people died there from the disease in 1701, eighty in 1720, 120 in 1740 and ninety in 1760. During the latter epidemic, inoculation was first practised in Shetland, but the fees of the operator were so high that only ten or twelve people could avail themselves of his services. In 1769 another outbreak occurred, by which time several people, professional and amateur, had become skilled in inoculation.

The greatest share of the credit in defeating this disease must go to an uneducated but very intelligent weaver of Northmavine, John Williamson, who discovered an improved method of inoculation. Unlike the record of others, including medical men, it was stated that Williamson had inoculated several thousands and never lost a patient. For a description of his methods we are indebted to the Rev Andrew Dishington, minister of Mid & South Yell:

> He is careful in providing the best matter and keeps it a long time before he puts it to use—sometimes 7 or 8 years. And, in order to lessen its virulence, he first dries it in peat smoke, and then puts it under ground, covered with camphor. . . . He uses no lancet in performing the operation, but, by a small knife, made by his own hands, he gently raises a very little of the outer skin of the arm, so that no blood follows; then puts in a very small quantity of the matter, which he immediately covers with the skin, that had been thus raised. The only plaister he uses, for healing the wound, is a bit of cabbage leaf.

The practice of bloodletting was carried out by native surgeons using an ingenious cupping instrument—the top of a ram's horn perforated at the tip. After making his incision the surgeon placed the horn over the spot, sucked out the air and with his tongue stopped the hole at the top. When half full of blood the horn would fall off.

For the state of health in the early nineteenth century we are indebted to the accounts of two medical men—Dr Edmondston writing in 1808 and Dr Hibbert in 1817. Among infectious diseases, measles and whooping cough were each carried to Shetland three times between 1779 and 1808, the latter being always fatal to many children. Scarlatina and influenza also followed soon after outbreaks in Scotland. Typhoid fever occurred occasionally in every parish.

Consumption was on the increase. Dr Edmondston noted that it was becoming more common through increasing contact with the mainland of Scotland, but he failed to realise that it was the lack of immunity in the islands that made it so deadly when once transmitted. As a cure for scrofula the people believed in the efficacy of the Royal touch, and in the absence of the actual living finger of Royalty, a few coins from the reign of King Charles I were kept and carefully handed down from father to son. In 1841 the minister of Mid & South Yell maintained that there were few localities in Shetland without one or more people who claimed to have been cured by this method.

In 1866 Robert Cowie, a medical student from Lerwick, submitted as his thesis for the degree of MD a study of health in Shetland. It was incorporated in his book *Shetland: Descriptive and Historical*, published in 1871, and provides a comparison between the state of health in Shetland and that in the rest of Scotland. Most interesting of his conclusions was that concerning longevity: he pointed out that over 33 per cent of Shetland people lived longer than seventy years compared with 18 per cent for Scotland as a whole, and 20 per cent in Shetland lived to be over eighty compared with 7·5 per cent in Scotland as a whole.

WELFARE

The traditional system of poor relief is described admirably by the minister of Unst in the Old Statistical Account. The island was divided into fourteen parts called quarters, through which the poor were dispersed, each quarter having its share of people to support. The poor went to each house in rotation and were maintained for as many days as the number of merks of land occupied by the family. When one circuit of the quarter was complete, the poor person began his round again. When anyone applied to be put on the quarter, the minister announced it from the pulpit, and if no one objected on account of the character or means of the applicant he received assistance immediately. The weekly offerings at church, and the more liberal collection taken at the celebration of the sacrament, were used to buy their clothes.

Children were expected to maintain their aged parents when they fell into extreme poverty, but the kirk session helped to buy clothes. Poor families not on the roll also received between 5s (25p) and £1 a year. Infants who had lost both parents were placed in charge of a family recommended by the kirk session, which provided £1 or more a year until the child was ten years old when it was considered part of that family.

When any sudden calamity befell a family or individual, the minister usually spoke on their behalf from the pulpit and appointed a day for a collection to be made. It was common to raise between £2 and £5 by this method. Greatest cause of hardship was the frequent loss of life at sea. In 1810 a Shetland Fishermen's Fund was set up for 'decayed fishermen and their widows', annual payment being 2s (10p) a year. Elderly fishermen thereby were entitled to 5s or 6s (25p or 30p) a year and widows 14s (70p) a year. In 1841 the fund stood at £2,485. After the great disaster of 1832 a sum of £3,000 was raised in England and Scotland, each widow receiving £3, each child under fourteen 10s (50p) and parents depending on a son £2, these continuing as an annual payment until 1843.

The only exceptions to this general spirit of humanity were the actions of some of the lairds. There were instances where, following the loss of a boat and crew, the laird seized a widow's cow from the byre as payment of her husband's debts.

In 1845 the old system of poor relief was abolished with the passing of the Poor Law Amendment Act, and thenceforth the poor were maintained by a parochial board financed by the rates. Assistance became far more impersonal, and one result was a great increase in the number of people seeking assistance. Expenditure on the poor increased from £250 in 1845 to £5,319 in 1869, which was shared by 1,309 paupers. As Dr Cowie pointed out in 1871, much of this was expended in management expenses, inspectors' salaries and law suits to determine the settlement of individual paupers, leaving only 6d (2½p)–1s 6d (7½p) each per week.

As late as 1870 Mr Hay of Hayfield gave evidence before the Poor Law Committee of the House of Commons urging the repeal of the Act and a return to the former system. He pointed out that the gross rental of Shetland after certain deductions was only £21,000, and that the maintenance of the poor was far too great a burden on the heritors.

CHANGES IN LAND USE

Throughout the nineteenth century pressure on the land increased with the rise in population, and a steady diminution of the arable land allotted to each crofter was the result. It was gradual, for under the run-rig system an additional tenant meant only a slightly smaller share for everyone.

A comparison of the two statistical accounts shows the gradual decrease in size of the crofts. The number of ploughs decreased, since the arable land could all be dug by spade; in Northmavine they fell from twenty-eight to twelve, and in Sandsting & Aithsting there were fourteen in the 1790s and none in 1841. The minister of Delting wrote that it was common to have four families on a farm which twenty years earlier had only one. It is unfortunate that the growth of the fishing industry retarded natural progress in agriculture; the population had increased to over 31,000 in 1851, far too many to be accommodated when the importance of agriculture was reasserted.

At the end of the eighteenth century came the first real attempt at land reclamation, when small farms known as outsets came into being. The method was to build a turf and stone dyke round a few acres of moorland, then turn the heather over by spade. Several thousand acres of arable land were cleared in this way, causing complaints from the crofters, who lost grazing land without compensation from the landlord in the form of reduced rent.

The outsets were not successful. They were generally given to a young married couple with no family to assist in the arduous work of land improvement and no funds to provide a stock of cattle, whose manure was absolutely essential to put the land in good condition. They remain today as patches of improved pasture among the hills.

One advantage noted was that, since they were free of run-rig and enclosed, they showed the possibility in Shetland of Scottish-type farming, with the growing of turnips for winter feeding of cattle. The landlords were not slow in applying this principle to the fields of the townships. They had their own fields planked or assembled in one part of the township round their own houses, and in 1841 the minister of Unst remarked that the work of enclosure had been going on 'in a very spirited manner' for the previous three years.

In the 1840s (earlier in a few places) the landowners discovered that farming could be more rewarding financially than fishing, and they started to abandon the system whereby fishing should be a condition of tenancy. No longer were people encouraged to settle on these estates; rents were increased to supposedly economic rates and the people started to move to districts where fishing was still important to the lairds. Vacated crofts were not relet but laid down as pasture for sheep. Even this process was not sufficiently rapid for the landlords, and many tenants were given forty days' notice to quit. When the valley of Veensgarth, Tingwall, was cleared in the 1850s to make a large sheep farm, twenty-one families were removed.

This preliminary policy of clearance met with little opposition from the tenants, for the people were accustomed to move at frequent intervals and few crofts had been held by one family for more than a generation or two. It was when the lairds laid claim to the common grazings that the people objected, and in a few places resisted fiercely.

A circular sent in 1867 to all the tenants of an estate in Unst shows the change of attitude on the part of the lairds following the removal of the scattald from the people. They would still be allowed to graze their animals as before, but charges would be levied of 9d (4p) for each sheep, 1s 6d (7½p) each for cattle and 3s 6d (17½p) for each horse.

Before the second half of the nineteenth century the scattalds were entirely open. The landowners believed they owned the hills, too, but the extent of each laird's share had not been determined. An old Scottish act of 1695 allowed a single landowner to force division of the commons by instituting proceedings in the Court of Session, but it was an expensive procedure, requiring the help of qualified surveyors to assign boundaries, and it had not been attempted in Shetland.

It was only when sheep-farming became a worthwhile proposition that the Shetland lairds asserted their claim to the hills, and as late as 1870, when Dr Cowie wrote his book, the commons had not all been divided. By this time several large farms had appeared with such innovations as fences, steadings, 'Scottish' ploughs, threshing mills and reaping machines. Dr Cowie's comment is valuable: 'In several districts farms have been formed of which the Lothians would not be ashamed, and of which we in Shetland would be more proud than we are were it not for the painful reflection that eviction was generally the first step in this progressive movement.'

The story of the clearances is one of the most neglected aspects of the history of Shetland. Contemporary writers either approved of the policy or mentioned it briefly, and to the laird it was a step, though a drastic one, towards bringing a measure of efficiency into the farming scene; but the social effects were appalling. There are no stories in Shetland of thatch burning over the heads of the tenants or of massive clearances, as in other parts of the Highlands and Islands. In some instances the people were moved only a short distance, at first, on to poorer land, but this was only a prelude to inevitable emigration.

In some cases those evicted were not given other accommodation. When the lands of Garth were cleared by the laird of Quendale in 1874, the houses were stripped and in some cases burned as soon as the tenants were out. Twenty-seven families were evicted at Martinmas and many went immediately to Australia or New Zealand. Not a living soul was left in Garth, Quam, Corston or Neeflan. Land which had been worked for 1,000 years was laid down to sheep, and the names of once populous townships were erased from the map.

The evils have been removed but the people have not returned. There are large areas of Unst, Fetlar, Northmavine and Dunrossness where only sheep now shelter from winter storms within the walls of ruined crofts.

4 MAKINGS OF MODERN SHETLAND

PERHAPS the greatest single factor contributing to the backward state of Shetland at the beginning of the nineteenth century was the lack of representation in Parliament. In theory Orkney and Shetland as one county returned a representative to Westminster, but Shetland had no say in affairs, since only a few Orcadian landowners enjoyed the right to vote. In 1781 Shetland lairds began to agitate for their legal rights, but every attempt was fiercely resisted by the landlords of Orkney, causing a great deal of animosity at this time between the two groups of islands.

This situation was remedied with the passing of the Reform Bill in 1832, which extended the franchise to all proprietors and tenants occupying lands of an annual value of £10. It must have been satisfying for local people to see one of their own countrymen, Arthur Anderson, returned in 1847 as the Liberal member for Orkney and Shetland.

ATTEMPTS AT IMPROVEMENT

The champion of Shetland at this time was Arthur Anderson, a man who rose to prominence in commercial circles in London, yet never forgot his native islands. He was born in 1792 at Gremista near Lerwick and his first job was that of beach boy at Bressay, tending the piles of drying salt fish. At the age of sixteen he joined the Royal Navy and saw much active service until the final defeat of Napoleon in 1815.

Anderson realised the importance of the fishing industry to Shetland, and the necessity of freeing it from the shackles of the laird-tenant relationship. In 1837, then a successful businessman, he started a fish-curing business on the island of Vaila, experimenting with improved methods of drying fish on wooden 'flakes' instead of on the beach. About five years later, this venture was wound up, probably as a result of a general recession in the industry in Shetland, but Arthur Anderson's other business ventures were more successful. He is better known as the co-founder of the Peninsular Steam Company which became the P & O Company in 1840 and is today the largest shipping concern in the world.

He long advocated the establishment of a mail service to Shetland by steamship in place of sailing vessels, and in 1837 offered to provide a regular service by one of his company's vessels. His offer was rejected but the idea was adopted, and in 1838 the mail contract was given to the Aberdeen, Leith, Clyde & Tay Shipping Company, whose paddle-steamer *Sovereign* had begun running experimentally in 1836.

In June 1836 Arthur Anderson started Shetland's first newspaper, *The Shetland Journal*, which continued until the end of 1837, when it was enlarged into *The Orkney and Shetland Journal*. The publication was edited and largely written by Anderson, and printed and published in London for circulation in the islands—an unsatisfactory arrangement, but there was no firm in either Orkney or Shetland that could undertake the operation. When the demands of the shipping company began to occupy more and more of his time, Anderson appealed in vain for someone to take over the journal, and reluctantly he had to cease publication. The failure of these projects was not due to any lack of ability in their founder, but to the lack of men in the islands with the ability to support him and develop his ideas.

In 1862 came Arthur Anderson's great gift to Shetland, the Anderson Educational Institute at Lerwick. As commendable was the erection of the Widows' Homes at Lerwick in 1865, three years before his death.

Arthur Anderson was not the first 'free' merchant in Shetland. Between 1820 and 1830 some of the lairds had abandoned their direct interest in the fishing industry, and other merchants set up business in their stead. Prices for fish, farm produce and knitwear became higher and demand was stimulated by the introduction of a regular steamer service; but the overall condition of the crofter remained the same and the system of barter remained fundamental to trade.

Not until 1872 was the first attempt made to investigate the social problems of the islands, when a commissioner visited Shetland to enquire into the relationship between merchant and tenant. The main concern was the extent of truck or barter as a settlement of wages, hence the name Truck Commission.

Every commercial concern within the islands was investigated and few lairds or merchants emerged with credit. There were still instances where the fishermen were bound to deliver their fish to the laird and if one dared sell to a free merchant the result was forty days' notice to vacate one's house and croft. Most common abuse was the reluctance of the merchants to pay cash for eggs and hosiery; they preferred to pay in clothing, and groceries, rounding off the odd pennies with sweets. If a knitter insisted on taking cash, a reduction was made at the rate of 25 per cent.

The Truck Acts that followed made this practice illegal but did not stop it entirely. As late as 1908 dealers at Lerwick were fined for making deductions in cash payments. The merchants pleaded that they had such small reserves of ready cash that they were forced to make payment in kind, and the general reduction in trade that followed these prosecutions tends to confirm the merchants' allegations.

Local government was next to be reorganised. In the 1880s Shetland was governed by the Commissioners of Supply, a body of landowners and other influential people, which since 1667 had collected the Scottish land tax and decided how it should be spent. There were also Justices of the Peace, the County Roads Trustees (set up by the special Zetland Roads Act of 1864) and the local authority under the Contagious Diseases (Animals) Act of 1878. Parish Councils administered the Poor Law and School Boards organised education in each parish. In 1889 came the important Local Government (Scotland) Act, which established Zetland County Council, a body of representatives elected by the people.

The ZCC took over many of the functions of local government, but poor relief, lunacy, education and licensing were left to their appropriate bodies, and the Commissioners of Supply remained in existence with reduced responsibility. Under the Local Government (Scotland) Act of 1929 all these other bodies were abolished and Zetland County Council was reconstituted.

The Crofters' Commission

Only eleven years after the investigations of the Truck Commission, crofters, lairds, merchants and ministers were again asked to give evidence before the Napier Commission, which visited Shetland in 1883 to make an investigation, long overdue, into the state of the crofters. Its report, like that of the Truck Commission, is a valuable account of the economic and social state of the islands during those troubled years.

There had been some improvements since 1872: accounts were settled more frequently by laird and merchant; cash was given more readily as payment for goods; the developing herring industry had given a boost to the commerce of the islands. But still the crofters suffered under an unjust system. The landlord could increase his rents at will and in some places still exacted his three days' unpaid labour and 'a fowl for each merk'.

Complaints varied from district to district. Poor housing conditions, the lack of security, the constant threat of eviction were charges made by some crofters. Others complained that instead of paying them for improvements made to house and land, the laird raised the rent since the property was more valuable. Most serious complaint was the removal of the common grazing from the tenants, which had reduced the numbers of sheep kept by the crofters, with less wool to make clothing, and less mutton to be salted for food in winter.

.The report of the Napier Commission led to the Crofters' Holdings Acts of 1886, which have often been called the crofters' 'Magna Carta'. Among other conditions they established security of tenure, compensation for improvements and a guaranteed fair rent. They also restored to the crofters the use of the scattald.

The Crofters' Commission was established to travel throughout the Highlands and Islands to listen to appeals of crofters against their landlords. It began sittings at Dunrossness on 24 August 1889—an event so important that word was sent to fishermen on the fishing grounds, who hauled their lines and made for the shore. A new spirit of expectancy and emancipation was in the air. The editor of *The Shetland News* recorded that the crofters 'gave their evidence as a rule in an unhesitating way, like men who knew their rights and meant to have them'.

A charge levied against the Crofters' Holdings Acts is that they perpetuated a system of uneconomic holdings, freezing the distribution of land in a position in which it has remained to this day. This is undoubtedly true, for although they established the civil rights of the tenants they did not solve the problems of agriculture in Shetland.

Further legislation was passed to reverse the process of enlargement, to increase the number of smallholders on some estates. The Smallowners (Scotland) Act of 1911 gave the Board of Agriculture power to establish smallholdings by agreement with the landlord, or compulsion if necessary. The Land Settlement (Scotland) Act of 1919 allowed compulsory purchase of land by the board.

Between 1915 and 1929, seventy-nine new holdings were created and 197 enlargements made, causing the resettlement of 315 people. Veensgarth farm was broken up in 1923 into nineteen new holdings and ten enlargements, largely restoring the situation of 100 years before. Today the Department of Agriculture owns the estate of Westafirth in Yell, bought in 1925, with the creation of four new holdings and twelve enlargements; the estate of Ordale in Unst, bought in 1928, and creating thirteen new holdings and seven enlargements; the estate of Cliff in Unst; and part of Fetlar, bought in 1964–5.

EDUCATION

Although a few primitive schools were established by the church after the Reformation they soon were abandoned. Education remained the preserve of the clergy and the lairds and they were slow in making it available to the people. In 1700 the Rev John Brand complained of the lack of education in Shetland, and suggested that a 'Latine School' be set up either at Scalloway or Lerwick; but more than twenty years were to pass before any action was taken.

On 14 November 1724 a meeting was called of all the heritors of Shetland, presided over by Thomas Gifford of Busta, steward and justiciar-depute of the islands. He pointed out that there was an act of government by which the landlords of each district were obliged to settle a fund for establishing a school in each parish. There was, it was pointed out, the added benefit that in each parish where a 'legal' school was set up the Society in Scotland for Propagating Christian Knowledge (established in

1709) would maintain a second school. It was agreed that such a fund would be provided, one half being raised by an extra imposition on the tenants.

In 1798 the Rev John Kemp of the SSPCK visited Shetland and was surprised to find that while the Society had erected nine schools, there were only two parochial schools. The SSPCK sent an ultimatum to the heritors of Shetland stating that unless they fulfilled their obligation, the Society would remove the schools it had provided. Within a few years each district had a parochial school, and the number of 'charity schools' also increased.

At the beginning of the nineteenth century there was a variety of schools in Shetland. Besides parochial schools and those maintained by the SSPCK, there were 'assembly schools' supported by special funds voted by the General Assembly of the Church of Scotland; and private schools, a few of which were run by ministers, providing tuition for the sons of gentlemen, which fitted them for further study at the universities of Aberdeen or Edinburgh.

A few schoolmasters could teach navigation and arithmetic, but as late as 1841 the minister of Lerwick commented that 'though conducted by estimable, zealous and right minded men, the mere attainment of reading and writing combined with the almost mechanical reading of the scriptures form the staple of the education'. Many children were taken from school when they could read a little. They had to learn to write by themselves in later years.

Whatever the limitations of the education received by the pupils, who walked barefoot to school each carrying a peat as his contribution to the heating system, it was in these little thatched schoolrooms that hundreds of Shetlanders received a basic schooling that enabled them to reach the rank of captain in the Merchant Navy.

Arthur Anderson played a great part in promoting education in Shetland. He provided a school and teacher for the then neglected islands of Out Skerries; he supported Lerwick Instruction Society, which was instituted in 1855 'for the Gratuitous Education of the Poor Children of the Town and Neighbourhood'; but the climax of all his philanthropic schemes was the building of the Anderson Educational Institute in 1862.

Mr Anderson proposed to provide a combined elementary and

upper school at Lerwick, the lower school to teach reading, writing and arithmetic to those children whose parents could not afford the fees of the parochial school. It was to be maintained by reduced fees and public subscription, and in order to receive government aid it was to be open for examination by government inspectors.

The higher school was to teach classics and the higher branches of education generally. It was supposed that parents who did not have to use the lower school for their children's education would be prepared to pay reasonable fees for their higher education, thus lessening the rates for the lower school. It was also hoped that the standard would be at least as high as that of seminaries on the mainland of Scotland.

Mr Anderson suggested that local aid might be forthcoming to run the school, but subscription lists at the school and at the Union Bank of Lerwick resulted in a trivial sum being raised and the donor of the school had also to finance its operation. The higher school of the Anderson Educational Institute was first to open on 4 August 1862. The opening of the lower school was delayed until the outcome was known of a bill before Parliament that would have excluded all elementary schools from public assistance unless under a parochial assessment. When the school eventually opened on 28 November 1862, sixty pupils enrolled immediately. The two sections remained until 1905, when the lower school was absorbed by Lerwick Central School.

The Education Act of 1872 had tremendous effects on schooling in Shetland. It made education compulsory and put the cost of education on the parish rates, assisted by the fees of the pupils. The most pronounced effect was the abandonment of the old thatched schoolrooms and the building of plain but commodious schools, many of which are incorporated in the enlarged schools of today. A further improvement was the Act of 1889, which made education free.

There were still problems to be surmounted in Shetland. In 1902 an inspector's report showed that at no fewer than twelve schools were there no pupils under seven years old, and that at seventeen of the sixty-three schools the average attendance was less than 75 per cent. Poor roads or their complete absence were the causes. Those were the days before school meals, when parents in winter were reluctant to send a child of five or six to a school perhaps 3 miles away over the hills, with a bere meal bannock carried in his school bag as lunch. The same report shows that forty-four of these schools presented 213 candidates for merit certificates, and 155 were successful, giving a pass rate of almost 73 per cent.

At first the Anderson Educational Institute was attended mainly by pupils from Lerwick and the immediate neighbourhood, for children in remote country districts could only benefit if they found lodgings in town; but this situation was remedied much later by two generous gifts. The first was the Brùce Hostel for girls provided by Robert Bruce, the laird of Sumburgh, which was opened in 1923, and was at that time the finest schoolgirls' hostel in Scotland. The second was the Janet Courtney Hostel for boys, almost completed in 1939, but not occupied by schoolboys until after the end of World War II.

HEALTH AND HOUSING

The living conditions of rural Shetland have been described in Chapter 3, but conditions in the working-class area of Lerwick were much worse. Rural poverty retains a certain dignity, but urban poverty quickly degenerates into squalor. In 1808 Dr Edmondston remarked that typhoid fever was endemic in parts of the town. The cause was obvious, for in 1885, when there was yet another outbreak in Lerwick, it was reported that sewage was lying in heaps on top of the sewers. Drinking water was proved to be affected and the old Baker's well, dear to many generations of Lerwegians, was closed.

The Public Health Act of 1897 provided for a sanitary inspector in Lerwick, with assistants in every district, but they could do little more than report what they saw. Not until after World War I did Lerwick start to tackle its housing problem and erase many of its eyesores.

In rural districts improvements came as slowly. In 1883 new houses were still being built with straw roofs, but one end was generally wood-floored and there were chimneys on both gables. After the Crofters' Commission brought security of tenure, crofters themselves began to carry out minor improvements. Emigration, too, eased the problem of overcrowding in many houses, and the average number of persons per room fell from 3·18 in 1861

Page 85 (above) The broch of Mousa, the best example of an Iron Age fort; *(below)* Jarlshof, showing post-broch 'Wheel-house'

Page 86 (above) An isolated croft, early twentieth century; *(below)* interior of an old croft house showing open fire and back-stane, early twentieth century

to 1·58 in 1911; but little real improvement was done until 1919, when the Housing Town Planning (Scotland) Act became law.

The task was formidable. Sanitation was practically non-existent; except in parts of Lerwick and Scalloway there were no drainage facilities and no public water supply; wells were shallow holes relying more on surface water than springs, and open to passing animals, including dogs, which it was believed were instrumental in the spread of hydatid disease. Efforts were made to line the walls with concrete and provide lids, and by 1923 this process was in full swing.

The public was strangely opposed to such innovations as sanitary conveniences of even the most elementary type. The authorities had power under the act of 1919 to insist on this provision, and the sanitary inspector could report with some satisfaction that in 1922 104 crofters had agreed to erect wooden closets.

In 1929 the sanitary inspector reported as follows:

> Generally thatched roofs have largely disappeared . . . walls have been heightened and are more waterproof, windows are larger and can be opened, earthen floors have largely disappeared, porches are being erected and box beds are mostly dismantled.

Unfortunately improvements in housing were not followed immediately by improvements in health. There was even the suggestion made that the smoke-filled houses of a previous generation kept tuberculosis at bay, and their eradication caused the terrible spread of the disease.

Infectious diseases such as scarlet fever remained endemic until the 1930s, at times assuming epidemic proportions with a peak of 243 notified cases in 1934. Typhoid fever, sometimes fatal, flourished in the insanitary conditions of the more densely populated districts like Lerwick, Sound and Hamnavoe. The fever hospital at Lerwick, built in 1888 at a cost of £1,500, was hard pressed to cope.

TB was for long the scourge of the islands, disturbing in that the Scottish deathrate declined steadily after 1900, but Shetland's remained alarmingly high. Even in 1924, when TB caused fifty-eight deaths in Shetland, the rate per 1,000 of population stood at 1·85 compared with the all-Scottish rate of 0·8. TB was by far the greatest killer, accounting in some years for one-fifth of all deaths. In 1933 it caused 25·4 per cent of all deaths between the ages of 1 and 65, compared with heart disease 13·1 per cent, and cancer 16·1 per cent.

By 1925 the encouraging work of the special wards of the fever hospital was being noticed, and in 1928 a sanatorium built at a cost of £15,000 marked a new era in combating the disease. As important were the improvements in housing standards and the greater efforts to isolate patients. Not until 1936 could the MOH report that Shetland had passed the crisis of the TB epidemic, with a death rate in line with that of the rest of Scotland.

Smallpox has been completely eradicated, but it is strange, considering the previous tragic history of epidemics, that the people of Shetland should be so opposed to vaccination. After the introduction of the 'conscientious objection' clause in the Vaccination (Scotland) Act of 1907 the numbers of children being protected fell steadily throughout Scotland, and in Shetland the practice was almost abandoned. In 1927 successful vaccinations were carried out on only 5·7 per cent of total births, compared with 57·2 per cent for the whole of Scotland. In 1937 the corresponding figures were 4·4 and 40·3 per cent. It is fortunate that the islands escaped so easily after World War II, for several Shetlanders returned from the East on ships that reported cases of smallpox on arrival in the UK.

Shetland's medical statistics are not all depressing. Longevity has already been commented upon, and even more outstanding is the low rate of infant mortality. In the early decades of this century, the rate for Shetland was frequently half that for the whole of Scotland: 1937 was typical with a rate in Shetland of 32 per 1,000 births compared to a national figure of 70 per 1,000.

The first real hospital in Shetland was not provided until 1902, when two sisters, Miss Inga Bain and Mrs Isabella Anderson, left money for the endowment of a hospital in memory of their brother. Thus was built the Gilbert Bain Memorial Hospital, costing £2,411, with accommodation for four male and four female patients. The first matron had a salary of £50 per year, out of which she had to pay her own board, though she did receive free firing and lighting. At first surgical work was carried out by general practitioners, and major cases were sent to Edinburgh by sea, a journey that proved fatal to many patients.

The work of the GB Hospital was improved in 1921 with the installation of an X-ray plant and electric lighting. Then in 1924 the first resident surgeon, Mr Rose-Innes, was appointed, his salary being paid partly by the Scottish Board of Health. In his first 13½ months at Lerwick he performed 350 operations and the number of patients forced to attend Edinburgh Royal Infirmary dropped from sixty-four in 1924 to only twenty in 1927.

After World War II further improvements were carried out; the hospital was enlarged slightly and in 1947 a full-time radiographer and physiotherapist were appointed. Specialists from the mainland of Scotland had already started to visit Lerwick under the auspices of the local authority. However, the inadequacies of the old GB were obvious and plans were afoot for a new hospital.

POPULATION CHANGES

A large population is not necessarily an indication of economic or social well-being. Although the population of Shetland stood around 30,000 for much of the nineteenth century, there was full employment only during the summer months and prosperity for only the most efficient of the merchant-lairds.

It had long been obvious that emigration was the only solution to the problem of the islands. Even in 1774, when the population was about 17,000, George Low wrote that the Shetlanders 'complain much of their landlords that they don't give them worth their labour for their fish . . .'; and adds, 'could they get themselves properly headed, I believe [they] would emigrate from most parts of the country in shoals'.

At this time it was in the interests of the lairds to encourage fishermen to remain on their estates, and the people themselves did not have even the resources to meet the cost of emigration; so Shetland did not participate in the hysteria of mass emigration that swept Scotland at the end of the eighteenth century.

A change in attitude occurred at the beginning of the nineteenth century, when thousands of Shetlanders were forcibly enlisted into the Royal Navy. For the first time they could compare conditions in Shetland with those in other parts of Britain and overseas. When peace was restored, many sailors did not return to Shetland; they emigrated or joined the Merchant Navy where, they now realised, their seamanship was highly valued.

The poor harvests of the 1830s and 1840s increased the trickle of emigrants. After 1851 the natural increase in the population was equalled by the rate of emigration, and in the three census years between 1851 and 1871 the population remained steady at over 31,000, with an all-time peak in 1861.

It is customary to place the blame for depopulation on the land policy of the lairds in the second half of the nineteenth century, but emigration had commenced a few decades before this. Certainly the clearances increased the flow of emigrants, to make it an uncontrollable spate before the end of the century. In some places the lairds actively encouraged emigration: in 1874, for example, when the Garth estate at Dunrossness was cleared to make a sheep run, the estate helped to arrange assisted passages to New Zealand. Emigration was also encouraged by the laird in Fair Isle. Some islanders went to Orkney in the 1830s, and in March 1862 came the blackest day in the history of the island when 148 inhabitants sailed on the first stage of a journey to St John, New Brunswick.

Between 1871 and 1881, 4,640 Shetlanders emigrated. The Crofters' Holdings Acts reduced the flow for a time, but the pattern had become established and encouraging reports from Canada, the USA, Australia and New Zealand induced more people to join their relatives.

The herring boom of the 1890s and early 1900s caused a tremendous improvement in the economy of the islands, reducing emigration to an average of under 200 a year. Men actually returned from the colonies and invested their modest savings in sailing drifters. At first the sailboats rewarded their owners handsomely, but soon they became obsolete, with the introduction of coal-burning steam drifters. The rate of emigration again increased, in direct proportion to the rate of decrease in the numbers of sailboats.

The decline in rural communities was even more marked than is indicated in the population graph (p 92). Lerwick actually increased in population at the end of the nineteenth century, though for many a move to the town was merely the first step in a move farther afield. The heavy losses during two World Wars aggravated the downward trend. It became so marked in some islands that insufficient young men were left to provide essential ferry services, thus causing the removal of entire communities.

Long after poverty had been abolished, emigration continued as a psychological phenomenon in the belief, then universally held, that the grass must be greener on the other side of the ocean. In the mid-1960s few Shetlanders emigrated to the Dominions, though many sought employment in the towns of Scotland. Only in the late 1960s was the downward trend halted.

From being a necessary step to alleviate a serious problem, depopulation became itself the most serious problem facing the islands. Until about 1913 depopulation was due to an excess of emigration over a diminishing natural increase, but later it was due to the combined effects of emigration and a more serious natural decrease.

Most of the emigrants were young single men and an excess of females over males was inevitable: the census of 1861 showed 18,600 females compared with 13,000 males, though this is partly explained by the absence of men at sea. A low marriage rate resulted: in the decade 1921–31, when emigration alone accounted for a loss of almost 2,500 people, Shetland's annual marriage rate varied between 3·8 and 5·1 per 1,000 compared with a rate of between 6·4 and 8·0 for Scotland as a whole. A low birthrate was the natural consequence: it dropped from 15·0 per 1,000 in 1921 to 12·1 in 1931, while the Scottish figures showed a drop from 25·2 to 19·0. It remained low for a long time, but since World War II the rate has gradually improved until it is now much nearer the Scottish figure.

With an ever-increasing proportion of elderly people, a high deathrate was also inevitable: in 1921 it was 16·0 per 1,000, compared with 13·6 for the whole of Scotland, and in 1931 the figures were 17·2 for Shetland and 13·3 for the whole of Scotland. This did not indicate a deterioration in the health of the community, for in 1931 66·5 per cent of all deaths were of people over 65 years of age.

The most noticeable effect of a century of depopulation is that some islands have become entirely abandoned, including South

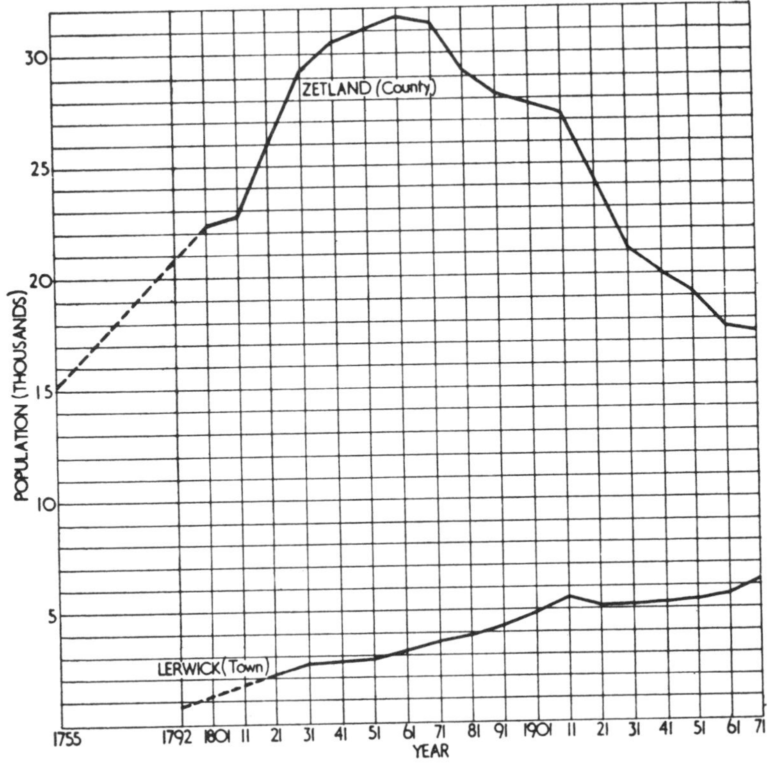

Population trends 1755–1971 for the whole county and for Lerwick

Havera, Hildasay, Papa, Linga, Oxna and Langa near Scalloway. These are all small islands that attracted residents only because they could support a few families, and settlement there indicates the extent of the pressure on the land in the early nineteenth century. More depressing is the decrease in population in large fertile islands such as Fetlar and Papa Stour, which in 1841 contained respectively 761 and 382 people but in 1970 only 106 and 26.

The thousands of Shetlanders who emigrated did not forget their native islands, since practically everyone in Shetland has relatives abroad with whom they correspond. There are Shetland Societies in the major towns of the Dominions and the USA, and young people often come to Shetland to locate the birthplace and relatives of a grandparent.

SHETLAND AND THE WARS

Long before the end of injustice and oppression, even before representation in parliament, Shetlanders had come to regard themselves as British, though with a Scandinavian heritage. This was first evident at the end of the eighteenth century when the nation was threatened by the military might of France. During the Napoleonic wars over 3,000 Shetlanders fought in the British armed forces; most of these were seamen pressed into joining the Royal Navy, but even then the tradition of voluntary service was well established.

Shetland's contribution to the British Navy is discussed more fully in Chapter 8. Its contribution to the land forces is as commendable, though on a much smaller scale. The history of voluntary military service goes back to 1760, when a corps known as the Shetland Invincibles was raised at Lerwick; it is not known how long it lasted, but between 1780 and 1815 volunteers again formed a corps, called the Orkney and Shetland Fencibles.

In addition to the Fencibles, who were enlisted for permanent service anywhere in Britain, men volunteered as part-time soldiers for local defence. At the end of the eighteenth century a battalion of Lerwick infantry was raised, and two companies were still in existence in 1808.

In 1860 the 1st Zetland Rifles were raised, reaching full company strength in 1866; but they were disbanded through waning interest, partly because of the popularity of the Royal Naval Reserve in attracting recruits. In 1900 the War Office gave permission for an infantry unit to be raised again in Shetland, and proposed that it be attached to the Seaforth Highlanders. When it was pointed out that Shetland was more closely associated with Aberdeen than with the Highlands, the War Office agreed that Shetland's infantry unit could be designated the 7th Volunteer Battalion, the Gordon Highlanders. The level of interest locally was amazing, and 300 men volunteered, including seventy from Scalloway alone.

In 1904 the German High Seas Fleet anchored off Lerwick, and the crews came ashore, ostensibly for recreation and sightseeing; but they caused much ill feeling among the Shetlanders by their arrogance and inquisitiveness, which contrasted sharply with the hospitality extended to them. Relations between Britain and Germany were rapidly worsening at this time, and it is almost certain that the Germans were spying in preparation for the inevitable conflict.

World War I

At the outbreak of war the two Shetland companies of Gordon Highlanders were posted to France. They took part in the various battles round the Somme, and suffered such heavy losses at the battle of the River Ancre that during later regrouping the special Shetland sections could not be formed. The survivors were posted to other units of the Scottish division.

As usual a far greater number of Shetlanders served at sea. Approximately 3,000 served in the Merchant Navy and another 1,560 served in the special Shetland section of the RNR, which was trained locally.

The islands themselves played a great part in the war. Since the English Channel was heavily guarded, enemy shipping could only gain access to the Atlantic by passing to the north or south of Shetland. Batteries armed with 6-in guns were placed on Bressay and the headland of the Knab to guard Lerwick harbour, and also on the island of Vementry. Catfirth became a base for seaplanes, and Swarbacks Minn, an inlet off St Magnus Bay, became an advanced naval base, subsidiary to that of Scapa Flow in Orkney. From Swarbacks Minn the 10th Cruiser Squadron, consisting of armed liners and fast destroyers, patrolled the northern seaways, intercepting enemy shipping and escorting neutral ships to Lerwick for examination. From Swarbacks Minn the 17,000 ton White Star liner *Oceanic* sailed on her last voyage, to be wrecked on a reef near the island of Foula.

In March 1917 the convoy system was introduced, and merchant ships from all parts of Britain were escorted to Lerwick before crossing the North Sea under the protection of armed trawlers and destroyers. In a period of less than a year, 4,500 ships of approximately 5 million tons sailed from Lerwick. Early in 1918, when the problem of the U-boats had been overcome, Lerwick ceased to be a convoy port.

Many ships were sunk by U-boats east of Shetland, their graves marked only with wreck symbols on the fishing charts of the North Sea. Fishing at this time was, of course, severely restricted. In one incident in June 1915 German U-boats attacked the herring fleet off Out Skerries and sank sixteen Scottish drifters, leaving one or two to carry home the crews, but only one fisherman died as a result of wounds.

After the war Shetland's contribution was recorded in *Shetland's Roll of Honour and Roll of Service*, which lists the names of the 621 men who died. This includes about ninety emigrants serving with the forces of the Dominions, but Shetland's actual share of over 500 is a greater proportionate loss than that of any other county in Britain.

World War II

Again in 1939 the islands were inundated with servicemen, and Shetlanders played their part in all three branches. Sullom Voe was established as an RAF base, and batteries manned by units of the Royal Artillery were built at the entrances to Lerwick and Scalloway harbours. With the fall of Norway the islands became even more vulnerable as possible stepping-stones for an invasion of Britain, and on several occasions such an invasion was believed imminent.

Civilians suffered more in this war than in its predecessor. Lighthouses were singled out for attack by enemy aircraft, the South Lighthouse on Fair Isle being especially unfortunate: a keeper's wife was killed by a shell fired through a window, and later the station was bombed and the wife and daughter of another keeper were killed. The lighthouse shore station at Out Skerries was bombed and a keeper's wife died of injuries. Floating mines exploding on the beaches were a constant menace, damaging houses and killing adults and inquisitive children.

Perhaps best known of all are the exploits of a small band of Norwegian patriots, based first at Lunna and later at Scalloway, who sailed their fishing vessels across the North Sea to their Nazi-occupied homeland, to land ammunition and saboteurs and return with refugees. Late in 1943 the US Navy lent three subchasers for this important work. Altogether 206 missions were sailed, 192 men and 383 tons of military stores were landed, 73 agents and 373 refugees were brought back, and 10 boats and 44 crewmen were lost.

Apart from these operations thousands of Norwegian civilians made their escape independently in tiny fishing vessels and even rowing boats, though many were lost on the way. Of the 5,000 who escaped to Britain, most came via Shetland. In 1941 alone, 1,881 refugees passed through Lerwick.

As for Shetland's own war losses, they were lighter than those of the previous war, but again no town or county in Britain suffered a greater proportion of men killed. At the end of the war Shetland mourned over 300 who would not return.

Effects of the Wars

Nothing could compensate for the tremendous loss of life inflicted upon the islands, for those who died were generally young men who might have rebuilt their islands had they survived. The wars created full employment for the islanders, however, and wages ran at levels never known before. After World War II Shetland shared in the changes that swept the whole country, to make the islands 'fit for heroes to live in', but real prosperity did not come until two decades later.

The scars of war remain in partly demolished fortifications at headlands near Lerwick and Scalloway, the wilderness of concrete gables at Graven, and the 'tank traps' at Mavis Grind and near Lerwick. There are still relics from World War I at Catfirth, and the big guns on the island of Vementry, still pointing across St Magnus Bay, are now of historic interest.

5 COMMUNICATIONS

ANNEXATION by Scotland made little difference at first to the islands, for they remained Norse in outlook and the old links with Norway remained strong. Growing trade during the sixteenth and seventeenth centuries also resulted in a considerable amount of contact between Shetland and North Germany. Each little port in Shetland traded directly with the Continent, whence the lairds and clergy ordered all their domestic supplies.

Shetland's European outlook was enhanced when Dutch herring fishermen came in large numbers during the seventeenth and eighteenth centuries. They arrived in May each year and the islanders were delighted to see them, not only on account of the tea, tobacco and spirits they smuggled ashore but also for news of the outside world after a long winter of silence. Even that dour Presbyterian minister, the Rev John Mill, writing in his diary in 1787 called their arrival 'an agreeable sight'.

Between Shetland and the rest of Britain communications remained very poor. It was popular to regard the islands as utterly remote and a journey there an ordeal. In 1700 the Rev John Brand wrote after his visit: 'It repents none of us of our voyage thither however dangerous it did prove'.

The diaries of the parish ministers describe the difficulties encountered in their efforts to attend the General Assembly of the Church of Scotland in Edinburgh each year. In 1733 the Rev James Grierson had to leave his manse in March to be certain of reaching Edinburgh by May. It is significant that he first took ship to Hamburg, thence to Leith; and it was not until the end of the eighteenth century that communications with Scotland became as important as those with Europe. From the Old Statistical Account it is clear that Leith was the usual terminus, with Aberdeen of secondary importance.

Although the transfer of information, whether by letter or newspaper, was hampered by the irregularity of the sailings, it must not be thought that Shetlanders were uninterested in or ignorant of foreign affairs. There were so many islanders in the British Navy, travelling to every corner of the globe, and so many foreign fishermen who made Shetland their base in summer, that the Shetlander was more accustomed to foreigners, more cosmopolitan in outlook, than the inhabitants of any other part of Britain.

ORGANISED SEA ROUTES

Although steam propulsion became established in the early nineteenth century, sailing vessels continued to play an important role for the next sixty or seventy years. Best known locally was the 107 ton clipper *Matchless*, owned by the Zetland New Shipping Company, which plied between Leith and Lerwick from 1846 to 1882. Built in Aberdeen at a contract price of £2,000, her length was 89ft, her beam 18ft, and her depth of hold 11·4ft. For accommodation she had a large fore-cabin or steerage, and a four-berth cabin (an innovation) for ladies. Her record time of twenty-four hours from Lerwick to Leith roads was never beaten by a sailing vessel. For many years the fare was 5s (25p) single.

For over a century a single firm has dominated sea communications between Shetland and the Scottish Mainland. Formed in 1810 as the Aberdeen, Leith, Clyde & Tay Shipping Company, it became the North of Scotland & Orkney & Shetland Steam Navigation Company in 1875. In 1953, with the predominance of motor vessels in its fleet, the old term 'shipping company' replaced 'steam navigation company'. In 1961 the company was taken over by Coast Lines, which is now part of the P & O Group.

The company's interest in steam began in 1825 with a paddle-steamer running between Aberdeen and Leith. Gradually the service was extended round the North of Scotland, and in 1836 the new paddle-steamer *Sovereign* included in her itinerary a fortnightly call at Lerwick during the summer. Built at Port Glasgow and of 378 tons gross, the *Sovereign*'s dimensions were 158·7ft × 24·7ft × 13·5ft, and her engines generated 240 hp. From the beginning, Aberdeen was the headquarters of the firm, while Leith occupied the secondary position of southern terminus.

In 1838 the company was awarded a government contract to carry mail to Orkney and Shetland by steamer once a week between April and October. During the rest of the year mail was still carried by sailing packets whose service was irregular and unreliable. In January 1852 the schooner *William Hogarth* was lost with all hands in a storm east of Shetland.

In 1858 a fortnightly winter run was started by paddle-steamer, but paddles proved unsuitable for winter conditions in this area, and only when the screw-driven SS *Queen* of 448 tons was acquired in 1861 was a reliable weekly winter service begun. A further improvement took place in 1866, when a mid-weekly call at Lerwick was added during the summer.

During this main period of expansion, the tradition began of naming the ships after saints with definite or supposed northern connections. The SS *St Magnus* of 618 tons appeared in 1867, the 641 ton SS *St Clair* in 1868 and the 787 ton SS *St Nicholas* in 1871. With the older *Queen*, these vessels constituted a first-class fleet.

At first the company's only port of call in Shetland was Lerwick, but in 1881 it was decided to increase the runs to three a week in summer and two a week in winter, the extra run to serve Scalloway and the other western ports of Shetland. This service came to an end in 1939.

It is not surprising, considering the dangers of this sea route, that several vessels were lost. Vessels wrecked this century include the SS *St Rognvald* in 1900 at Orkney, the SS *St Giles* in 1902 north of Aberdeen, the SS *St Nicholas* near Wick in 1914, and the SS *St Sunniva* on Mousa in 1930. It is remarkable that no lives were lost in any of these ships.

In wartime the story was different. In World War I three vessels were lost and seven crew members drowned. In World War II casualties were much heavier. Several of the company's vessels were commandeered by the Admiralty, the SS *St Magnus* serving at Narvik, and the SS *St Clair* taking part in the occupation of Iceland. The SS *St Clement* and SS *St Fergus* were both lost, one by enemy action, the other following a collision. The 'new' SS *St Sunniva* disappeared with all hands in the Bay of Fundy while serving as a rescue ship for a North Atlantic convoy.

On the normal route between Leith and Shetland, the SS *St Rognvald* and SS *St Magnus* were both attacked by enemy aircraft but survived. Not so fortunate in the end was the SS *High-*

lander: on 1 August 1940 her guns downed two enemy aircraft, and she steamed into Leith with the wreckage of one of them on deck; but this heroic deed received too much publicity and she was marked for revenge. Her name was changed to *St Catherine*, but to no avail, and on 14 December 1940, on her way to Lerwick, she was sunk by a German aeroplane a few miles north of Aberdeen with the loss of thirteen crew members and one passenger.

Many changes have occurred in the last few decades. The first motor vessel was the *Earl of Zetland*, built in 1939, and in the years following World War II the entire fleet was replaced by motor vessels. In 1971 the port of Leith was dropped from the itinerary, all cargo for Shetland now being handled at Aberdeen; the last vessel to operate the indirect run Leith-Aberdeen-Kirkwall-Lerwick was the MV *St Ninian*, sold to Canadian owners in April 1971.

The mid-1970s saw the replacement of the company's fleet of conventional vessels by modern roll on/roll off ferries. The Aberdeen-Lerwick route is now served by the 4,467 ton car ferry *St Clair* which was built in 1965. With an overall length of 404ft and a beam of 58ft she can carry 735 passengers and 230 cars. She was introduced in 1976 and inaugurated a new era of comfort for passengers. Powered by two Pielstick engines each generating 2,000 bhp, her speed is 19 knots. She is assisted on this route by the 1,205 ton *St Magnus* which was built in 1970. The latter is 318ft long with a beam of 51·8ft; she can carry 120 cars and has accommodation for 12 passengers. The company's third vessel, *St Ola*, operates across the Pentland Firth between Scrabster and the Orkney port of Stromness. Of 1,345 gross tons she can carry 400 passengers and has room for 98 cars. In October 1975 the company's name was changed to P & O Ferries (Orkney and Shetland Services) and early in 1976 the vessels' buff-coloured funnels were repainted bright blue to conform with the rest of the line.

The MV *St Clair* is larger than her counterparts of a century ago because of the increased weight of cargo and the increased number of passengers today. Shetland is now far from self-supporting, and all food supplies with the exception of fish, some meat and some vegetables are imported. It is interesting to compare the freight charges: in 1873 a lamb could be sent to Leith for 1s 3d (6p), but in 1970 it cost 57p. Fares have also increased greatly—from £3 Aberdeen-Shetland first-class return in 1939 to £12·60 in 1971, and to around £37 in 1978.

Competitors have attempted to operate more cheaply than the 'North Company' but none has lasted long. Biggest challenge was made by the Shetland Islands Trading Company, Ltd, formed in 1903, whose ship SS *Norseman* of 407 tons, with accommodation for 105 passengers, ran from Leith and Aberdeen to Lerwick and the North Isles of Shetland between 1904 and 1907. It is significant that the competition caused the larger company to reduce its charges three times in one year.

Internal sea routes

From the time of the Norsemen until the end of the nineteenth century, transport within Shetland showed little variation. The sea was the highroad linking the islands, and, though people walked long distances, sea transport was always preferable.

During the seventeenth and eighteenth centuries, while the old Country Acts were recognised, a definite scale of charges was drawn up for each sea crossing, the charges for a six-oared boat being proportionately greater than for those with four oars. When the Acts fell into disuse, the system of ferries continued but with greatly increased charges. For instance, the crossing from Unst to Fetlar cost 10d (4p) in 1770, but by 1808 it had risen to 2s 6d (12½p), both charges being for a six-oared boat.

The scale of charges was fixed, but there were no timetables. The traveller had first to find a boat and crew willing to convey him, and the duration of the trip depended on the weather. At the height of the summer fishery it was occasionally difficult to obtain transport, but for most of the year the people regarded a hire as a godsend.

Because of the large number of boats available and the large number of relatively short crossings, communications were probably better in Shetland than elsewhere in the Highlands and Islands. But travel was dangerous and uncertain, and there was frequent loss of life through sudden squalls striking the sail. One tragedy, much publicised because of the prolonged legal proceedings that followed indirectly, occurred in May 1748, when the four sons of the laird of Busta were drowned while crossing Busta Voe.

From the mid-nineteenth century, sailing smacks operated between Scalloway and the other western ports, and from Lerwick to the North Isles and to Dunrossness. They were more dependable than open boats but still not free of incidents. In 1886 an elderly woman, Betty Mouat, the only passenger on the packet *Columbine*, sailing from Grutness to Lerwick, drifted alone across the North Sea to Norway, after the two crew members had launched the rowing boat to go to the aid of their skipper, who had been knocked overboard, and could not return to their ship.

As with external communications, steam brought fixed timetables to the major internal sea routes. In 1881 the 'North of Scotland' company added the western run to their itinerary: leaving Leith on Monday morning the little *Queen* called, via Aberdeen and Stromness, at Scalloway and Walls, with less frequent calls at Spiggie, Reawick, Brae, Voe, Aith and Hillswick. In the peak years of the herring fishery calls were also made at Ronas Voe.

The last major route to survive was that between Lerwick and the North Isles. The first sailing vessel to ply regularly between Lerwick and Unst was the *Janet* in 1839, and larger vessels followed; but the greatest improvement came when the Shetland Islands Steam Navigation Company introduced the steamer *Chieftain's Bride* in 1868. In 1876 a new company was formed, with capital of £6,000, half the shares being held by the 'North Company', to provide a better service on this run with the SS *Lady Ambrosine*.

In the past 100 years two vessels have dominated this route, both named *Earl of Zetland*. The first 'Earl' was built at Paisley in 1877, and ran a service twice weekly between Lerwick and Unst, calling at intermediate ports. She also paid a weekly visit to Out Skerries and the ports on Yell Sound, at first calling at almost every little village.

The slow nature of this voyage, with delays while goods were ferried to and from the shore, caused the service to lose trade to its rival, the inter-island overland ferry route to Unst, which began in 1932; and attempts were made to speed it up by dropping the smaller ports and building piers at the larger. The Yell Sound run ceased after World War II in favour of a third run each week to the North Isles.

Page 103 (above) Shetland sheep penned for 'rooing', removal of the fleece by hand; *(below)* a Dunrossness yoal secure in its naust at Boddam

Page 104 (above) SS *Earl of Zetland* in 1939. Built in 1877, she provided a service from Lerwick to the North Isles until 1946, when she was replaced by the second holder of the name; *(below)* arrival of SS *St Magnus* at Lerwick in 1924. Of 1,591 tons, she was then the largest vessel ever owned by the 'North of Scotland' company. She was sold in 1960. The smaller vessel is the SS *St Sunniva*, built in 1887, wrecked in 1930

The first 'Earl' was an iron screw steamer of 253 tons, and her dimensions were 144·8ft × 26·2ft × 8·9ft. She remained in service for sixty-eight years, during which time she was three times stranded or partially sunk. She was extremely popular, partly because of the skill of successive captains and crew, who provided a reliable year-round service in a region notorious for its winter gales and heavy seas. Her passenger accommodation was, however, hopelessly inadequate.

A new *Earl of Zetland* was built at Aberdeen in 1939 but had barely started running when war broke out. The new vessel was requisitioned for service on the Pentland Firth, and the old *Earl of Zetland* was recalled to serve another six hazardous years, in which she twice survived attacks by enemy aircraft.

The second 'Earl' was a very efficient ship, of 548 gross tons, with a length of 154·9ft and breadth of 29·1ft. Her high ratio of beam to length compensated for the shallow draught of 13ft required on this route. As built she catered for two classes—saloon amidships and second class forward—but later she was made a one-class ship. Cargo was handled by a single derrick and electric winches.

The service was popular with visitors in summer but for most of the year it made a loss. Finally, in February 1975 the *Earl of Zetland* was withdrawn from service following the introduction of car ferries on the shorter inter-island routes.

The smaller inhabited islands are served by vessels whose dimensions depend not on the length of the crossing or the weather conditions but on the facilities at the island terminal. For example, the Foula mailboat, which has to cross 18 exposed miles of the Atlantic, must be small enough to be lifted out of the reach of the sea after her weekly trip to Walls. Foula has no sheltered inlets and the tiny pier is built in what is little more than a geo. The service is irregular in winter, and it is not uncommon for the people of Foula to be cut off from the rest of Shetland for a month or more.

Fair Isle has a more dependable service, the MV *Good Shepherd* running regularly once a week to Grutness for most of the year, and twice a week between May and October. There are also daily services across Yell Sound and Bluemull Sound, incorporated in the overland service to Yell and Unst, and between Lerwick and Bressay. Before the opening of the Trondra-Burra bridges three operators ran services between Scalloway and Burra.

ROAD TRANSPORT

The earliest roads were footpaths twisting across the countryside in an attempt to find the driest route among peat bogs and marshes. The Shetland pony was used as a mount and as a beast of burden. Peats and manure were carried in special baskets strapped to its back, but heavy loads were also carried by the people, who tramped long miles. The wealthy had larger ponies, and in 1733 a horse could be hired at the rate of 'one shilling (Scots) the mile and something for the boy'.

The first real road in Shetland was a gun track from Fort Charlotte to the headland of the Knab, constructed in 1781. The first non-military road, running from Lerwick inland to the agricultural valley of Tingwall, was completed in 1797.

When the links with Scotland were strengthened and Lerwick was chosen as the only port of call for the new steamer service, visitors and landowners began to agitate for proper roads. The chance for large-scale roadworks came with four consecutive years' failure of the potato crop coinciding with a similar period of poor fishing. To prevent famine, the government, through the Board for the Relief of Highland Destitution, began in the late 1840s a programme of roadbuilding, and from the mode of payment these roads came to be called 'meal roads'. Between 1849 and 1852, 117 miles of road were constructed to link the north, south and west Mainland with Lerwick and to connect Burravoe and Cullivoe in Yell. At this time the difficult section between the North Sea and the Atlantic Ocean at Mavis Grind was blasted out of the hillside.

In 1864, by the passing of the Zetland Roads Act, the main roads were taken over and maintained on a district basis. Existing roads were improved and extended, and the first roads appeared in the islands of Unst, Fetlar, Whalsay and Bressay, to give a total mileage of 328 by 1901. The roads required constant repair; after heavy rain or severe frost followed by a rapid thaw the narrow rims of cartwheels caused deep ruts, which were filled with gravel and stone chips from roadside quarries. There were horse-drawn carriages on the roads in the 1860s, but in 1880 Tudor stated that 'driving is more a name than a reality'.

The poor surfaces of the roads and their narrow width retarded the introduction of motor cars, but by the end of 1911 there were a dozen on the Mainland, most of them for hire.

Until the mid-1930s the roads were merely single track carriage-ways with water-bound surfaces, dusty in summer, muddy and pot-holed in winter. In 1935 the Crofter Counties Scheme allowed the Council to begin improvements with 100 per cent grants, and by 1942, when the Scheme ended, some 63 miles of Class 1 road-way had been widened to 16ft and surfaced with bitumen mac-adam at a cost of £160,000. Some further reconstruction was carried out during the war, but many less important roads deteriorated through lack of maintenance.

Since World War II lack of finance has been a serious prob-lem, for the main roads of Shetland are not classed as trunk roads, and consequently do not receive 100 per cent grants for improvement as do those in most parts of Britain. Improvements have been carried out with grant aid received under normal maintenance and minor improvements, and assistance under the Congested Districts Act.

By 1969 Shetland's road network had increased to 502·14 miles, of which 144 miles were designated Class 1. Most of the remainder consisted of single-track roads with passing places, but 96·35 per cent of the mileage was surfaced with tarmacadam.

The numerous gates on second-class roads have now been replaced with cattle grids. The original type of grid prevented cattle and sheep from straying but did not deter Shetland ponies, which frequently sustained injury in attempting to cross. Now a modified type is in use, with wider spacing between the bars to allow a pony's hoofs to reach the floor of the grid pit. In 1962 there were 132 cattle grids, and in 1970 162.

Since Shetland's road network extends over twelve islands, difficulties are met in maintenance and snow-clearing. Heavy in-vestment in plant and vehicles is necessary. The ZCC Roads Department was for long the largest single employer in the islands, the numbers employed fluctuating between 280 in the summer and 160 in the winter of 1962, while in 1970 the maximum was just under 300.

A few of the islands are separated from the Mainland or from a neighbouring island by narrow bridgeable sounds. A wooden footbridge connected the islands of Burra as long ago as 1791, and the two largest islands of Out Skerries were so connected in 1901. In 1905 an iron and concrete bridge was built to link Muckle Roe and the Mainland: 360ft long and 5ft wide, the contract price was £1,020, of which 75 per cent was provided by the Congested Districts Board and the remainder raised by public subscription. The bridge at Out Skerries was rebuilt and widened in 1955. In 1969 work began on the most ambitious project so far—the linking of the prosperous isles of Burra via Trondra to the Mainland at an estimated cost of £500,000—the money being provided by the Scottish Development Department (Roads Division). This scheme was completed in October 1971.

A feature of postwar years is the enormous increase in the number of motor cars. Ironically this sign of increasing prosperity is causing problems in rural areas, for it means less trade for private bus operators. Services from Aith and Sandness to Lerwick have been abandoned, causing great inconvenience to non-motorists and tending to hasten depopulation in those two areas. The number of cars rose from 1,146 in 1938 to 4,741 in 1970—giving a ratio of one car to 3·6 people and making Shetland one of the most car-minded counties of Britain.

AIR TRAVEL

Shetland figured in the exploration of the North Atlantic air-route. The Americans Cramer and Pacquette arrived at Lerwick in 1931, but they and their seaplane disappeared mysteriously on the next stage of their flight. August 1933 saw the Lindberghs at Lerwick after a flight from Faeroe. Hopes were raised that Shetland might be included in the transatlantic route, but the days of the seaplane were over as far as long-distance communications were concerned.

The first aeroplane to land at Shetland, a De Havilland Dragon of the Scottish Motor Traction Company, came down in a field at Sumburgh in 1933. Highland Airways was already planning to extend its service beyond Orkney, and in November 1934 made the first flight from Aberdeen to Shetland via Orkney with three commercial travellers as passengers; but the firm waited until direction-finding equipment was provided at Sumburgh before starting a regular passenger service, on 3 June

1936, in a De Havilland Rapide. In fact a rival company, Aberdeen Airways, later incorporated in Allied Airways, stole the show by starting its own service a day earlier.

On account of this rivalry, Shetland, before World War II, had three return flights every day except Sunday. Allied Airways flew the route Shetland-Orkney-Thurso-Aberdeen (Dyce), and Scottish Airways, incorporating Highland Airways, provided two flights daily, linking Shetland with Orkney, Wick, Inverness, Perth and Glasgow on one route, and with Orkney, Wick, Inverness and Aberdeen (Kintore) on the other. The Rapides continued to fly during the War, unarmed and with almost complete radio silence, without mishap.

In 1947, following the Labour government's policy of nationalising civil air transport, BEA took over the services. For a time ex-German JU 52s were used, but they were then replaced by Pionairs (Dakotas). In 1962 came the first Dart Herald, and in 1966 the Viscount. More attention is now certainly paid to safety, but the services are much more frequently interrupted by weather conditions than were those of the early pioneers, who operated a cheap service and made a profit. Winter gales, summer fog and crosswinds can stop the present service; and cancelled flights and the obligation to find accommodation for passengers cause the service to be uneconomic.

Although Shetlanders, with their tradition of reliable overnight sea-crossings to and from Aberdeen, are not so air-minded as the people of Orkney, interest in air travel is increasing. In 1970 Loganair began an inter-island air service between Sumburgh and Unst, with charter flights to Fair Isle, Foula and Papa Stour, where simple airstrips have been levelled by the islanders themselves. Loganair claims that its efficient performance is due to the use of Islander aircraft suited to conditions in this area.

Sumburgh airport has developed rapidly. The runways were laid with tarmacadam during World War II and in 1966 were extended by 600ft to accommodate Viscounts. Since 1971 the airport has played an important role in oil exploration. Rig crews are flown to Sumburgh by chartered aircraft and flown to and from their rigs by helicopters based at Sumburgh. In 1973 there were 9,114 aircraft movements compared with 1,062 in 1965, and in the same period the number of passengers increased from just under 20,000 to 94,312.

POSTAL SERVICES

There was a post office at Lerwick as early as 1736. Letters were carried by the masters of trading vessels, and the small sailing vessel *Isabella* of Lerwick made a voyage south once a year for mail and general cargo. The volume of mail was negligible, however, for few of the people could read or write.

In 1760 the government awarded a trading consortium in Leith an annual subsidy of £60 to carry mail to Lerwick five times a year. The grant was inadequate, so the mail became of secondary importance, and the sloop called at several Scottish ports, often taking six months to reach Shetland. In 1794 a firm in Aberdeen offered to take over this service and increase the number of sailings to ten a year if it was granted an annual subsidy of £120. The Postmaster-General refused to grant more than £60, but a similar sum was contributed with great reluctance by the clergy, heritors, 'and other principal inhabitants of the islands'.

As late as the 1820s the correspondence of Wesleyan missionaries shows the unsatisfactory state of the mail service, for a letter of 21 March 1825 reads: 'It appears that all our preceding letters for some months have been lost; a little vessel that had sailed from Leith . . . about two months ago having never been heard of since'.

Rapid improvements followed the introduction of a mail service in 1838, though a reliable weekly service was not provided until 1861. The introduction of the penny post in 1840, together with the spread of education and a greater tendency to travel, increased the volume of mail. In 1847, according to the records of the Post Office, there were twenty receiving offices in Shetland.

Payment to sub-postmasters was paltry and subject to periodic review. In 1890 the postmaster at Sullom had his salary increased from £5 10s (£5·50) to £6 a year, but the unfortunate holder of the post at Tresta had his reduced from £8 9s (£8·45) to £7. The postmaster had also to provide the premises for carrying out his duties. Even at Lerwick a proper Post Office was not erected until 1910; before that a different building was used by each newly appointed postmaster.

At first the mail was carried to rural post offices by foot messenger. The earliest route was a private postal service between

Lerwick and Unst in the 1820s, taken over by the GPO soon after 1840. On the section between Lerwick and Mossbank one Robert Laurenson was carrier between 1839 and 1863. Outwards on Monday and Thursday he left Lerwick at 4am arriving at Mossbank at 1.40pm. His return journey was made on Tuesday and Friday. After twenty-four years' service, in the words of a contemporary, 'he was turned adrift because of the mails being conveyed by gig and to live or die as he best could without pension or other aid'.

The coming of the horse-drawn vehicle brought great improvements to most parts of Shetland. Before the end of the century mail gigs replaced foot or mounted letter carriers on three further routes—to Scalloway, Dunrossness and Walls. The Lerwick firm of Ganson Brothers took over all of these services operating four times a week. In 1910 the first motor, a 15hp Albion, was used to carry mails, and by 1916 all horse-drawn vehicles had been replaced by motor vehicles. The firm had four services running three times a week, covering 80,000 miles a year, for a payment latterly of £1,120 a year, which also helped to provide an otherwise uneconomic rural bus service. In 1947 Ganson Brothers' mail contract was terminated and their service taken over by the Post Office, which now provides a daily delivery to most parts of the Mainland.

Although rapid improvements followed the inauguration of the first weekly mail, the people of Shetland have never been satisfied with their service. In 1887 they complained to the Treasury and to the steamship company, pleading unsuccessfully for a daily service between 1 April and 31 September and a thrice-weekly service the rest of the year. Orkney, it was pointed out, had then a daily service throughout the year.

During World War I the public accepted irregularities in the mail service due to the presence of submarines in the area, but in 1921 another complaint was presented to the GPO. It was not until the inauguration of an air service in 1936, however, that a daily service was seen to be feasible. Zetland County Council, after urging the government to instigate such a service, received the reply that an opportunity would be given to tender.

In January 1937 for a period of nine days no steamers were able to leave Shetland on account of stormy weather. The isolation was ended when the GPO chartered a plane, which landed

1,000lb of mail at Sumburgh. The regular airmail service was inaugurated on 23 November, a thrice-weekly service with the promise of a daily service in summer. Since then first-class mail and daily newspapers have been carried by air, parcels and weekly newspapers by steamer.

The flat rate for postal charges is very important in Shetland, where freight charges are so crippling. There is a considerable postal trade in hosiery, in which the Shetland knitter can compete with her counterparts elsewhere. Mail-order firms also have a considerable trade with customers in the islands. Most parts of Shetland have a daily mail service (Sundays excepted) while Lerwick has a twice-daily delivery and in some of the smaller islands the frequency is as low as once a week weather permitting.

TELEGRAPH AND TELEPHONE

Between 1868 and 1870 the Orkney and Shetland Telegraph Company Ltd, floated with a capital of £20,000, laid a telegraph cable from Caithness to Boddam in Shetland; but it was subjected to strong tides and broke three times within the first year. In 1876, when it cost 13s 6d (67½p) to send a telegram of twenty words from Shetland compared with 1s (5p) from elsewhere in Britain, the struggling company was taken over by the General Post Office. In 1885 the latter laid a new cable between Sinclair Bay, Caithness, and Sandwick Bay in Shetland, and direct communications became possible between Lerwick and Aberdeen. Shetland also played a part in the linking of Denmark and Faeroe. In 1906 telegraphic communication was established between Shetland and Faeroe using automatic high-speed morse, a service later extended to Iceland.

Internally the first telegraphic link was opened between Lerwick and Scalloway in 1870. Gradually the service was extended to other areas so that in 1888 there were seventeen telegraphic offices, in 1893 twenty-seven and in 1906 thirty-five.

During World War I telegraphic cables were laid to Papa Stour and Foula, but they were soon abandoned, the former being the less satisfactory. A radio station was built near Lerwick to provide communications for the naval authorities, and after the war it was turned into a Meteorological Station.

The first private telephone in Shetland was installed in 1883 between Hay & Co's premises at South Esplanade and Hayfield House, but the GPO did not provide a network within Lerwick until 1907. In June 1909 the telephone was extended to the important herring centre of Sandwick, where there were initially ten subscribers, and a few weeks later, to Scalloway, where there were also ten subscribers. A call from Lerwick to Scalloway then cost 2d. Progress was steady throughout the Mainland, and in 1935 the service was extended by cable to the North Isles. Radio-telephone links were supplied to Out Skerries in 1934, and to Papa Stour and Foula in 1937, all three links for telegrams only.

An ultra-short-wave radio station was set up in 1938 on the Hill of Quarff with the aim of furnishing trunk telephone communication with the rest of Britain. Then World War II broke out and the sending of messages, even those by the GPO, came under the control of the senior naval officer. Not until after the war was Shetland fully incorporated in a nationwide telephone circuit.

A separate development was the laying in 1940 of a co-axial cable via Fair Isle to the North of Scotland; it posessed twelve speech channels, provided a teleprinter service for telegrams, and linked Lerwick and Fair Isle by telephone.

Progress has been rapid since World War II in accommodating increased demand on these services. In 1953 a new radio-telephone link with Out Skerries allowed for private telephones there, and by 1955 this service had been extended to Foula and Papa Stour. In 1958 the beam-radio station at Hill of Quarff was closed and a new improved telephone circuit was provided via radio stations at Shurton Hill near Lerwick and Scousburgh, Dunrossness.

In 1978 there were 6,351 telephone subscribers in Shetland compared with 3,256 in 1971. They were served by thirty-three local exchanges, all of them automatic, with group switching centres at Lerwick and Mid Yell. All inter-island submarine cables have now been replaced by radio links and the new exchanges in Unst, Yell and Whalsay are linked to the main switching centre at Lerwick by a system of super-high-frequency 300-channel radio links. The smaller exchanges at Fetlar, Out Skerries, Foula, Fair Isle and Papa Stour are linked to the switching centre by small capacity six-channel VHF radio links. Between Lerwick, where a new exchange has been built, and the main radio terminal at Shurton Hill, the circuits are routed in a four-tube small-bore coaxial cable, each pair of tubes having a capacity of 960 telephone circuits. The aim of all these developments was to extend subscriber trunk dialling facilities to the islands of Shetland by the end of 1974.

These developments were part of a modernisation scheme originally planned in 1966, long before North Sea oil was found, and it was indeed fortunate that they were carried out in time for the unforeseen demand of recent years. But the quickening pace of oil-related activities is putting a severe strain on telephone services, and there are now plans to augment all the exchanges likely to be affected by oil developments and to augment radio and cable links to carry the further increase in traffic that is expected.

To serve oil rigs and platforms outside the normal range of radio links a new system of 'tropospheric scatter' has been set up. Stations at Scousburgh in Shetland and at Mormond Hill near Fraserburgh now give the rigs access to the public trunk network.

6 AGRICULTURE AND FISHING

UNTIL sixty or seventy years ago the men of Shetland combined the occupations of farming and fishing, hence the apt compound—crofter-fishermen. It is not so simple nowadays. There are still fishermen with crofts and crofters with boats, but in general the two occupations have become separated, and the proportion of the population engaged in these activities has declined with the growth of service industries.

AGRICULTURE

The Shetland farmer has many difficulties to face. The geographical position of these islands accounts for such diverse problems as late harvests and high freight charges, and imposes limits on what can be grown. The small size of the average holding is another problem peculiar to Shetland—a legacy of the Norse system of land tenure, aggravated by the nineteenth-century fragmentation of the crofts.

Perhaps the greatest obstacle is the blanket of peat that covers most of the islands. Yet this has been reduced in many areas by drainage and the use of fertilisers, and lime has overcome its acidity. Today the process of surface seeding, encouraged by government grants and the availability of machinery, has created thousands of acres of good pasture from land formerly covered by heather and wild cotton grass. In the total acreage reclaimed and regenerated between 1957 and 1970, Shetland had the best record of the seven crofting counties.

Shetland gains certain advantages from its maritime situation: severe frosts and prolonged snow are comparatively rare, and the islands grow good grass, with the consequent dominance of sheep-farming.

The Crofter

One of the least understood individuals in Britain today is the crofter of the Highlands and Islands—a man who prefers to live and work in an isolated community with few amenities, the only doubtful advantages being an open-air life and independence. To be successful he has to combine the skills of carpenter, stonemason and boatman, yet he enjoys an annual cash income often less than £500 per year.

A proper understanding of the crofter defies even those concerned directly with the future of agriculture in this area. The first report of the Highlands and Islands Development Board states simply :

> . . . crofting appears to be a form of living and working which gives deep satisfaction to those who follow it. It does not and cannot except in rare cases support the crofter as a full time pursuit . . . (yet) if one had to look for a way of life which could keep that number of people in such relative untractable territory, it would be difficult to contrive a better system.

It is this realisation that has produced the vast amount of legislation that protects the crofter. Shetland comes under the Crofting Acts, which govern land tenure and even land use : the crofter thereby enjoys security of tenure and a fair adjudicated rent. He also has the right to transfer tenancy of his croft, and, should he decide to leave it, he is entitled to compensation from the owner for any improvement made during his tenancy.

The crofter is eligible for a wide range of grants and subsidies for improving houses and steadings, for drainage, for erecting new fences and for reclamation of rough grazings. Since March 1971 the crofter has been eligible for legal aid in all proceedings in the Scottish Land Court.

The requirements for membership of this select body are few. Under the Crofting Reform (Scotland) Act of 1976 a crofter is defined as the tenant of a holding of which the area does not exceed 30 hectares, not including common grazing, or a holding of which the annual rent does not exceed £100.

Traditional Agriculture

Until the end of the last century the main purpose of the croft was to provide food not income for the family; as much food as possible had to be home-produced and the area under cultivation 100 years ago was more than twice what it is today. The crops, grown in a sort of rotation, were oats, potatoes and bere; then the land was left ley or fallow for a year, which did not clean it, for oats sown the following year had to compete with a colourful profusion of wildflowers. Bere was more important than oats, since it gave a greater yield in grain, though its straw was inferior as fodder; it was always heavily manured, and a large part of the best ground, the infield, was reserved for it every year. Cabbages were also grown for food, the seedlings being raised in round stone-walled enclosures. Seaweed was used as fertiliser but never so extensively as in Orkney, since Shetland's steeper beaches made it less abundant. The strongest manure accumulated in the byre during the winter; layers of dung were covered by layers of turf carried from the scattald, to absorb moisture, and further dung accumulated, then further turf layers were added, and so on.

The people were poor and their implements had to be as simple and inexpensive as possible. The Shetland plough drawn by four oxen was small and inefficient, easily broken by stones or a stiff furrow. More commonly used was the Shetland spade, with a 4ft wooden handle, iron shoe and a step to drive it into the earth. When the crofts became smaller and it became necessary to cultivate even steep and rocky parts, almost all the land was dug by teams of three or four women. In 1840 those who had to employ labour could have an acre of ground dug for 8s (40p) at a rate of 6d (2½p) a day for each woman.

Ponies were used to carry home dried peat from the hills, but a large amount of peat, like manure and seaweed, was transported on the backs of women in homemade baskets known as kishies.

The domestic animals were poor specimens, stunted by severe winters and inadequate feeding. In Aithsting in 1840 a typical croft of 3–4 acres kept four to six milking cows, with their calves and yearlings—a total of twelve to fifteen head to keep alive during the winter. In addition there were two or three ponies, thirty to forty ewes, one or two pigs, fifteen to twenty hens and large numbers of geese.

Visitors to Shetland invariably condemned this system of husbandry. There were no restrictions on the right of commonage, the main limit to the number of animals kept being the need to provide a few handfuls of straw or hay to keep them alive in the winter. Crofters came to rely too much on the scattald. Inevitably the recurring cycle was one of overstocking followed by disaster. In the winter of 1784, which was exceptionally severe, the minister of Delting recorded the deaths of 4,506 sheep and 427 black cattle, 'besides horses, of which no accurate account could be obtained'.

When the crops were lifted at harvest the gates on the hill dykes were opened and the sheep and cows were allowed to roam at large over the fields of the entire township. Since the fields were in general divided under the run-rig system, it was impossible for anyone to experiment with new crops such as rye-grass and turnips, for they could not be protected from the animals. The system of common grazing was in itself detrimental to the quality of the stock—inferior lambs were not castrated and best lambs were usually sold because they were worth most.

There were several reasons for the conservatism of the crofter-fishermen: they were too poor to risk experiment; their arable acreage was too small for other than food-producing crops; and they were at the mercy of the landlord, with no security of tenure. Finally the people were more interested in fishing than crofting because the landowners depended more on that section of the economy. As the population increased, the crofts became smaller and smaller. Disaster was inevitable, and it came when the fishing industry showed signs of collapsing in the 1840s. Then the lairds began to turn their attention to the land, and their tenants were seen merely as an embarrassment.

The Improvers

Among those who constantly advocated improvements were the parish ministers of the Church of Scotland. It was easier for them than the crofters, for they were in constant contact with their fellow ministers in Scotland and with agricultural developments there; they could afford to experiment, and, perhaps more important, the glebe was usually the best land in the district.

The Rev John Turnbull, parish minister of Tingwall 1806–67, was the most famous of the early improvers. He experimented with sown grass and clover, and, about 1808, introduced field turnips to Shetland; he even tried unsuccessfully to grow wheat. He also imported agricultural implements from Scotland and persuaded Shetlanders to build stone walls in place of turf dykes.

Another minister deeply interested in the improvement of agriculture was the Rev John Bryden of Sandsting & Aithsting, who sought an alternative to the universal black oats, *Avena strigosa*, then in use. In the late 1830s a number of his parishioners experimented with Angus-shire early oats obtained from the glebe, which they agreed was 'superior to the other in grain and straw'.

The landowners were themselves active in improving their own farms and the quality of their livestock. The Shetland cow was a good milker for her size but when fattened for slaughter gave a carcase weight of only 1½–2cwt; but by crossing with Aberdeen Angus or Shorthorn bulls a greatly increased carcase weight resulted.

The main innovation in the early part of the nineteenth century was the adoption of a definite crop rotation, with sown grasses instead of ley to clean the ground, and the growing of turnips for winter feeding of cattle. As early as 1818, Mr Ogilvie of Quendale was rotating turnips, bere, clover and oats. Crop rotation and the growing of roots for winter feeding entailed enclosure. In 1839 Christian Ployen visited the estates of Mr Hay at Laxfirth and Dale and described the new development as follows:

> The portion of land belonging to each house is regularly enclosed and divided into five equal parts, which it is made encumbent on the tenant to cultivate with a fixed rotation of crops. . . . The tenants are everywhere discontented with the regulations introduced, so that besides the expense, Mr Hay has much trouble from the attachment of the people to their old system. He, however, carries out his plans with a high hand, and the refractory tenant is turned off without mercy, which is easily done from the nature of the bargain between proprietor and cultivator.

Enclosure was anathema to the crofter, for the fences prevented his cattle and sheep from obtaining fodder on the seashore, and hindered the traditional practice of grazing on the stubble fields and ditches of his neighbours. Sooner or later, however, everyone came to regard enclosure as an essential step in the improvement of agriculture, and probably the crofters' initial reluctance stemmed from mistrust of the landowners. They may have foreseen the next step, from enclosure to the eviction of the tenants and the establishment of sheep-farms, a process that marred the second half of the nineteenth century and caused great distress among the population.

Days of Change

For centuries the prices for livestock in Shetland showed little variation. The Dutch fishermen from the seventeenth century onwards bought a few sheep and cattle at inflated prices, but there was no dependable way of getting stock to markets outside Shetland. In 1774 Low noted the price of Shetland ponies as £1 to £2 10s (£2·50), but in 1839 Christian Ployen recorded prices of £5 or more for 'wretched little animals'. This increase in price was due directly to the inauguration in 1836 of a fortnightly steamer service between Lerwick and Leith.

In 1839 the trade in small cattle was reported as being very brisk. It was no longer essential to sell cattle at Martinmas to merchants in Lerwick to be killed and salted, for they could be exported alive to fetch a better price. In 1841 the parish minister of Mid & South Yell noted a rise of 50 per cent to £3 15s (£3·75) in the price of black cattle 'owing to the great facility of transport now afforded by steam'.

Eggs rose in price from 1½d to 7d a dozen between 1838 and 1872, but more important still, because of its far-reaching effects, was the increasing demand for sheep. The sheep exported in 1824 and 1825 numbered sixty-nine and seventy-six respectively, and as late as 1839 Christian Ployen spoke of seeing many cattle but few sheep in his travels through Shetland. The 1840s, however, saw rising prices for sheep and wool, and Shetland was now in a position to benefit. Blackface and Cheviot sheep were imported from Scotland to graze on the best pasture and used for crossing with native Shetland ewes to give greater wool yield and carcase weight. While a Shetland sheep produced a fleece of 2lb weight, a cross sheep often produced 5lb.

The clearances and the growth of sheep-farming dominated the social and agricultural scenes for the next forty years. Not all the land was given over to sheep, since mixed farming also developed with the spread of new ideas; but the agricultural statistics tell the story of increasing numbers of sheep and decreasing numbers of crofts as the people left Shetland for the colonies.

Henry Evershed visited Shetland in 1873 and found agriculture in a state of turmoil. He met the class of crofter-fishermen practising the traditional form of agriculture, which he called 'the most primitive and unproductive example of husbandry that can be found in Britain'. Their numbers were still decreasing

Page 121 (above) Shetland sheep showing ear marks; *(below)* Shetland pony

Page 122 (above) A herring station at Lerwick between the wars; *(below)* drift-net fishermen at Scalloway preparing for sea. In the background, flying the Norwegian flag, is one of the first purse-seiners to fish in Shetland waters

before the onslaught of so-called improvement, and large sheep-farms and Scottish-type mixed farms were taking the place of the crofts.

As an example of a sheep-farm Evershed described that of Mr Bruce at Veensgarth, which carried 600 Cheviot and 600 Blackface ewes crossed with Leicester tups on 3,000 acres of hill pasture. Every year an average of 1,200 lambs were sold for shipment to Leith, the price in 1873 being £1 7s 6d (£1·37½) each when Shetland sheep were selling at Lerwick for 5s (25p). Winter feeding was provided from 25 acres of hay. There were also 200 acres of arable land in Veensgarth valley which Mr Bruce intended to lay down to permanent pasture for 300 more ewes.

An an example of a mixed farm Evershed described that of Mr Umphray of Reawick, which consisted of 90 acres mainly under sown grass for summer grazing and turnips for winter feeding of cattle; 75 of those 90 acres had been reclaimed from moorland since 1860. Ten Shorthorn cows were kept for milk, butter and breeding, and their calves were reared.

The island of Unst was in the forefront of improvements. Here Evershed met the first of a new class of crofter—the man who was prepared to devote his attention to agriculture rather than fishing—in Peter Smith of Westing, who had a croft on Major Cameron's estate. Smith was the occupier of 22 acres, 10 of which were arable. The rent was high at £7 per annum plus 7 per cent of the outlay on a new slate roof, which had cost £30. Crop rotation enabled Smith to keep crossbred cattle, including four milking cows; and sheep, ponies and young cattle were kept on the scattald for a payment of 4s (20p) for every £1 of rent.

Smith was apparently fortunate in having a landlord and factor who tried to improve his living conditions, but, even more important, he was willing to comply with the new ideas of improved husbandry. Others did not fare so well, for Unst was one of the islands worst affected by clearance. Evictions continued until the Crofters' Holdings Act was passed in 1886, following on Lord Napier's Commission of 1882.

Agriculture Today

It is perhaps ironic that the present prosperity of Shetland's agriculture is based on sheep, with lambs for export and wool for

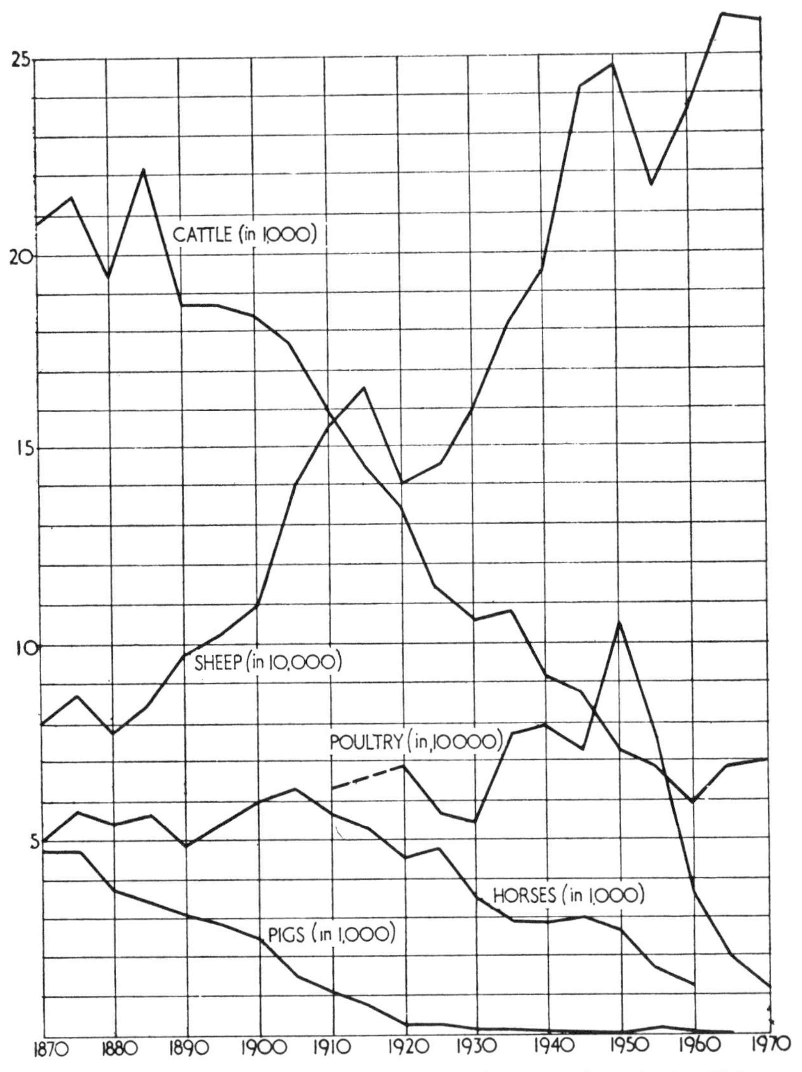

Stock figures 1870–1970, based mainly on the research of Heinz Heineberg, 1969

Shetland knitwear. The days of unlimited grazing have almost gone and the crofter's share of stock on the common grazing—the souming—is strictly regulated, except on a few scattalds.

The accompanying graph shows the increase in sheep stocks since 1870. At first the increase was due to the growth of large sheep farms, but then the crofters also realised that sheep were easier to keep than cattle. Shetland's summer total of 300,000 ewes and lambs is much higher than the total for Orkney and about the same as that of Caithness (which has a very much larger area). The numbers fluctuate considerably, heavy losses being sustained periodically among hill sheep in severe winters; the losses during the winter of 1967–8 were reflected in a drop of almost 30,000 in the June figures. Each autumn some 60,000 lambs are shipped south, the increasing number of heavier cross lambs being an important feature. Cheviot and Suffolk tups are most commonly used in crossing.

These developments could not have taken place without the provision of improved hill pasture. Since 1886 the crofter has enjoyed the right to apply for his share of the scattald to be apportioned for his exclusive use, but until recently few had done so. Notable exceptions were the fourteen crofters at Hillwell, Dunrossness, who, soon after World War II, applied to the Land Court for permission to apportion 150 acres. This was approved, and within two years most of the land had been fenced and reseeded.

In 1955 the government established a scheme of special grants to crofters, including grants for reclamation of hill land, and between 1957 and 1970, 688 successful applications were made in Shetland involving 16,985 acres, and over 8,500 acres were reclaimed or regenerated. For comparison, in Inverness-shire, during the same period, there were 364 applications for 11,943 acres, and just under 6,500 acres were improved.

Cattle stocks declined drastically until about 1960, but recently there has been an upward trend. The quality is much improved, for Herefords, Shorthorns and black-polled animals have replaced the traditional Shetland breed. In 1965 an artificial insemination sub-centre of the Aberdeen Milk Marketing Board was set up at Scalloway. The Shetland breed of cattle may still have a future, for in the 1960s successful efforts were made to save the breed from extinction in the belief that Shetland cattle are best suited for milk production on poorer crofts. Their immunity to bovine tuberculosis was important in the past.

In general the crofter no longer keeps a cow to supply milk; dairying and beef production are now in the hands of those with larger holdings. The 1981 total of 5,103 cattle includes 593 dairy cattle, and milk for Lerwick, Scalloway and Burra comes from Dunrossness, Tingwall and the outskirts of Lerwick. A few years ago insufficient milk was produced to supply local needs and 30,000 gallons a year were imported from Orkney, but this situation has been largely remedied. The islands are now self-sufficient in milk in the summer time. In January 1980 some 18,000 gallons of milk were brought in from Aberdeen but in January 1982 the figure was only 6,000. Shetland was the first county in Britain to free itself from bovine tuberculosis.

The demand for Shetland ponies is extremely variable. Following the introduction of a steamer service there was a demand for ponies for use in British coalmines, and in 1851 thirty were bought for South Hetton pit in Northumberland at a price of £4 10s (£4·50) each. Thereafter the price rose rapidly, and even when machinery replaced ponies in the main roads of the pits, a use was found for the 'Sheltie', since it could draw a load along a passage little more than 4ft high. High prices prevailed for a time after World War I, when Russian ponies were no longer available; but then the demand fell, and in 1936 it was stated that the price was too low to justify breeding. Since World War II prices have increased greatly, as ponies are now in demand for children's pets in Britain and on the continent. A record price for Shetland of £598 was obtained at Lerwick in 1968.

Poultry-keeping does not flourish in Shetland, which has the second lowest total in Scotland—12,870 in 1970. Only Bute has fewer. Geese, once kept in large numbers, are now rarely seen. Chicken hatcheries and egg-producing units were started after World War II, but high freight charges on feeding stuffs and falling egg prices made them uneconomic. In 1951 egg production was at a level of over 5 million per year, 80 per cent being exported to Scotland, but today not enough eggs are produced to satisfy home demand.

As regards the area under cultivation it is difficult to compare the statistics for 1970 with those of a century ago, for different criteria are used in subdividing the various types of grassland. The area under food crops (bere, oats, potatoes and turnips) has fallen from just under 15,000 acres to 3,500, but the area under sown grass has increased from 440 acres of rotation grass to over 17,000 acres of grass for pasture and mowing. This shows the change from subsistence farming to stock raising. The breakdown of the figures in the former group is revealing. Bere and barley have fallen from 2,352 acres to 45, and oats from 9,173 to 2,177; the latter is now used almost entirely for stock feeding. Potatoes have dropped from 2,902 acres to 659, showing the dependence on imported supplies, though there is large-scale growing at Dunrossness for sale in Lerwick and Scalloway. The main advocate of improvement today is neither landlord nor parish minister but the North of Scotland College of Agriculture, which since 1904 has tried to improve crofting methods by advice, lectures and demonstration.

One of the drawbacks of the first Crofters' Holdings Acts of 1886 was that they perpetuated holdings that were not and never could be economically viable. Today one of the functions of the Crofters' Commission is the reshaping and enlarging of holdings to steer available land into the hands of young energetic men. In 1968 there were 2,550 holdings in Shetland compared with 3,973 in 1870. Of the former figure half had under 5 acres of arable land and only eight had more than 100 acres of arable. It must be pointed out that a crofter may run two or more small units together, in which case it is possible to obtain a reasonable income; but crofting is often only subsidiary to another job, the annual subsidy of £6 or so per ewe being the biggest source of croft income.

The number of crofters is still falling as a wider choice of other jobs becomes available. The land is agglomerating into economic units for those who wish to make crofting or farming a full-time occupation. At the moment agriculture is in a state of transition as many crofters are now the owners of their holdings and still more are negotiating a purchase. Some of the scattalds are still run on a communal basis while others have been apportioned among the various crofters who hold grazing rights in them and who are now going ahead with their own improvement schemes. Hay is still cured for winter keep but silage making is increasing in popularity being far more dependable in this wet climate.

The annual value of agriculture to Shetland is difficult to estimate since so much of the produce is consumed in the home. Most experts agree that it must be at least £5 million including subsidies.

FISHING

From earliest times fishing has been an important occupation in Shetland. At first it was carried on solely for food, but then came fishing for trade. Hanseatic merchants from Hamburg and Bremen were the most numerous traders, though in 1633 Captain John Smith encountered a few English and Scottish merchants. In 1712 came the salt tax, which forced the lairds to take over control of the industry.

At first there were plenty of fish near the shore, but in the latter half of the seventeenth century, perhaps on account of climatic changes, the fish migrated to deeper water. The fishery that then developed became known as the haaf fishing (from Old Norse *hav* or sea) as opposed to the earlier inshore fishery.

The Haaf Fishing

The haaf fishing began in the early eighteenth century, rose to a peak in the mid-nineteenth, and declined rapidly after the disaster of 1881. Stations were selected as near the fishing grounds as possible. A good beach covered with flat rounded stones was more important than a good anchorage, for the boats were hauled ashore at the onset of bad weather. There were stations all over the islands, but the main parish was Northmavine, where there were nine; the island of Unst also had nine haaf stations.

Preparations began in April each year, when the lodges of the fishermen and curers and the booths of the merchants were repaired and re-roofed with turf. The actual haaf season lasted from 20 May to 12 August, the period during which the fishermen were bound by agreement to fish for their landowner.

In winter, when fishing with handline was carried on mainly for home consumption, only those who were in debt after the summer season were still bound to deliver their surplus to the laird. In practice most fishermen were never out of debt.

The boats used were direct descendants of the old Viking longships. The earliest type of fishing vessel of which we have knowledge is the yoal, still surviving at Dunrossness and Fair Isle, but the boat developed specially for the haaf fishing was the larger 'sixern', so called because she was rowed with six oars. She was clinker built, 18–22ft on the keel with 6ft beam, and double-ended, with a rake in stem and stern. A boat measuring 19½ft of keel was 30ft overall. In both yoal and sixern the sail was a dipping lug, hoisted on a mast set almost amidships.

According to Dr Edmondston, writing in 1809, the men of Northmavine and the west side of Shetland used a longer fleet of lines than others—120 bughts of line each 50 fathoms long with hooks 5 fathoms apart baited with haddock, herring or coalfish. When tied together and laid on the sea-bed, the lines stretched almost 7 miles. To haul them in by hand was a formidable task.

A sixern, the most common type of fishing vessel in the nineteenth century

The boats made two trips a week, Monday to Wednesday and Thursday to Saturday. While at sea sleep was impossible, the only food a little oatmeal bread, but a little cheap smuggled spirits helped to restore warmth. The fishermen rowed or sailed up to 40 miles from land and generally shot and hauled their lines three times each trip in depths varying between 50 and 100 fathoms. Only ling, cod and saithe were marketable; worthless fish such as skate and halibut were reserved for the use of the fishermen and their families.

At the station the fish were first weighed, and then they were split open and their backbones removed before salting. After three days in pickle they were spread out on the beach, carefully tended by beach boys, and when a white bloom of salt crystals appeared on them they were piled into stacks and protected from damp by tarpaulins. When drying was completed, they were stored to await shipment to Spain, Hamburg and Ireland.

The price of fish remained low for centuries. In 1633 ling fetched 3d each and cod 2d. In 1774, when Low visited Shetland, ling were 4d each and cod 1d or 2d, 'which low price', he declared, 'occasions vast grumblings among the fishermen, who complain that they are forced with their children to sea in all weathers, exposed to every danger, forced to buy their boats and every material at the highest price and after all their expense and toil have no reward for their labour'.

In 1809 a typical season's catch for a sixern was 106cwt, worth £21 4s (£21·20). Out of this the crew of six had to pay £7 10s (£7·50) for hire of boat and gear, plus the cost of their food while at the station, leaving £1 12s (£1·60) as each man's profit. At this time the profit to the merchant on each cwt of cured fish was 5s (25p), and, since 2¼cwt of wet fish was the equivalent of 1cwt dried, the total profit from each boat was almost £12. In defence of the merchant it must be pointed out that the demand for salt fish was extremely variable, and losses were incurred during wet summers when an inferior article was produced.

Prices were much higher when J. R. Tudor visited the islands in 1882. The price for the season was not declared until the returns for dried fish were known in the autumn. The cost of curing and the curer's commission, each 2s 6d (12½p) per cwt, were first deducted, and the remainder was halved between crew and boatowner. Assuming with Tudor a market price of £1 3s (£1·15) per cwt for dried fish, the fishermen were paid 8s (40p) a cwt. Enormous quantities of fish were exported during the era of the haaf fishing: in 1790 800 tons, in 1809 1,075 tons, and by 1875 the haaf fishing was responsible for exports of 3,500 tons. The haaf fishing was arduous and extremely dangerous. When the weather deteriorated, the men were reluctant to cut their lines and run for shelter, for at one stroke they could lose the whole profits of the season. In days when there were neither barometers nor weather forecasts, personal observations were not always reliable. Sudden storms that caught the fleet of tiny undecked sixerns at sea 30–40 miles from land caused many disasters, the worst still spoken of today. On 16 July 1832 thirty-one boats were lost; the crews of fourteen were picked up by Dutch herring busses but 105 men perished. Another disaster occurred on 20 July 1881, when ten boats and fifty-eight men were lost.

It was partly the dangers involved that brought the haaf fishing to an end. Young men, freed after 1886 from the restrictions of the landlords, realised that a better life could be had outside Shetland, in the Merchant Navy and in the colonies. It appeared, too, that herring was going to be the fish of the future, for good catches were being made by decked sailing boats from the late 1870s on. The sixern was not a good herring boat; she could not carry more than ten or twelve nets and she could not deliver her catch in good condition to the curers.

Nevertheless the sixern has an honoured place in the history of Shetland's fishing industry. In the hands of a capable crew she was a good seaboat for her size; and no other craft could have made a profit for fishermen who received so little for their fish. Some sixerns were still fishing after 1900 manned by middle-aged and elderly men who had survived the changes ashore and afloat, but few people mourned the passing of the haaf era in spite of its bustle and activity. Now all that remains are the silent beaches and the lichen-covered walls of the lodges at places like Fedeland and Stenness.

The Smack Fishery

Since the sixteenth century at least Dutch fishermen had fished the Shetland banks successfully in large seaworthy sailing vessels, but not until the early nineteenth century did Shetlanders start to follow their example. Dr Hibbert estimates that the Shetland smack fishery began in 1805 or 1807 with a few vessels of between 6 and 35 tons and carrying six to eight hands. The real stimulus to this fishery was the establishment of a tonnage bounty in 1820 for large vessels engaged in ling and cod fishing. In 1821, there were twenty-four smacks fishing from Shetland; in 1829, the last year of the bounty scheme, the number had risen to eighty and their success guaranteed the future of this fishery.

For 100 years the cod smacks put Shetland right in the forefront of British deep-sea fishing. An assemblage of yachts, revenue cutters, lighthouse tenders, and Baltic traders were bought and converted into cod fishers to accompany English-built smacks and vessels built locally in a sea-fever that the islands had never known before. Companies were founded to send out smacks and secure their share of the export trade. Names like Hay & Co and Nicolson & Co continue to the present day. Fortunes were made but not by the fishermen.

At first operations were confined to the home banks, then in 1833 Hay & Co sent three vessels to fish on the Faeroe banks, where good catches were taken. In the 1840s Shetland smacks fished regularly in the Davis Straits, where the cod (of poor quality) were so numerous that they could be jiggered on bare hooks. Thereafter the fishing was confined to the Faeroe banks with occasional trips to Iceland and Rockall.

The smacks were owned by the curers, and the crews joined them at the end of March, They made three or four trips out every season and 20–30 tons were regarded as a good catch. The fish were hauled on handlines with shellfish as bait. Some smacks were provided with 'wells' or tanks which allowed free circulation of seawater, whereby they could carry live bait, generally mussels and large white whelks known as buckies.

The catch, mainly cod, was cleaned, split and salted on board, and drying was carried out back on the beaches of Shetland. On the last trip of the season, the 'well' smacks filled their tanks with live cod, and after discharging the salt part of the cargo at Shetland, the live fish were sold at high prices at Hull or Grimsby, where the smacks had their annual refit. During the winter some smacks were 'laid up' in Shetland ports, and some were used to carry cargoes of dried fish to markets on the Continent.

In 1864 the largest fleet of smacks set sail from the islands—107 ships, of 4,362 tons, manned by 1,185 men. In 1870, 1,638,604 fish were landed from smacks alone, amounting to 2,488 tons of cured fish. The best combined haaf and smack fishing season was in 1875, when 3,458,799 fish were caught and 5,593 tons of dried fish were exported.

Although the smacks provided greater comfort and safety for their crews than did the sixerns, they were engaged in a dangerous occupation. Many smacks were lost—three in 1878, when the *Gondola* and *Harriet Louisa* sank off Iceland and the *Telegraph*, homeward-bound, was lost with her own crew and eight men previously rescued from the *Gondola*.

The factors that contributed to the death of the haaf fishing (see p 131) meant the end of the smack fishing. In addition, competition from Faeroese fishermen in their own waters ousted the Shetlanders, and from 1880 onwards the smacks were sold in increasing numbers to Faeroese owners. In 1896 twenty-four smacks sailed from Shetland, in 1899 only seven. The last cod fishers were the *Buttercup* belonging to Hay & Co, Lerwick, and the *William Martin* owned by Nicolson & Co, Scalloway. In March 1908 the *William Martin* began her last season for Shetland owners. No young men were then entering the industry and her owners had to send to Faeroe for a skipper and complete crew. In the autumn of that year she was sold. It is to the credit of the English yards which built these smacks that some were still afloat in Faeroe in the late 1960s.

The Herring Fishery

Shetland has long been recognised as the centre of the richest herring grounds in the North Sea, perhaps first by the Dutch, who were catching herring here in the sixteenth century and for over 300 years remained dominant.

Successive British governments, jealous of Dutch success, tried to start a British herring fishery by legislation but without success. In 1750 The Society of the Free British Fishery was formed in London and four busses fished the first year, two of them at Shetland. All had a successful season. On 27 September 1750, at the Royal Exchange Coffee House, one barrel and six half-barrels of Shetland herring fetched the colossal sum of £75 11s (£75·55).

A big building programme began and in 1753 thirty-eight British busses fished in Shetland waters. Thereafter a rapid decline set in, for which mismanagement and corruption were largely responsible. In 1772 the Society's assets came under the auctioneer's hammer and realised only £7,000.

In 1808 yet another attempt was made to develop the herring industry by state aid. A bounty of £3 per ton was offered for all vessels of 60–100 tons engaged in herring fishing. The result was almost negligible, for in 1809 Dr Edmondston recorded that only one Shetland vessel claimed the bounty that year and the season's cure was a paltry 300 barrels.

As in the case of the ling and cod fisheries, development of the herring industry in Shetland was due to the efforts of the merchant landowners, who, as Captain Halcrow states, 'after having exploited line fish and fishermen to the utmost, turned envious eyes on the Dutch.' The only boats available in the islands were sixerns and these tiny open boats constituted the first Shetland herring fleet. Their catching power was limited. Although between 1820 and 1830 there were 450 sixerns in the islands engaged mainly in the haaf fishing, the annual export of cured herring was less than 3,000 barrels a year.

In the 1820s, incentive came in the form of a bonus of 2s (10p) on each barrel of herring cured and a further 2s 8d (13½p) on each barrel exported. The landlords began to invest in slightly improved types of craft—the two-masted Fifie and Scaffie of the East Coast of Scotland. They had a keel length of 25–35ft, but the most outstanding innovation was the addition of a foredeck covering about one-third of their length. At first the half-deckers were bought secondhand from Scotland, but later they were built at Lerwick in the yard of Hay & Ogilvy, who themselves operated a fleet of over 100 vessels.

The improved catches of the period demonstrated the success of the half-deckers. The catch rose from 10,000 crans in 1830 to 36,000 crans in 1833. (One cran equals 3½cwt.) In 1834 55,000 barrels of cured herring were exported, the main markets being the rest of Britain and the West Indies. Some crews met with outstanding success, and fishermen, formerly never out of debt, found themselves with money in the bank. In 1839 Christian Ployen noted the case of five men who in three years had paid off the purchase price of a boat and gear costing £120 and had besides earned £22 a year from the herring fishery.

Then came two severe setbacks. In September 1840 a great storm caught the fleet at sea, causing the loss of thirty boats, at least five of them with all hands, the rest suffering catastrophic loss of nets. In 1842 came a disaster of another kind—the collapse of the fishermen's bank at Lerwick. The crews were unable to obtain credit and dozens of half-deckers were hauled ashore and left to rot.

In the late 1870s the industry again began to develop: new markets were found in Germany and later in Russia and a new race of merchants, mostly Scottish, took over. The real impetus,

A 'Fifie' sailing drifter of the late nineteenth century

however, came from the adoption of large decked herring smacks built in Scotland. As the boom got under way, curing stations sprang up all over the islands. In 1885 the production was 370,000 barrels, but this was nothing to the record year of 1905, when more than half the entire Scottish herring catch was landed at Shetland. A fleet of 1,783 vessels, with crews numbering 12,500 men, landed 645,000 crans worth £576,000, and 1,024,044 barrels were cured. Most of these vessels were English and Scottish drifters, but Shetland's share was considerable—300 sailboats manned by 2,000 fishermen.

The trade was soon centralised in Lerwick, Baltasound, Scalloway and Sandwick, following the introduction of the auction system of sales. A new pier and fish market were built at Lerwick in 1907, and the gradual replacement of sailing vessels by steam drifters, to whom the extra miles to Lerwick were unimportant, presaged the end of the other ports.

The decline of the industry after 1905 was as rapid as the rise immediately before. Some people blamed the developing Norwegian whaling industry; more likely it was caused by a change in the movements of the herring shoals. By 1914 there was still a large fleet of 643 boats based at Lerwick, but World War I destroyed traditional markets and interrupted the activities of the herring fleet. There was a temporary revival in 1919 and for some years a fleet of 300–400 steam drifters operated from Lerwick, landing 200,000–300,000 crans annually to retain for Lerwick the title of premier herring port in Britain, though with a drastically reduced local fleet.

Improved Techniques

One of the reasons for the periodic upsurge of the herring industry after a period of stagnation and decline is the adoption of some innovation either in vessel type or gear. Often this brings far-reaching effects in its wake. Usually it entails greater expense, and the poorer fishermen, unable to copy or compete, must drop out.

Just as the large decked herring boat of the 1880s meant the end of the sixern, so the coming of the steam drifter started a decline in the numbers of sailing drifters and practically ended the local herring fleet, for few crofter-fishermen could afford the greater capital outlay. In 1910 only eight out of 310 British steam drifters based at Lerwick were Shetland-owned. In times of over supply it was always the steam drifter that reached port first and secured the best price, and she was also independent of the wind. In days of light wind, many a fine shot of herring had to be shovelled overboard as the sailing boat lay becalmed a few miles from port.

The Shetland fleet of sailing drifters declined steadily—thirty-eight in 1928, fourteen in 1932, one in 1937. The numbers of crofter-fishermen fell, too—between 1911 and 1931 from 2,263 to 938. Those who had large crofts concentrated on the land, others emigrated or joined the Merchant Navy.

Herring prices remained low. From an average of 3s 9d per cwt in 1901 the price had risen to only 8s 9d by 1931. The coal-burning drifters were expensive to run and in poor seasons could not meet their expenses. Then their numbers also declined and the great days of Lerwick as a herring port were over.

With the introduction of the paraffin engine, some of the old sailing boats got a reprieve. Owned chiefly by crews from Burra and Whalsay, they kept alive the tradition of herring fishing in Shetland, and in 1939 the fleet numbered fifty. Then came World War II, with the loss of Continental markets for a second time. Men and boats were required for the war effort. Some boats and many men did not return.

The postwar drifter was far more efficient than the drifter of twenty years earlier. She was equipped with echo-sounders for locating herring shoals, radio-telephone and the latest navigational aids. But the drift net, though made from modern man-made fibre, was almost identical to that used by the Dutch 500 years before.

In 1965 the full force of modern technology struck Shetland when a fleet of Norwegian purse-seiners, quickly increasing to 500 in number made Lerwick their base for operations 12–40 miles east of Shetland. They were large vessels equipped with sonar (similar to asdic, which was once used for spotting enemy submarines). The nets were equally modern : large nylon purse-seines to trap an entire shoal and hauled by hydraulic power blocks. Again there was an upsurge of interest and the first British purse seiners appeared in 1966. For some years the herring catch rose as the purse-seine fleet grew in size. Then a slump set in as the herring suffered from overfishing and eventually fishing was banned to save the stocks.

The Modern Fleet

Today the main effort is concentrated not on herring but on white fish, mainly haddock and whiting for the fresh-fish market in Aberdeen and local processing plants. The practice of sending fish cleaned and packed in ice to Aberdeen and Leith began in the late nineteenth century. Tudor records the beginning of the fresh-fish trade as 1876, when 60cwt were shipped south. This was nothing to the vast amounts being salted and dried, but by 1879 it had risen to 1,000cwt and by 1881 to 10,000cwt. Tudor forecast that the fresh-fish trade would develop into a 'very profitable business'—a prediction that was not really fulfilled until after World War II.

The salt-fish industry was practically over by 1900. The new but much smaller fresh-fish trade was developed by men from Lerwick, Scalloway, Burra Isle, Whalsay and Skerries, and several fishermen from north-east Scotland settled in Lerwick at this time. Almost all the landings were high quality haddock caught on 'small lines', and the tedious job of unravelling and rebaiting the lines was performed by the women of the family. In some districts the dredging of mussels for sale as bait was a profitable occupation.

In 1909 the first motorboat was purchased, several more were added in 1910, and in the line fleet, too, decked craft began to add a little more comfort. But between 1900 and 1939 the white-fish industry, like the herring industry after 1905, showed one long steady decline. The industry was hampered by the rising cost of carriage to the mainland, the lack of a local ice factory (not provided until 1946) and by the activities of Aberdeen trawlers poaching within the 3 mile limit. In 1938, though herring landings had declined, too, white fish accounted for only 8 per cent of the total earnings. In 1939 the haddock line fleet totalled forty-one vessels all under 50ft long.

The 'shot in the arm' was the adoption of the seine net, which was used by Lerwick inshore fishermen as early as 1926 for flats. In 1927 1,500cwt of flats were landed, worth £3,600, but seining did not become an important method of fishing until a net suitable for catching haddock was evolved. In 1939 lining accounted for 32,754cwt, and seining for only 629. The changeover took place during the war, and in 1944, while small-line landings had dropped to 4,873cwt, seine-net landings totalled 19,411cwt.

Since 1945 successive governments, through their statutory bodies—the Herring Industry Board and White Fish Authority—have taken an increasing interest in the fishing industry. In that year a loan and grant scheme was set up to enable fishermen to invest in better craft. Loans are repayable with interest over periods up to twenty years but generally fishermen repay this debt within 3–10 years.

More recently the Highlands and Islands Development Board, realising the special importance of fishing in their area, have given

Still knitting in spite of advancing years. Mrs Colvin died in 1978 aged 102. Jo Grimond, whose long career as MP for Orkney and Shetland ended in 1983, appears to give advice from his photograph on the wall

Page 140 (above) Shetland pony used for carrying baskets of peats in nets known as meshies. This practice survived longest in the island of Fetlar; *(below)* peat-cutting, 1970. The tushkar, unique in Shetland, is still in common use

grants for the purchase of good secondhand boats, and have helped to revive the industry in islands where it had almost died out. The result has been the transformation of the fleet: boats are no longer laid up for the winter nor is fishing suspended while croft work is attended to in spring and autumn. The capital involved in acquiring a modern vessel demands year-round fishing in nearly all weathers.

The modern fleet can be divided into four main groups. At the top are the nine purse seiners, large vessels up to 140ft long, which fish for herring and mackerel and spend most of the year at the other end of Britain, fishing off Cornwall. Next come the white-fish vessels, forty of them in the 50–80ft range which land their catches of haddock and whiting for processing locally. The largest regularly land their catches at Aberdeen after a round trip of up to 400 miles.

In the inshore range, 35–50ft, there are thirty-one multi-purpose vessels equipped for seining, creel-fishing for shellfish and occasionally lining for halibut, dogfish, or haddock. In November 1968 one of this class pioneered scallop-dredging in Shetland waters, and this has quickly developed into an important fishery.

These two groups are manned by full-time fishermen, but there is also an important group of forty-eight vessels in the range 20–35ft which fish almost full time for shellfish but suspend operations during winter. In addition there are over 200 small open or partly decked boats used occasionally for creel- and line-fishing.

The system of fixed prices for white fish that continued successfully throughout most of the 1960s was replaced in 1973 by the auction system leading to greatly increased prices. Today minimum prices for each species are fixed under Common Market rules so that even in times of over-supply, when part of the catch is bought for conversion to fish meal, fishermen receive a fair price.

Within recent years there has been a remarkable increase in the landings of shellfish. Lobster-fishing was reported at the end of the eighteenth century; and in 1808 three English smacks arrived, supplied the local fishermen with creels and bought their lobsters at 2d each. The scheme was not a success and even in 1909 the total catch of lobsters numbered only 700, worth £62. By 1947 the total value of shellfish landed by part-time fishermen was still under £3,000, but by 1960 shellfish landings were worth £60,000. In 1962, however, some of the larger vessels were forced by poor catches of white fish to try creel-fishing, and they boosted the value of lobsters to £110,000 for the year. In the same year crab-fishing began, and by 1968 the catch had risen steadily to 8,900cwt, valued at £22,200. This fishery has caused a revival at West Burrafirth and Ronas Voe, ports that had been deserted for almost sixty years.

The creek returns for 1977 showed a total of 485 full-time fishermen, 136 part-time fishermen and 27 crofter-fishermen. There are fewer boats and fewer fishermen than there were fifty years ago, but total catch, total value and average earnings have never been higher. 1982 was a record year for the industry with a catch worth more than £10 million.

7 OTHER INDUSTRIES

IN the past when the islands were practically self-supporting the Shetlander had to be a master of several trades. The minister of Northmavine could write at the end of the eighteenth century: 'The province of the men is managing their small farms, the fishing, boatbuilding and cutting their peats . . . besides they are generally tailor, shoemaker, weaver etc. to their own family and many are smith and wright'. This versatility was commendable, but many writers bemoaned the lack of a manufacturing industry at which the men could be gainfully employed during the long winter, as were the women with their knitting. The problem remained unsolved until the late 1960s, when the growing importance of knitwear and fish-processing filled the void.

THE WOOLLEN INDUSTRY

With crofting and fishing, knitting can be regarded as the third strand in Shetland's economy. In the past the croft supplied the basic food for the family, the profit from the fishing season paid the rent, and knitting was the most important source of ready cash. It was rarely regarded as a primary occupation, but fitted into slack periods in the cycles of housework and crofting. The minister of Sandsting & Aithsting, writing in 1791, unwittingly testifies to the industriousness of Shetland women: 'The yarn is generally spun at night when they would be otherwise idle, and when carrying dung, or travelling on the road, they are always knitting'.

A century and more later the crofter's wife still knitted as she walked to the shop or from the peat hill with loaded kishie on her back. Even today, when a lesser sense of urgency drives the knitting needles, the great tradition is maintained, as a study of the prize list at the annual Royal Highland Show reveals.

The soft wool of the native sheep, being more suitable for

knitting than for weaving, was an important factor in deciding the form of the early industry. As long ago as the sixteenth century there was a vigorous demand in Germany for Shetland stockings; then Dutch herring fishermen took over the market, and at the end of the eighteenth century, the value of this trade was £17,000 a year. It was a bitter blow to Shetland when the Napoleonic wars interrupted the activities of the Dutch herring fleet, and in 1808 the trade was worth only £5,000.

In the early days of the industry little attention was paid to quality, so the price was low. One minister writes of the wool being 'destroyed in coarse stockings which can hardly bring the value of the wool'. In the 1790s the stockings were bartered in Lerwick for tea, snuff and tobacco, and fetched only 5d a pair. For stockings carefully made there was a good demand, and in Unst at this time the stockings were 'much valued for softness and warmth' and fetched 1s 4d to 2s 6d a pair. Unst has long been famous for fine knitting, particularly of lace shawls so fine that a specimen 6ft square, containing 1½ miles of wool, weighs only 2½oz and can be pulled through a wedding ring.

In 1837 Arthur Anderson, trying to popularise Shetland knitwear in England, presented some fine stockings to Queen Victoria and the Duchess of Kent. Two years later the hosiery dealer Edward Standen began marketing Shetland knitwear in London. By 1893 the industry was worth about £25,000 a year, rising to £50,000 in 1910 and almost £100,000 in 1920.

The rapid rise after World War I was due to the increasing popularity of Fair Isle patterns in pullovers, scarves, berets and gloves. The Royal family again helped to foster this fashion when in 1921 the Prince of Wales wore a Fair Isle jersey while playing as Captain of the Royal and Ancient Golf Club at St Andrews.

Fair Isle

It has been claimed that knitting was introduced to Fair Isle by shipwrecked Spanish seamen in 1588. This is only a legend that tries to account for oriental features in patterns which are basically Scandinavian. There is, however, one story commonly told in that island of how a young woman, inspired by the cross painted on the bow of the wrecked galleon, used it as the basis of a pattern that is still knitted today.

The knitting of patterned garments is not confined to Fair

Isle, for although the art was preserved there, it was later introduced to the other islands. The art of using homemade dyes also survived there longest. Elsewhere in Shetland more use is made of natural colours from grey, white, brown and black sheep.

Methods of Manufacture

The methods of manufacture have changed over the years. At first all the wool was carded and spun by hand, the upright Scottish type of spinning-wheel probably being a later introduction than the elongated Norwegian type. Dyes were once derived entirely from native plants, but in 1840 the botanist Thomas Edmondston wrote that madder, indigo and logwood were in general use, and listed five or six plants still used for making dyes. Some required an almost witch-like mode of preparation. To make red dye the lichen *Lecanora tartarea* was scraped off the rocks; it was steeped in stale urine for three weeks, exposed constantly to gentle heat; then it was taken out, divided into cakes about ¾lb in weight, wrapped in dock leaves and hung up in peat smoke to dry. Nowadays chemical dyes are used universally except in Fair Isle, where some traditional shades cannot be reproduced by chemicals. Most yarn, however, is bought ready dyed.

As the demand for knitwear increased, it became impossible to produce enough yarn by hand, so the practice began about 1900 of sending wool to Brora and later Inverness for spinning. By the late 1930s practically all the wool for Shetland knitwear was spun on the mainland of Scotland, a situation that has often been deplored. Eventually the demand for Shetland knitwear could not be met by hand-knitters and the main revolution in the industry occurred with the introduction of the hand-flat knitting machine.

It is almost certain that the first knitting machine was introduced by Messrs Pole Hoseason of Mossbank about 1925. About 1930 three other firms, Messrs T. M. Adie of Voe, Mr John Tulloch of Urafirth and Mr L. J. Smith of Sandwick, bought their first machines. In the early 1950s home-knitters themselves began to invest in the smaller domestic-type machines then available, but the real boom in knitwear began in the 1960s, when Continental and particularly French markets became important; then the number of home-owned machines increased accordingly.

Machine-knitting now accounts for over 90 per cent of production. Almost the entire output consists of plain jumpers, but a distinctive Shetland touch can be added by the incorporation of hand-knitted Fair Isle patterned yokes. Small factories have been opened in several islands, having the advantage of greater control by management over the quality and the quantity produced, but the industry remains essentially cottage-based and part-time.

Generally all the members of the family help in their spare time in the various processes of winding yarn on the cone, the knitting and the finishing, by sewing together body, neck, cuffs and waistband. The earnings of machinists and finishers are far greater than those of women who still ply the knitting needles. The average income in the early 1960s was estimated at £4–5 a week though some women managed to earn up to £12 a week and run their homes at the same time.

The value of Shetland knitwear rose to £800,000 in 1966 and £1,150,000 in 1968 owing to the greatly increased output of machine-made garments. In 1969, when there was a turnover of almost £1½ million, the industry supported over 2,000 home-knitters working regularly and perhaps 1,000 working less regularly for 35 local merchants, most of whom also operated a knitting unit with up to 50 full-time employees. The total number of full-time workers was 350. France was then Shetland's most important customer outside Britain, buying in 1969 one quarter of the islands' total production.

That was before the oil construction boom when for the first time there were highly paid jobs for women. The home-based knitting industry was badly hit and production fell sharply. Since then a recovery has taken place and the industry's turnover in 1981 was estimated at £4 million.

There is still a small trade in traditional hand-knitted garments sold direct to shops in Lerwick or to private customers. It is difficult to see a future for this sector unless the purchaser starts to realise the time needed to make these garments and pays a better price.

Shetland Tweed

Tweed manufacture is now relatively unimportant, though in the seventeenth and eighteenth centuries the weaving of 'claith' was universal. As late as 1808 there were weavers in every parish who wove blankets and a kind of cloth 'for the ordinary wear of the country people'. In 1881 John R. Tudor found websters in Northmavine, Delting and Lunnasting, but the census of 1911 showed only thirty-six weavers in the whole county.

There was a strong demand for Shetland tweed from the American market during the early 1950s, though there were only two or three firms geared to take advantage of it and operations were factory- rather than home-based. The whole British woollen textile industry and the expanding Japanese industry were pouring their goods into the USA, so the Americans imposed a quota system, followed in 1956 by a punitive tariff that almost killed the revitalised Shetland tweed industry.

New markets have been found since then, and Shetland tweed is produced by five firms of which the largest is at Sandwick. The value of this section of the industry was estimated at £90,000 in 1969.

Trademark

The lack of an effective trademark was one of the most serious drawbacks of the woollen industry. The failure of all applications to the Board of Trade to have the name Shetland reserved for garments knitted in the islands meant that the name was applied merely to a type of knitwear manufactured in places as far apart as Hawick and Japan. The eagerness with which those manufacturers capitalise upon the name shows its high reputation. Unfortunately, by producing an inferior article, they often do untold damage to the island industry.

In 1921, when alarm was raised at the amount of imitation Shetland goods manufactured beyond the islands, the Shetland Woollen Industries Association was formed to protect the industry by applying a certification mark to garments knitted in Shetland, but it failed through lack of support. In 1947 the SWIA was revived, and in 1956 the certification mark of the Society was extended to cover the description 'Made in Shetland', to be used for knitwear produced on hand-flat machines and hand-woven tweed. In 1983 Shetland Knitwear Trades Association was set up with more than thirty firms as members. It has a distinctive trademark attached to all garments produced by its members.

The relationship between Shetland wool and knitwear made

in Shetland is hard to define. During spinning on the mainland of Scotland, much of the fine Shetland wool becomes dispersed, and what returns is merely a blend of wool, only part Shetland.

A small wool mill, said to be the most modern at that time in Scotland, was started in 1946 by A. Sandison & Sons, Baltasound, and lasted till 1951. The establishment of a large mill to handle the islands' wool clip is one of the recommendations of the report published by the Highlands and Islands Development Board in 1970. The total amount of yarn used in knitwear and tweed manufacture in 1969 was 400,000lb.

FISH-PROCESSING

Before the practice developed of preserving fish by freezing, most of Shetland's catch had to be cured before export. Up to the end of the nineteenth century this created a considerable amount of employment in salting and drying cod and ling; and an even greater source of employment ashore was the herring fishery, which developed in the 1880s.

Several hundreds of men were employed as coopers, assembling wooden barrels, and for the heavier jobs round the station, but most of the labour force consisted of women working in crews of three and paid as a team on piecework rates. They gutted and packed the herring with salt in barrels, developing amazing dexterity. The hours were long and they had to stand in the open in all weathers, their cut hands and fingers smarting from the ever-present salt.

In 1905, 2,500 shore workers were employed at thirty-six stations at Lerwick, 2,840 were employed at forty-eight stations at Baltasound and thousands more assisted at ninety stations distributed among dozens of smaller ports. The industry declined quickly at the small ports, however, though at Lerwick the summer fishery continued to be a major source of employment until the late 1930s. In 1935 there were 1,850 shore workers there.

Curing was the main outlet for the catch, but as early as 1905 new trends were apparent. In that year three firms operated kippering kilns and steamers ran regularly to Hamburg with cargoes of fresh herring packed in ice to be smoked in Germany. Both these outlets grew in importance. Kippering developed into an important industry at Scalloway, where by 1930 there were five kilns in operation, and the name Scalloway had become famous for a product of high quality.

After World War II freezing became important, and a factory was built at Lerwick by the Herring Industry Board. In 1960, out of a total catch of 31,000 crans, freezing absorbed 13,000 crans, compared with 12,000 for curing and 4,000 for meal and oil. Although landings have improved consistently since then, the amount sold for human consumption has remained static. There is no longer an insatiable market for salt herring, since the Baltic countries now have their own fleets catching and curing herring. In 1970, out of a total catch of 77,000 crans, freezing accounted for 12,600 crans, curing for 13,000, and the meal and oil factory for 36,000 crans. Of the remaining 15,400 crans, most was bought by buyers in Fraserburgh and transported there in carrier vessels for processing, and a small amount was kippered locally.

The new white-fish industry did not at first create much employment ashore. The catch, chiefly of prime quality haddock, was packed in ice and despatched by steamer to customers and parent firms in Aberdeen and Glasgow.

Greatest problem after World War II was the decline in the number of local white-fish buyers. In 1946 there were fourteen firms, but rising freight charges forced one after the other out of business until in 1958 there was only one major firm left, a company that rented part of the Herring Industry Board's factory at Lerwick for filleting and freezing white fish. The price paid to fishermen dropped through lack of competition, and in 1957 the average was less than 30s per cwt.

To overcome this local lack of buyers the fishermen had to consign their fish by steamer to Aberdeen fish market, though freight and handling charges, which soon reached £1 per cwt, reduced profit considerably. The larger boats solved the problem by carrying their catches direct to Aberdeen. In 1963 40 per cent of the islands' white-fish catch was landed at Aberdeen and a further 33 per cent was consigned there by steamer, leaving only 27 per cent to be processed locally. The detrimental effect on Shetland's economy was obvious: all the fish could have been filleted and frozen locally, creating jobs at a time when unemployment was a serious problem.

Then local businessmen began to realise the potential of Shetland's fishing industry. First locally owned factory was that of

Iceatlantic (Frozen Seafoods) Ltd at Scalloway, which opened in 1960, followed within a few years by a second firm at Scalloway and two at Lerwick. By 1965 70 per cent of the white-fish catch was being processed locally, with full-time employment for 200 filleters and other employees.

In the late 1960s, with assistance from the Highlands and Islands Development Board, the fish-processing industry expanded and diversified. There are now five factories at Lerwick processing white-fish and herring, and one of them handles all varieties of shellfish. Scalloway has three factories processing white fish, herring and some shellfish. One of the Scalloway factories converts all its white-fish offal into high-grade meal for animal feeding.

Even more remarkable is the rate of these developments in rural districts, especially in areas where decline has been progressive for almost seventy years: the island of Yell has a cannery and a shellfish unit with storage for live lobsters: a factory was built at Graven on Sullom Voe to handle shellfish and small amounts of white fish and herring. It has now closed—a victim of the oil era. The islands of Out Skerries, Whalsay and Burra each have a small white-fish processing plant.

Fish meal and oil production have long been important at Bressay, the island that shelters the harbour of Lerwick. A plant was set up at Heogan in 1883 to utilise surplus herring; and in 1912 a second plant was established at Aith Voe, but it closed in 1933.

The output of meal and oil decreased with the decline in the herring industry between the wars, but it received a boost in the 1960s with the expansion of the white-fish industry. Unsold fish and offal from processing plants were shipped from Lerwick to Bressay. A bigger boost still in the late 1960s was the landing of herring and pout by Scandinavian vessels engaged in the controversial industrial fisheries. Foreign vessels landed 20,000 tons of fish in 1968 and over 16,000 tons in 1970. In that year the factory produced 6,250 tons of fish meal and 3,000 tons of herring oil which is used in the manufacture of margarine. Its full-time labour force numbered 32.

The factory at Heogan has been expanded progressively to cope with increased supplies. In 1974 Shetland vessels discovered another species to fish, the humble sand eel which is too small to be used as food although it sustains larger species of fish as well as seabirds. In 1981 this catch reached 40,000 tonnes and the Norwegian-British consortium who own the factory decided to erect new premises with greatly increased capacity.

The numbers employed in fish processing increased from 200 in 1965 to just over 600 in 1970 including 120 employed only during the herring season. The loss of the herring fishery in the late 1970s came as a blow to students and others who had come to depend on herring processing for summer employment. In 1981 it was calculated that Shetland's fishing industry provided jobs for 1,265 people—542 fishermen, 480 employed in fish processing and 243 in ancillary industries. These figures emphasise the importance of fishing and fish processing to Shetland. The success of both sectors accounted largely for the revival of Shetland's economy in the 1960s and they remain as important today.

BOATBUILDING

The import of small fishing boats from Norway continued for centuries after the severing of Shetland's political ties with that country. The main centres for this trade were small towns around Bjornafjord, south of Bergen. The planks were assembled with very few nails, numbered and taken apart for shipment and reassembly in Shetland. Boats of the same design were also constructed in Shetland.

The first purely Shetland boat was the sixern, an enlarged and improved version of the typical Norwegian model, and as early as 1740 boats of 18ft keel were in use at Northmavine. It is probable that the first sixerns were commissioned in Norway, for a Norwegian county prefect's report refers to larger 'Shetland boats' still being built at Tysness between 1836 and 1840. But as greater skill was acquired locally, imports declined, and ceased altogether about 1860.

The start of the cod fishery in fully decked smacks was a great impetus in establishing boatbuilding concerns. Between 1820 and 1850 smacks and sloops were built at Lerwick, Scalloway, Delting, Reawick, Walls and Skeld, while Hay & Ogilvy at Lerwick also built schooners and brigantines. Activity increased at this yard with the adoption of partly decked herring boats in the 1830s, before the collapse of the herring fishery in 1842.

In the 1880s, when the herring industry revived with the use of fully decked Scottish-type sailing smacks, the boatbuilding industry also revived, with yards at Lerwick, Scalloway and later at Sandwick. The last sailing drifter to be built in Shetland was the *Swan*, built by Hay & Co, Lerwick. With an engine installed she was still fishing after World War II. After 1910 boatbuilding was confined to small fishing vessels, motor haddock boats (the successors to the sixerns), four-oared boats and a few yachts. There were several notable builders and two firms—A. Sandison & Sons, Baltasound, and W. Duncan, Hamnavoe—continue to the present day.

In 1946 an attempt was made to resume building larger vessels by David Howarth at Scalloway, which yard built some fine vessels up to 65ft in length before it closed in 1951. Since then all the new dual-purpose fishing vessels that have been added to the fleet have been built in Scotland, with the exception of four of the largest, which have been built in Norway.

It is in the building of small wooden vessels that island craftsmen are most renowned. The Norse influence is still pronounced in the clinker-built Shetland boats, which are tapered to both stem and stern.

In 1962 Shetland Marine, a federation of local builders, was formed to explore the possibility of entering the main British small-boat market. In the 1960s Shetland-built pleasure craft were exhibited regularly at the International Boat Show in London, and several orders were secured in this way. Most small boats nowadays are mass-produced, but Shetland boats are still built by craftsmen, and this feature has accounted largely for the favourable comments from experts and general public alike. The intention of Shetland Marine was to build large fishing vessels in addition to pleasure craft and although boats up to 40ft long were built at Lerwick the group's main ambition was not realised and it was disbanded. Nevertheless small fishing boats and pleasure craft are launched regularly from boat building sheds at Baltasound and Hamnavoe.

The craft of boatbuilding is not confined to organised yards and professional boatbuilders; in every district there is a carpenter or a crofter who builds boats as a sideline or as a hobby. Often surprising results arise from unpromising materials: in 1964 a previously undistinguished Shetland-model boat, 18ft long overall and built by a crofter in Foula seventy-three years earlier made a successful crossing of the Atlantic under sail. Plans are now afoot to preserve her as a splendid example of her class.

MINING AND QUARRYING

In spite of the great variety of minerals found in Shetland, few occur in sufficient quantity to warrant extensive exploitation. However, the history of quarrying and mining on a small scale is long and varied.

The beautiful red and green-tinged granite of Hildasay was quarried at the end of the nineteenth century for building stone and ornamental purposes, being shipped south for polishing. The best building stones occur among the sedimentary rocks on the east of Shetland. At one time the Bressay sandstones were quarried extensively, especially at the cliffs of Ord Head and Bard Head; in 1841 a dozen men were so employed, earning up to 1s (5p) a day each. Bressay also produced roofing slates, and Mousa produced flagstones for the streets of Lerwick. Lerwick sandstone was worked for building material until well into the twentieth century, but for the last thirty years practically all new houses in Shetland have been built of imported brick or concrete blocks produced locally.

Before the introduction of tarmacadam to the roads of Lerwick in 1933, and rural Shetland in 1936, the roads were surfaced with gravel and pebbles obtained from roadside quarries. Today stone is crushed by machinery at quarries at Scalloway, Unst and Yell, producing 40–50,000 tons of hard core, aggregate, bitumen macadam and dust per year.

The hard blue-grey limestone of the Mainland and Unst has been quarried for building stone and road metal, but its most important use is the production of agricultural lime. A century ago there were numerous stone-built kilns situated along the limestone bands. Limestone and peat were placed in alternate layers to fill the kiln, which was then lit; later the burned lime was separated from the peat ashes, then slaked with water. A typical burning yielded 30–36 barrels of lime, approximately 2½ tons, and a kiln might be burned three times a year.

In 1936 there were two kilns in operation at Fladdabister and Girlsta, and operations continued at the latter until 1969, when the quarry was closed. At present agricultural lime is imported from Banffshire, but, since limestone is so abundant in Shetland, it is to be hoped that production will be resumed locally.

Copper and iron ores

Outcrops of copper with associated iron are found at several places in the parish of Dunrossness. Dr Hibbert mentions iron ore once worked at Fitful Head and a vein of iron pyrites worked at Garthsness at the end of the eighteenth century. Only at Sandlodge, however, have there been concentrated efforts to recover the ores. At the end of the eighteenth century Welsh miners sank shafts and raised £2,000 worth of copper ore. In 1803 a shaft was sunk 132ft, following a vein 9–10ft wide and dipping at an angle of 50–60°, but work stopped in 1808. In 1872 crushing and washing apparatus was installed, and in 1880 the lease was sold to the Sumburgh Mining Co, but work was suspended the same year. To this date the mine had produced 1,995 tons of copper, valued at £5,814, and 10,000 tons of iron, which were sold to gasworks as a desulphurising agent. In 1907 a west shaft was sunk, following a zone of siderite, oxidised to within 100ft of the surface to limonite and haematite, giving assays of 64 per cent iron with rich pockets of copper pyrites. Below the oxidised zone the assays were 35 per cent iron and 5–6 per cent copper. The mine reopened in 1920 and work continued sporadically until it was finally closed a few years later.

Magnetite occurs at Sullom in an irregular lenticular ore body. A detailed investigation carried out between 1939 and 1945 proved the ore to be of excellent quality, with assays of 63 per cent iron. Ore reserves were estimated at 20,000 tons down to 72ft below ground level, but only a few thousand tons of magnetite were produced in the 1950s before the mine closed in 1959.

Chromite and Talc

Although an outcrop of soapstone or steatite, a form of talc, was worked at Cunningsburgh from Iron Age to medieval times to produce cooking vessels and receptacles, recent exploitation has been limited to the North Isles of Shetland. Chromite was once worked in Fetlar and Haaf Grunay, and soapstone was shipped in sacks from Fetlar during World War I, but all these workings are small compared to those of Unst.

Chromite or chromate of iron was discovered in Unst in 1817

by Dr Hibbert. Exploitation began in 1820, when scattered lumps were gathered and small quarries opened, the ore being shipped for the manufacture of chrome pigment. A larger high-grade ore body was then discovered at Hagdale, and in 1857 the quarry gave employment to 100 men. It operated until 1865, producing an estimated 30,000 tons of ore. Quarrying continued in other parts of Unst until about 1875.

About 1907 quarrying was restarted on a minor scale, a small shipment of ore was made in 1909, and by 1913 regular cargoes were being shipped to Liverpool. During World War I there was increased demand for chromite for hardening steel, since supplies from abroad were difficult to obtain, so the old quarries were pumped dry and output was increased.

After World War I a concentrating mill was erected, mainly to cope with the huge spoil heaps, and in 1920 the quarries were giving part-time employment to 50 or 60 men, but with renewed imports of high-grade ore from abroad the Unst quarries closed in 1927. An English company took over the lease in 1937, and several shipments of fairly low-grade chromite ore were made, until operations finally ceased in 1944. An estimated 50,000 tons of chromite have been produced since 1820.

Mining of talc began in a small way in 1939, but developed rapidly after 1945. Current production is around 17,000 tons per year produced by five men, and the operation is highly mechanised to enable the Unst product to compete with imported talc. It is used mainly in the production of fertilisers and also in the ceramics industry.

Peat

Shetland's most abundant mineral is peat, which has been dug and dried for fuel from the time of the earliest colonisation of the islands. Peat ash is found even in Neolithic sites, and only recently has peat become less important than imported coal and oil. Tradition has it that Torf Einar was the Earl who first showed the Norse settlers how to cut peat; more likely it was he who introduced to Shetland the Norse implement known as the tushkar, which is unique among all peat-cutting districts of Britain.

The strip of moor to be worked in early summer must first be cleaned or 'flayed' by removing the covering of heather or moss. An implement known as a ripper is used to make a cut parallel to the face of the peat bank and about 2ft in. Undercutting of the surface layer is performed with an ordinary garden spade.

When the peat has been exposed the tushkar is used in digging out the slabs. In all other peat-cutting areas two workers are required in the digging process—one cuts the turf with a spade while his helper carries away the wet slabs to be laid flat for drying—but in Shetland only a single operator using a tushkar is needed. He forms the slabs, untouched by hand, into a dyke, with regular spaces to allow the wind to pass through. Not until two weeks later, when the first stage of drying is complete, are the peats handled and set up in small pyramids for the second stage of drying.

When drying is complete, the peats are transported home and carefully built into a weatherproof stack. In most districts they are bagged and carried to the nearest road for transport by motor lorry or by tractor and cart, and in a few places they are ferried by boat. At one time ponies were used universally to 'lead' home the peats, a practice that survived longest in Fetlar.

From being an essential annual chore, peat-cutting has now come to be regarded by many office workers as healthy exercise in the open air. It is common to see a dozen or more expensive motor cars lining the sides of the peat road in the hills above Lerwick, while their owners are busy cutting peat.

It has long been a dream in Shetland to harvest the expanse of peat by mechanical means as is done in Eire. Experiments carried out beside the Loch of Brindister in the early 1950s proved that Shetland peat has a high wax content, but attempts at drying artificially disappointingly proved that the milled peat process is impracticable in Shetland.

Vast deposits remain practically untouched; for instance a survey of the Kames bog in Pettadale estimated that there were 670,000 tons of dry peat solids, of which 400,000 might be used for fuel. It has been calculated that this amount would keep a 3·5MW power station running for 25 years. The estimate for Yell was approximately 200 million tons of raw peat or 16 million tons of peat solids.

TOURISM

Until near the end of the nineteenth century, accommodation for visitors consisted merely of small inns at Lerwick and Scallo-

Page 157 (above) Aerial view of Scalloway and its harbour; *(below)* Scalloway castle overlooking Blacksness Pier and the fish market

Aerial view of Lerwick in 1977 showing fishing vessels and craft used in the oil industry berthed at the quays

way. The only people who could provide comfortable lodgings for visitors were lairds and ministers, and it is to the credit of both groups that they never failed to do so. The common people also gave what they had, so that the extent of Shetland hospitality was the biggest surprise to visitors of the eighteenth and nineteenth centuries.

In the 1880s and 1890s, when Shetlanders realised that strangers were eager to visit the islands, several hotels and boarding houses were opened. A guidebook of 1900 listed eight hotels in Lerwick, Scalloway, Unst and Clousta, thirty-three boarding houses, including several at Dunrossness, and five inns.

The number of tourists increased very slowly. Cruise liners began to call in summer, but they mainly benefited the knitwear shops in Lerwick. In the first half of this century the chief promoter of tourism was the steamship company, which organised package tours with a stay in its own hotel, opened at Hillswick in 1900. Other package tours did not develop until the 1960s, when Wallace Arnold, Midland Red and Scotia Tours provided stays in Shetland of from twenty-four hours' to two weeks' duration.

Biggest rise in the number of visitors (54 per cent) occurred between 1958 and 1962—14,500 to 22,400—according to annual figures provided by the Scottish Tourist Board. Thereafter the numbers remained static or decreased slightly, since available accommodation was fully utilised.

In 1966 there were only three hotels in Lerwick, with 90 beds, and 104 beds were available in boarding houses. For the whole county the total number of beds available for visitors was just under 500. In addition there was a youth hostel at Lerwick and a hostel attached to the bird observatory at Fair Isle.

Since then the Shetlanders have realised the potential of tourism as an industry. Existing hotels have been extended and seven new hotels have been opened, including the large twenty-six bedroom Lerwick Hotel, opened in 1970 and costing £150,000 to build. Fetlar now has a guesthouse and a new hostel has been built at Fair Isle. Some crofters are providing partly furnished accommodation in disused croft houses, and the number who provide bed and breakfast is increasing. The value of the tourist industry in the late 1970s was around £2 million a year.

Numerous bus tours are available and a few sporting amenities and some entertainment have been provided, but much remains to be done in catering for visitors. Shetland Tourist Organisation is aware, however, that large numbers of visitors are town dwellers who appreciate the peace and quiet of Shetland as it is. Such people include bird watchers, anglers, archaeologists and simply people who love islands.

Outside Lerwick there is a tremendous need for better information regarding the many attractions—the sites of special scientific interest, the archaeological sites and the scores of islands which can be visited, each with its own special interest. Hitherto the tourist season has been largely confined to three months a year, but recently attempts have been made to extend the season by promoting sea angling, with an international competition in September. The festival of Up-Helly-Aa in January is now attracting more visitors and is certain to increase in popularity.

SEAWEED-PROCESSING

In the second half of the eighteenth century, the making of kelp from seaweed for use in the glass and soap industries became an important occupation in Scotland. About 1760 several of the Shetland lairds invited an expert from Orkney to assess the seaweed potential here, and he reported that under proper management the output might be as high as 40 tons of kelp a year. Cutting and burning seaweed began soon after, and the first year produced 80 tons. Output rose steadily, to over 600 tons in 1808.

Each landowner, exercising his supposed rights to the foreshore, employed a man to supervise the work, paying him £2 to £2 10s (£2·50) a ton, while the latter hired women and boys at trifling wages. In the 1790s the average wage was 7s 6d (37½p) a month or roughly '2d a tide'. The seaweed was first allowed to dry, and was then burned in pits, fresh material being added from time to time until the pit was filled with gelatinous kelp, which was allowed to cool before handling.

In 1808 rising prices tempted the people to make their own kelp from seaweed (*fucus serratus*) and tangle (*laminaria digitata*) growing below low-water mark and cast ashore after a storm. This produced better quality kelp and accounted for over 100 tons of the total for that year. The price rose as high as £20 a ton but fell quickly after the end of the Napoleonic wars. The great rival to kelp in the glass and soap industries was Spanish barilla, a carbonate of soda made from plant ashes, which had an alkali content of 23½ per cent compared with one of only 2½ per cent in Shetland kelp, and increasing imports of barilla ruined the kelp industry. This was a blow to Shetland, but the effect was far more severe in Orkney and the Hebrides, where certain districts had founded their whole economy on seaweed.

A revival took place in 1870 for the production of iodine and bromine, and in 1880, according to John Tudor, a few hundred tons of kelp were produced in Unst, Yell and along the Mainland shores of Yell Sound. For many visitors their most lasting impression of Shetland was the little kelp fires burning along the shore. The industry had almost died before the end of the century.

In 1965 tangle gathering began on a small scale in the Sumburgh, Bigton and Sandness areas, organised by local agents, for Alginate Industries (Scotland) Ltd of Inverness. For some years a small amount of dried tangles was shipped to a factory at Loch Boisdale. The price in 1969 was £16 5s (£16.25) per ton or roughly 1d per tangle.

8 THE SEA AROUND US

AN account of Shetland is incomplete if it deals only with the islands and the islanders. The influence of the fishermen extends over a wide circle round about, and much of the special character of the group is derived from the sea and the chance visitors it brings.

SHIPS AND SHIPWRECKS

The only records of shipwreck before the mid-sixteenth century are three incidents described in the sagas, but after 1567 information is abundant. In that year the Earl of Bothwell, fleeing from Scotland, called at Shetland on his way to Norway. He found a German merchant, Geert Hemelingk, carrying on his trade at Grutness and chartered his ship *Pelikaan*. The pursuers almost caught Bothwell in Bressay Sound, for as the *Pelikaan* sailed out of the north entrance, the *Unicorn*, commanded by Sir Wm Kirkcaldy of Grange, sailed in the south entrance. Bothwell had a local pilot who cleverly steered the *Pelikaan* close to a sunken rock a few miles farther north, and the pursuing vessel, following almost the same course, struck violently and sank. The reef is known as the Unicorn rock to this day.

In 1588 the ships of the defeated Spanish Armada escaped in disorder round the north of Scotland, and one of them, *El Gran Grifon*, was wrecked at Fair Isle. It was easy in later years to classify all unidentified wrecks as those of Spanish ships, but there is no doubt about *El Gran Grifon*. Her commander was Admiral Don Juan Gomez de Medina. Her crew, numbering about 200, spent six or seven weeks on the island, causing near famine among the islanders as they tried to support their uninvited guests. In 1970 the wreck was located, and some interesting relics, including an 8ft long bronze gun and a large amount of lead shot and cannon balls, were recovered.

With the development of trade in the eighteenth century much traffic proceeded along the east coast of Shetland from ports between Archangel and South Norway bound for Britain and the Low Countries. The North Atlantic trade was also becoming important, with cargoes of timber and tobacco for Europe sailing eastwards past Sumburgh Head.

When the English Channel was under the command of a hostile power, ships trading to America and the Far East preferred the northerly route in spite of its natural dangers. Many were wrecked, including some with valuable cargoes. One of these was the Dutch ship *De Liefde*, a vessel 160ft long, built in Amsterdam in 1698. In October 1711 she left Amsterdam, one of a fleet sailing to Batavia and Ceylon. The War of the Spanish Succession was at its height and the English fleet controlled the Channel, so the fleet chose the northern route. On Sunday 7 November the people of Out Skerries returned from church to find a solitary Dutchman wandering about in a daze—the sole survivor of *De Liefde*. He had been on lookout duty in the crow's nest and had been flung ashore when the ship struck the rocks.

Reports that she was carrying 700,000 Dutch florins instigated several attempts at salvage. None was successful until 1965, when a group of divers located the wreck, and, in 1967, recovered 4,000 silver coins as well as finds of historical importance. Among other treasure ships were the Dutch *Kennemerlandt*, wrecked at Out Skerries in 1664, and the Swedish *Vandela*, wrecked at Fetlar in 1737.

In later years emigrant ships from Europe bound for America used the northerly route, and one was wrecked at Fetlar in 1765, with the loss of all passengers and crew. No lives were lost, however, when the German ship *Lessing*, carrying 465 passengers and crew, was wrecked at Fair Isle in 1868.

The Shetlanders have shown contradictory attitudes to shipwrecks. Only those who live in a treeless island can understand how eagerly the beaches are scanned even today for useful bits of timber cast ashore from a deck cargo lost at sea. In former times, when basic commodities were scarce and luxuries practically unobtainable, a wreck or goods washed ashore were regarded as gifts from Providence.

The Stewart earls laid claim to all wrecks and a large proportion of the cases in Earl Patrick's court book for the years 1602–4 deal with pilferage. The first entry concerns 'twa barrelis pick [pitch] cassin in about the bankis [cliffs] of the Skerreis, ane lispund yrne [iron] taine out of ane peice of ane brokin schip'.

For centuries ships have continued to be 'brokin' and have continued to provide fuel and building material. In 1700, John Brand tells us, the people of Out Skerries relied on driftwood for much of their fuel. After the wreck of the *Kennemerlandt*, a quantity of spirits was recovered, and it was reported that the people of that island were in a state of intoxication for the next twenty days.

It became the practice for wrecks to be sold and the proceeds divided into three shares, 'one thereof to the proprietor of the ground, one to the salvor, and the other to the proprietor if any appeared, which failing to the king, with the best anchor to the admiral'. This arrangement did not satisfy the Earl of Morton when he received rights of admiralty: he refused the owner of the ground anything more than damage to his property, while the salvors had to content themselves with what they could carry off and hide. This rapacious attitude was extended even to the undamaged cargoes of stranded vessels. In 1761 the Rev John Mill was concerned that a number of his parishioners had robbed two Dutch vessels stranded at Sandwick. Even in the nineteenth century this attitude prevailed, the people of the west and northwest coasts of Shetland having the worst reputation.

In their treatment of shipwrecked seamen the Shetlanders appear in a different light, for no effort was too great in providing help and shelter for the survivors. John Brand, so critical of the morals of the people, could say in 1700, 'Such a kind and generous Reception, Merchants and Mariners meet not with in many places upon which they are unhappily cast'.

FOREIGN FISHING FLEETS

Shetland lies in the midst of some of the best fishing grounds in the world. Temperature, salinity and ocean currents combine to promote an abundance of plankton, food for herring and shoals of small fish, which in turn provide food for other species. Strangely, Britain has let other nations reap the benefit of this area. There were between seventy and eighty English vessels, mainly from Southampton, fishing here as long ago as 1532, but by 1547 their numbers had dwindled to nine. In the early seventeenth century line fishermen from Fife were active; but from the time of King Henry VIII the activities of British fishermen were completely overshadowed by those of the Dutch, fishing with lines for cod and with drift nets for herring.

The Dutch herring fleet rose to a peak in the mid-seventeenth century, when as many as 2,200 busses were said to put in at Lerwick at one time, and one could walk from Lerwick to Bressay across a sound ¾ mile wide on a bridge of moored vessels. This was before the wars which interrupted the Dutch fishing industry.

Visitors to Shetland continually urged British governments to take their share of the ocean's wealth. In 1774 George Low reported St Magnus Bay to be teeming with herring. 'But', he added, 'this is nothing to the swarms which are around the coasts and never come into the bays. These are the armies which enrich our neighbours while we look tamely on.' Not until 100 years later did British fishermen begin to exploit the herring shoals.

Today ships of more than a dozen European countries fish round Shetland and on the banks to the east (Bressay Bank, Viking Bank and Bergen Bank). Some nations once had larger fleets, but some are still expanding their fishing industry. At one time Swedish vessels fishing for ling to the north-west of Shetland called in such numbers at Baltasound that a Swedish church with resident pastor was opened there in 1910. At Lerwick the Dutch were for centuries the most numerous of visitors, but in 1936 for the first time their numbers fell below those of the Swedes. Since World War II the Norwegian fishing fleet has been most active in this area, fishing with lines for ling and dogfish, harpooning whales and basking sharks and later purse-seining for herring.

Throughout the 1960s Russian vessels became more numerous, reflecting the development of the Soviet fishing industry. Most frequent Russian callers are tankers ferrying fresh water to the fleet at sea, but ocean-going tugs also arrive with disabled trawlers in tow. During bad weather large numbers of Russian trawlers, factory ships and transport vessels seek shelter in the wide firth between Fetlar and Out Skerries. Trans-shipment of fish and stores is carried out with the approval of the British government.

In spite of so many nationalities being represented on the fishing grounds, harmony usually prevails. Co-operation is most marked when a vessel requires help. The Russians were at first suspicious and sometimes refused assistance offered to their vessels in distress. Careless dumping of refuse between Fetlar and Out Skerries led to complaints by Shetland fishermen, who had nets torn or lost. Misunderstanding over their use of red flares for signalling led to unnecessary trips by Lerwick lifeboat. All these difficulties have been resolved.

After years of fishing in this area the Russians became much more friendly, seeming anxious to assist whenever possible. In 1968 and again in 1971 during periods of drought a small Russian water-tanker took an emergency supply of water to fill the reservoir at Out Skerries. The Russians have reason to be grateful for our own assistance, for in October 1958 three men were rescued by Lerwick lifeboat from a wave-washed rock after their trawler had been wrecked on the Holm of Skaw, Unst. In another incident twelve Russians were rescued by breeches buoy from their trawler ashore at Tresta Wick, Fetlar.

Since the extension of Common Market fishing limits in 1977 very few Russian fishing vessels have called at Shetland ports.

CONSERVATION

There has long been concern lest intensive exploitation of any species of fish might result in over-fishing, dwindling stocks and the loss of men's livelihood. One of the earliest forms of control was the establishment of a close season, a period in which fishing for a certain species was banned. It was with conservation in mind that the great Dutch fleet sailed for Shetland under strict orders 'that no-one shall wet their nets in the sea before the Feast of St John The Baptist' (June 24). In 1774 George Low complained of the activities of other fleets in this area, which he believed broke the shoals by starting before this date.

Shetland, too, had dates fixed for preserving stocks of inshore fish, to be fished only in winter, when it was difficult and dangerous to go far afield. One of the old Country Acts prohibited fishing in any voe between Beltane and Allhallowmass, ie between 1 May and 1 November each year.

Lines and old-fashioned drift nets were selective in their operation. The real conflict of interest only arose at the end of the nineteenth century, when steam trawlers from Aberdeen began operating round Shetland. When they began poaching inside the prohibited 3 mile limit and even in the voes, ill-feeling became open hostility. A Society was formed to keep watch and report cases of illegal trawling, with a reward of £5 offered for information leading to arrest. The fishermen of Fair Isle were the most vigilant—perhaps they suffered most—but the high prices obtained for inshore fish more than compensated for an occasional fine, and skippers of Aberdeen trawlers made frequent appearances in Lerwick Sheriff Court, thirteen being fined or sentenced in one day in May 1907. It should be pointed out that opposition was only extended to illegal trawling, and when lives were in danger all bitterness was forgotten, for, also in 1907, the crew of the Aberdeen trawler *Strathbeg* were rescued by the men of Fair Isle.

Sailboats and lines eventually lost the battle against steam vessels and otter trawls, and Shetland fishermen, too, began to modernise their fleet. They invested in small motorboats, and, about 1926, began fishing with Danish seine nets for plaice and other flatfish. When Shetlanders themselves began to appear in court for violating the 3 mile limit, they agitated to have all Shetland waters opened for seining by vessels under 50ft long. A special byelaw to this effect was passed in 1927, but the ban on trawling within 3 miles of the shore continues.

It is for reasons of conservation that international agreements govern the mesh size of nets and state a minimum size for each species below which fish must be returned to the sea. Other countries often flout these regulations, and Denmark especially has built up an important industry using small-meshed nets to catch fish of all sizes purely for reduction to meal and oil. The extent of industrial fishing by foreign vessels is a cause of worry to many people who fear that harm will be done to our own fishing industry.

It is important to distinguish between conservation and conservatism. With every new invention critics have come forward to claim that through over-efficiency it would destroy Shetland's fishing industry. The introduction of the seine net was regarded in this light, but it marked the beginning of unprecedented prosperity. Similarly when purse-seines appeared, fears were expressed for the future of the herring industry.

Of course there are limits to what we can take from the sea without endangering the future of a species. Halibut have become scarce through extensive trawling. The catch rate of lobsters has declined after the period of heavy exploitation between 1962 and 1966. When the Norwegian herring catch slumped in 1969, overfishing was suggested as the cause and a herring-tagging experiment was started in 1970 to assess the effects of industrial fishing in the northern North Sea. In 1971 a close season was applied to the herring fishery in this area to last during the two main periods of spawning. This and other measures proved ineffective and in 1978 herring fishing was banned by the British government.

WHALING

The unfortunate history of whaling shows what can happen when a species is over-exploited. Shetlanders have never drawn their just share of this wealth, for they never had a properly organised whaling industry of their own and were later content merely to serve on the whaling vessels and shore stations of others.

The only native whaling industry was the sporadic driving ashore of caaing whales (*Globiocephala melaena*) between 8 and 20ft long, which continued until the beginning of the present century, the blubber being stripped and boiled for oil. The Shetlanders did not regard whales as a source of food, though in 1741, a time of great famine, they were eaten from necessity by the people of Northmavine. In that year, a single drive resulted in 360 whales being forced ashore at Hillswick, yielding between two and four barrels of oil each. The record caa was at Quendale on 22 September 1845, when 1,540 were killed within two hours.

There were frequent disputes between the Earl of Morton, the landowners, and the fishermen as to how the spoils should be divided. In 1739 a meeting was held between the Earl and about twenty heritors where it was decided that the proceeds should be divided into three parts—one to the Earl of Morton, who enjoyed rights of admiralty, one to the laird on whose ground the whales were flenshed, and one to be divided among all the men participating in the kill.

Lord Dundas, who succeeded the Earl of Morton, waived his right to a share in the whales, donating his third to the fishermen; but the lairds continued to demand their share in spite of frequent protests from their tenants that the whales were killed below low-water mark, outside the laird's property. It was only after the Crofters Commission removed the threat of eviction that the tenants dared stand up for their rights.

On 14 September 1888 over 300 whales were driven ashore at Hoswick. None of those participating could have realised that this slaughter would lead to the famous Hoswick Whale Case. The whales were auctioned for £450 and the two landowners concerned claimed their third as usual. The men refused and the case was taken to court in Lerwick, where Sheriff MacKenzie concluded that the landowners had no right to any share of the proceeds. The landowners then took their case to the Court of Session in Edinburgh, where it was feared that the fishermen would have little chance of success, and might be faced with heavy expenses. A fund was established, and contributions were received from abroad, especially from New Zealand. But the fishermen's fears were groundless : the Court of Session upheld the decision of Sheriff MacKenzie, that all proceeds from the sale of whales should go to the captors alone. Unfortunately never again was a kill of such extent made in Shetland. This form of fishing still continues in the Faeroe Islands.

From the mid-eighteenth to the late nineteenth century Shetlanders found employment on whalers from Hull, Dundee and Peterhead. In 1752 there were forty British whaling vessels, and in 1788 there were 255. Many called at Lerwick to complete their crews before proceeding to the Arctic. In 1808, when 600 Shetlanders were so employed, an estimated £7,000 was paid out at Lerwick as wages on their discharge. In 1825 1,400 Shetlanders were serving on about seventy whalers. At the end of the eighteenth century £2 a month or £12 for the season could be earned in the Arctic. At the end of the nineteenth century £24 was considered an excellent payment for the season.

To extend the season as long as possible the journey north and return home were made at stormy times of the year. The Old Statistical Account is sprinkled with references to 'Greenland Ships', not all British, wrecked on the shores of Shetland. Conditions in Arctic waters were far worse. Nineteen vessels were lost in 1830. Many vessels were trapped in the ice at the early or sudden onset of cold weather. Most famous was the *Diana* of Hull, twenty-six of whose crew of fifty-one were Shetlanders, the youngest a lad of fourteen years. In 1867 she more or less drifted into Ronas Voe after fourteen months absence from home, having been trapped in the ice for six months with adequate provisions for only two. Thirteen of her crew had died, including nine Shetlanders, and only two men were still able to go aloft.

In the 1860s the Greenland whaling industry declined through over-exploitation, but sealing among the icefloes in the early part of the season caused a temporary respite. In 1874 there were still between 600 and 700 Shetlanders employed on whalers, but in 1888 only seven vessels called at Lerwick to complete their crews, and by 1907 the industry was dead.

With the invention of the explosive harpoon in 1868 and its adoption by the Norwegian whaling industry in 1880, the hunting of Norway's whales also began in earnest. When the whales there were nearing extinction, and after protests and violence from Norwegian cod-fishers, who feared that damage was being done to their industry, the Storting in 1904 banned whaling on the Norwegian coast. About this time Norwegian companies received permission from the British government to establish whaling stations at Shetland, and two began operating at Ronas Voe in 1903, and one each at Collafirth and Olnafirth in 1904. The whales sought included the blue whale *Balaenoptera musculus* and the sei whale *Balaenoptera borealis*.

Although there was some employment for local men, there was much opposition from the public on account of the stench and pollution of the beaches. The herring fishermen were particularly bitter, maintaining that the killing of the whales would mean the end of the herring fishery; but there was no obvious connection between the two industries and no one heeded this prediction. In 1907 large anti-whaling demonstrations were held, and in 1908 an appeal was made from Zetland County Council direct to Mr Asquith, the Prime Minister.

The industry assumed major proportions. In 1908, with eleven vessels operating and 326 men employed ashore, including 142 British citizens, it caught 651 whales—yielding oil, whalebone, cattle food, and other products worth £63,000. In 1914, with thirteen ships operating, its catch of 599 whales produced £61,500. As the whaling zones became exhausted, the Norwegians were given access to waters ever nearer Shetland, until by 1928 the whaling industry in Shetland was extinct. Strangely the decline in the herring fishery coincided almost exactly with the start of whaling.

In modern times whaling is carried out in this area by small wooden Norwegian vessels catering for a relatively small demand for whale meat in Norway.

The most lucrative period in the history of whaling for Shetland was the development of the industry thousands of miles away in the Antarctic. Christian Salvesen & Co of Leith began operations in 1908 in the Falkland Islands and a year later at Leith Harbour, South Georgia, where the number of Shetlanders employed increased steadily to a peak of 200 a year between 1945 and 1963. Wages were high considering that the season lasted only six or seven months, and by 1950 the industry was worth about £200,000 a year to Shetland in wages. Then the southern stock of whales also showed signs of over-exploitation, and by 1963 it was no longer economically possible for a British expedition to operate in the Antarctic.

SHETLAND AND THE BRITISH NAVY

Shetlanders have long had the reputation of being among the best seamen in the world. Their love of the sea coupled with lack of opportunity at home has resulted in many thousands finding employment in the Royal Navy and the Merchant Marine. At the end of the eighteenth century, when each district of Britain was expected to 'furnish upon any extraordinary emergency' a quota of men for the Royal Navy, Shetland had no difficulty in finding her share of 100. The parish of Delting was expected to supply six men, but we read in the Old Statistical Account that on the outbreak of war sixteen men volunteered.

Unfortunately the Navy was not content only with Shetland's quota, but sent its 'press gang', which began to terrorise the islands, intercepting whaling ships returning from Greenland, seizing men at sea, even breaking up weddings and carrying off boys from school; for the Navy realised in the words of one captain that 'every Shetland man and boy understands how to handle an oar and manage a boat'. Such naval tactics led the people to hate the Navy, and they did their utmost to avoid capture. Dr Edmondston wrote in 1808 that 'some have perished on the rocks in their attempt to escape from this dreaded severity and others have had their health irrecoverably ruined by watching and exposure during inclement weather'.

Between 1793 and 1801 1,100 Shetlanders were enlisted; but in 1803 HMS *Carysfort* arrived at Lerwick to recruit still more. Her commander, Captain Fanshawe, wrote to the principal landowners proposing to leave the islands in peace if they furnished their usual quota of 100 men. That was after the vessel had been cruising for almost two months and had already seized sixty-five men.

In 1808 an estimated 3,000 Shetlanders were serving in the Navy out of a total male population of about 11,000. Wages sent home that year were in the region of £3,500, but many of these men never returned. Several died in the West Indies.

In the winter of 1861–2 a unit of the Royal Naval Reserve was established at Fort Charlotte in Lerwick. The RNR came into existence to provide a body of seamen trained in gunnery, ready for an emergency. Reservists had to undergo four weeks' training annually, and were paid £10 a year, with a pension of £12 a year after the age of 60. In 1870 400 reservists drilled at Lerwick, and the numbers increased until between 1,000 and 1,400 reported every winter, providing a valuable source of income for Lerwick's landladies. The closing of the training centre in 1910 was a great blow to the islands and to Lerwick in particular. After that island reservists had to undergo annual training at centres in England until the outbreak of war in 1914, when a base was again established in Shetland.

In peacetime the Merchant Navy has for long been a source of employment for Shetlanders, the tradition really starting during the poor fishing seasons of the mid-nineteenth century. By the end of the century the Merchant Navy was extremely important to Shetland. Between the wars the number of Shetlanders serving at sea rose to a peacetime peak of 2,500, alternating periods at sea with periods at home helping on the family croft. The Merchant Navy is still important to the islands, though far fewer Shetlanders now sail in it.

At the beginning of the nineteenth century many schoolmasters included navigation in their curriculum, and in 1808 Dr Edmondston remarked that after a single voyage to Greenland most young men spent the winter engaged in further study of the subject—which explains why so many Shetlanders attained the rank of Captain. One of the best known was Captain John Gray of the SS *Great Britain*, which was recently towed back to England from the Falkland Islands. In 1906 it was estimated that 300 ships in the British Merchant Navy were commanded by Shetlanders. Four Shetlanders rose to the rank of admiral in the Royal Navy.

Shetland has for long had close links with Leith Nautical College, especially since 1944, when courses for Deck Ratings began on board the training ship *Dolphin* moored in the East Old Dock, Leith.

SAFETY AT SEA

How many ships have been lost in this area we shall never know. Shipwrecks were recorded only when someone survived to tell the tale or when a piece of broken timber bearing the name of the stricken vessel was cast ashore. In the absence of lifeboatmen, fishermen and others had to render what assistance they could as they still do today. Shetland has its own heroine of the sea in a young woman named Grace Tait, from Snarravoe in Unst, who in 1856, with her aged father-in-law, rescued two men clinging to an upturned boat. For this she was awarded the medal of the Royal Humane Society.

The first lighthouse was that of Sumburgh Head, established in 1821. Others were built to serve naval traffic during the Crimean War. Those of Out Skerries, Muckle Flugga and Bressay were all built between 1852 and 1858. Later Shetland shared in the general improvement of British coastal lights. Fair Isle South light was established in 1892, Fair Isle North in 1893, Vaila in 1894 and Balta Isle in 1895.

There are now twenty-two lighthouses in Shetland, seven of them manned. Most are on the east side of Shetland, denoting the greater traffic near Lerwick, while the west side is badly lit, with only one major and four minor lighthouses. There are still isolated islands dangerous to shipping, such as Papa Stour and Foula, which have no warning lights. Fog signals are supplied at Fair Isle, Sumburgh Head, Bressay and Out Skerries, and radio beacons at Bressay and Muckle Flugga.

Shetland is covered by the system of electronic navigational aids, one of the Decca Navigator Stations being sited near Lerwick. Another at Cunningsburgh was opened in 1968 as a link in the Norwegian chain of twenty-one stations. In that year, too, the US Coastguard Service opened a Loran monitor station at

Scatsta to serve its international chain of stations in North Europe.

The first lifeboat based in Shetland was that supplied to the people of Fair Isle by the Board of Trade in 1878. The islanders had received much publicity on account of their splendid services in life-saving: in 1868 they rescued 465 passengers and crew from the German ship *Lessing*; and in 1876, in more difficult conditions, they rescued the crew of the German brig *Carl Constantin* of Stralsund. In that year four ships were wrecked on Fair Isle, one of them, the Norwegian brig *Hertigen*, being lost with all hands.

The Board of Trade lifeboat was carefully maintained by the islanders and replaced by a new boat in 1911. In 1924 a motor lifeboat was introduced to the station, and it was not withdrawn until after World War II, when it was replaced by rocket life-saving apparatus. By this time two modern lifeboats had been stationed by the RNLI on the Mainland of Shetland, and these were capable of covering the Fair Isle area.

The loss of the Aberdeen trawler *Ben Doran* in 1930 demonstrated the need for better lifeboats with a greater cruising range. Lerwick's first lifeboat, *Lady Jane and Martha Ryland*, arrived in July 1930, and by the end of 1931 had rescued thirty-four lives from three vessels. In all she made fifty missions and saved ninety-three lives. The second lifeboat, *Claude Cecil Staniforth*, arrived in August 1958. Altogether she made ninety-five missions and saved thirty-two lives including three Russian seamen saved in October 1958 from the Holm of Skaw, Unst, a feat which brought recognition to the coxswain John Sales in the form of the RNLI silver medal for gallantry, an addition to the bronze medal awarded for a previous rescue. Even the number of lives saved does not demonstrate fully the service provided by Lerwick lifeboat. In March 1969 during a terrific storm the lifeboat escorted three Norwegian vessels to safety, a feat for which the entire crew received recognition from the RNLI. The present vessel, *Soldian*, a 52ft Arun class lifeboat was commissioned in 1978.

Aith lifeboat station was opened in 1932. An old open boat, the *K.T.J.S.*, motor-driven but assisted by a large sail, was supplied as a temporary measure in 1933. In 1935 a 52ft Barnet-type lifeboat named *The Rankine* (the family name of the donor)

Aerial view of Sullom Voe oil terminal in March 1982 showing process area (centre), loading jetties and crude-oil storage tanks (far right)

Page 176 (above) Modern crofting scene at Dunrossness—threshing and baling oats at Brake, Quendale; *(below)* progress in education, the new primary school at Dunrossness

was built at the Isle of Wight for Aith station; and she was replaced in 1961 by the *John and Frances Macfarlane*, another 52ft Barnet-type vessel, with twin Gardner diesel engines giving a speed of over nine knots. In all, 104 missions have been carried out from Aith and eighty-five lives have been saved. Both Lerwick and Aith lifeboats are equipped with radar, echo-sounders and radio-telephone.

An important role in life-saving is played by men of the coastguard service, who have twenty-one stations, though only at Lerwick, the district headquarters, is a regular watch maintained. The other stations are manned by 230 auxiliary coastguard men, all volunteers, and a watch is kept at twelve stations during bad weather.

Lerwick Life-saving Company was formed in 1906, and rescues include that of January 1964, when the crew of thirteen of the Aberdeen trawler *Rangor* were rescued by breeches buoy. The Company was awarded the MOT shield for the best wreck-service of that year, shared with Port Ellen and Mull of Oa.

To illustrate developments in methods of life-saving and incidentally the great improvements in communications, it is interesting to compare the events following the stranding of two Aberdeen trawlers in the same area but thirty-five years apart. On Friday 28 March 1930 the ST *Ben Doran* ran aground in fog on Ve Skerries, a dangerous ridge of reefs west of Papa Stour, The sea was moderate and the men could have been quickly rescued if they had possessed means of informing other vessels of their plight, but radio was not then in use in fishing vessels and their flares were not seen. They were spotted next day by the crew of another trawler, but rough seas prevented rescue. Rescue attempts by Lerwick Life-saving Company, and independently by the crew of the line boat *Smiling Morn* of Burra, began at first light on Sunday. It was now blowing a gale and the sea round the wreck was a confused mass of breaking waves. Nine of the crew could be seen standing in the rigging.

The nearest lifeboat, 120 miles away at Stromness, was then called out. She arrived at the scene on Monday, only to find that the *Ben Doran* had broken up and that there was no sign of survivors. Three bodies were recovered, and two of them were interred at Sandness Churchyard, where the *Ben Doran* memorial now stands.

In order to prevent a recurrence of the tragedy, a lighted buoy with wave-operated whistle was anchored near Ve Skerries and lifeboats were stationed by the RNLI at Aith and Lerwick. Since then tighter safety regulations have been enforced and electronic devices make fishing safer, but still trawlers and other vessels occasionally find themselves in trouble around Shetland. On 2 February 1967 the MT *Juniper* heading for Aberdeen was steaming between Papa Stour and Ve Skerries, her Decca Navigator and radar equipment both out of order but her skipper confident of his course. Unfortunately he failed to allow sufficiently for the strong tide and the trawler ran aground on Papa Stour. The calls for help were quickly answered and Aith lifeboat was soon on the scene.

The rescue operation was extremely difficult, and only intimate knowledge of the region made it possible. The heavy sea caused the lifeboat to rise and fall as much as 15ft alongside the wreck, and it was estimated that at one time there could not have been more than 1ft of water under the lifeboat. But the crew of twelve were saved, though the *Juniper* was a total loss, and Coxswain John Nicolson of Aith was later awarded the RNLI's silver medal for gallantry, with an extra award for the bravest rescue of 1967. Each member of the crew was awarded a vellum for bravery.

In December 1977 the Ve Skerries figured in yet another drama when the Aberdeen trawler, *Elinor Viking*, ran aground during a storm. Aith lifeboat was quickly on the scene, her crew willing to attempt rescue although it is doubtful whether they could have succeeded. The seamen were snatched from their badly listing vessel by the crew of a helicopter from Sumburgh, a feat which won widespread acclaim as the most daring rescue ever carried out.

9 THE PEOPLE

CONSIDERING the past history of the islands, it is not surprising that the islanders themselves are of very mixed ancestry: Norsemen, Scots and shipwrecked Germans have all contributed towards the mixture and added to the list of surnames. Broadly speaking Shetland surnames fall into three groups: there are the old Norse surnames such as Isbister and Halcrow and those ending with the suffix -son; there are many Scottish surnames brought by immigrants of the sixteenth and seventeenth centuries, such as Sinclair, Moncrieff and Mowat; and lastly there are surnames brought by small numbers of recent immigrants from Norway and Britain, such as Syversen and Hansen, Owers and Caldwell, names unknown a generation ago, now very much part of the Shetland scene.

The vague concept of a 'Shetland way of life' is difficult to define. Some people maintain that Shetland is basically a Scottish county with an unusual history now largely forgotten, but there are still fundamental differences between Shetland and Scotland, some difficult to pinpoint. There is no regret in Shetland for the passing of Norse rule, and no antagonism towards Scotland for the mistakes of 300 years ago, but there is still a feeling of separateness that is stressed quietly in innumerable ways. For instance, the Shetlanders consider themselves British rather than Scottish, and refuse to participate in the friendly rivalry between Scots and English. The environment itself has also caused differences in the attitude of the people, and these add greatly to the charm and individuality of Shetland.

CRIME

Shetland is now one of the most law-abiding parts of the UK, without serious crime; it is significant that there has been only one case of murder this century. It was not always so. The

Stewart era was marked by lawlessness, and murder was by no means uncommon. An improvement occurred soon after, but theft remained a common offence, the people having no qualms about helping themselves to a neighbour's sheep or a few fish from his drying skeo. The penalty was severe, even banishment for persistent offenders. Law enforcement and crime prevention lay in the hands of the ranselmen. A list of their instructions given in Thomas Gifford's *Description of Zetland* of 1733 shows how wide were their powers.

Domestic morals, the rates charged by tradesmen, the problem of 'idle vagabond persons' all fell under the care of the ranselmen. They were to enquire 'who sits from kirk on the Sabbath day and from diets of catechising'. Such a heinous crime was liable to an on-the-spot fine of 20 shillings Scots (about 8p), of which two-thirds was to be given to the poor, and the remainder kept as an incentive by the ranselman. The last recorded case of the appointment of ranselmen was at Fair Isle, where two were sworn in as late as 1869 following a series of petty thefts.

In 1972 the islands' police force was twenty-one strong, eighteen being stationed at Lerwick, one at Scalloway and one each in the islands of Unst and Yell. Since then a policeman has been stationed in the island of Whalsay. In 1969, in accordance with a nationwide reorganisation of the police service, the police force of Shetland was amalgamated with those of Orkney and Caithness as the Northern Constabulary, with a Chief Constable based at Wick.

The incidence of crime rose considerably during the oil construction boom when thousands of workers came to the islands. The total number of crimes reported to the police went up from 578 in 1972 to 2,349 in 1980 of which nearly half related to motor vehicles.

MORALS AND RELIGION

In spite of the excessive restraint practised by the church a century ago, religion still plays a great part in the lives of the people. In Lerwick alone there are twelve places of worship, run by as many different denominations. Even those who attend no church have a respect for religion, and Sunday is observed more strictly than in most parts of Britain, but without the severity of the Lord's Day in other parts of the Highlands and Islands. Most commendable is the religious tolerance shown in all the isles of Shetland.

RECREATIONS AND SOCIAL LIFE

In the past most social activities were reserved for the winter. Summer was the season for working the croft, for fishing six days a week, for sailing to the far Greenland whale fishing; but in winter merry-making relieved the monotony of long dark nights. Even weddings took place mainly in winter—weddings to which the whole community was invited and whose festivities were spread over two days and nights. Weddings of this type are still held in the islands of Whalsay and Out Skerries, and provide a welcome break in the strenuous life of the fishermen.

Dancing played a great part in the life of the islanders. Until the late eighteenth century, songs known as visecks formed the accompaniment to dances which must have resembled the ring dance still performed in Faeroe. The visecks were forgotten, however, and most of the old dances, too, and in 1774 George Low commented that the Scottish-type reel had taken their place. There are local variations of the reel, most popular being the Foula reel and the Shetland reel. One ancient dance survives in the Papa Stour sword dance, its tune having definite Scandinavian characteristics; it is performed by seven male dancers representing the seven Saints of Christendom.

Shetland's musical heritage consists mainly of fiddle tunes, with words set to a few of them. The tunes fall roughly into three groups: wedding tunes, such as the Bride's March from Unst; 'trowie' tunes, pieces of music reputed to have been learned near the haunts of trows or fairies; and reel tunes, the most popular being 'The Merry Boys o' Greenland'. Some reel tunes are based on Scottish, English or Irish traditional tunes, but changed so as to be barely recognisable.

From Norse times comes the tradition of guizing or attending a party disguised with a mask, the aim being to withhold one's identity for as long as possible. The tradition is maintained by children guizing for pennies at Hallowe'en and on Christmas Eve, and in some districts, by 'first-footers' on New Year's Morning. More important is the annual festival of Up-Helly-Aa held at Lerwick on the last Tuesday of January.

In traditional Shetland life, whenever possible, hard work was combined with pleasure. The men of the township used to form a group to cut the year's peats for each family in rotation and were lavishly entertained by each house in turn. At the beginning of this century cardings were still held, when young women met to prepare wool for spinning; the social aspect of this gathering was important, too, for the young men of the district invariably gathered as well, and when the work was done a dance was quickly organised.

Nowadays communal entertainment takes the form of dances, concerts and whist drives, often in aid of a deserving organisation such as the Royal National Lifeboat Institution, the Red Cross or Oxfam. The old Nissen huts that served many districts in the years of austerity following World War II have generally been replaced by handsome public halls and community centres. The monthly meetings of the Scottish Women's Rural Institute, with lectures, demonstrations and competitions, are well attended in every district. For many years after World War II the debates held by the Althing Social Group at Tingwall were well attended, until the introduction of TV in 1964. The film shows run by the Highlands and Islands Film Guild in rural halls also ended soon after the arrival of TV. Drama is attracting greater numbers of enthusiasts in all parts of the islands. The year's highlight is the drama festival held in the Garrison Theatre at Lerwick, with teams competing in several sections, including one for plays written in the Shetland dialect.

Outdoor sport enjoys only a short summer season, for the climate is too damp for much of the year. Football, originally a game played at Christmas with the bladder of a pig for a ball, has now developed into a well organised sport, with four teams from Lerwick, one from Scalloway, one from Dunrossness and one representing the RAF competing in a senior league for five different trophies. In addition teams from rural districts compete for the parish cup and there are junior, school and even Sunday-school leagues.

A senior inter-county competition is held each year between Orkney and Shetland featuring football and hockey. The junior inter-county is of wider scope, comprising football, hockey, net-ball, athletics and aquatic sports. With Orkney and Faeroe, Shet-land competes in a triangular football league for the North Atlantic Cup. There are virtually no winter sports, since snow seldom lies long enough and the lochs seldom freeze thick enough.

The 'king' of summer is undoubtedly yachting, once exclusively in Shetland models, but now with faster though far less graceful dinghies competing in their own section. Each district has its own regatta, which is usually the biggest event of the year. The climax is the inter-club regatta held at Lerwick in September, when up to fifty boats compete in teams.

For those interested in agriculture there are annual shows at Cunningsburgh and Walls and sheepdog trials at Tingwall. Like the regattas each of these events is concluded by a concert and dance.

Greater importance is attached to Christmas in Shetland than in other parts of Scotland, but this does not detract from the importance of the New Year celebrations. To prolong the festivities, some districts still hold additional celebrations eleven days later to mark these festivals according to the old Julian Calendar, which was abandoned in 1752. Even when these are over, the Shetlander can still look forward to Up-Helly-Aa.

FOLKLORE

The early crofters had many difficulties to surmount in their everyday lives, so it is little wonder that they had to invent supernatural beings to account for their trials and family tragedies. Underground in hills and knolls lived the trows or demons, little creatures with material bodies but having the power to make themselves invisible. The people feared them. It was dangerous to offend them even by a careless word, and they were always referred to as 'the guid folk', in case any were listening. Sometimes the trows carried away a human child, replacing him with a poor ailing child of their own. They stole milk from the byre, and sheep and cattle lost in the hills were believed to end up at trowie banquets.

Most evil of all supernatural beings were witches, who, though having mortal shape, were under the control of Satan. They could take away the profit of the farm, cause a cow to lose her milk and even cause the loss of boats at sea.

There was no clear division between the natural and supernatural. Things might not be what they seemed—a seal might be a normal animal whose skin could be flayed and sold or it might be one of the forms of a merman or merwoman. These creatures frequently visited the world of men, casting off their sea dresses, but they had to be careful not to lose their sea clothes or they would become inhabitants of the earth.

The church claimed credit for driving the trows and evil spirits from the islands, but probably the advent of pressure paraffin lamps played a great part in lighting the dark shadows of the house and of the minds of its occupants. Then the ubiquitous motor car ended the long journeys on foot over bleak cheerless roads, and improvements in the standard of living removed the number of personal disasters needing explanation. What remains of superstition are a scattered collection of amusing stories, a few place names like Trollhoulland, once the haunt of the trows, and perhaps here and there an old person who believes there are things on earth not seen by mortal eyes.

FAMOUS SHETLANDERS

Of the thousands of emigrants, most famous was Sir Robert Stout. Born in 1844 at Lerwick he emigrated as a young man to New Zealand, where, after teaching for a few years, he decided to study law and qualified as a barrister. In 1875 he was elected a member of Parliament, in 1878 he became Attorney General and minister for Lands and Immigration, and in 1884 he became Prime Minister of his adopted country.

Most unusual of emigrants was John Clunies-Ross, who organised a settlement in the formerly uninhabited Cocos Islands in the Indian Ocean, becoming undisputed 'king' of the islands. Before his death in 1854 a prosperous trade had been built up in copra, and the islands are still ruled by one of his descendants.

Among the families of the lairds were several notable scholars whose achievements did not receive due recognition within the islands. The Edmondston family of Unst was outstanding. Arthur Edmondston wrote in 1808 what was then the best account ever of the islands. His brother, Dr Laurence Edmondston, a distinguished naturalist, was first to recognise the snowy owl, and the glaucous, ivory and Iceland gulls as members of the British fauna. The latter's son, Thomas, was an outstanding botanist, and at the age of twenty became Professor of Botany at Glasgow

University; but less than a year later he was killed accidentally by gunshot while serving as naturalist on an expedition to the Pacific.

The Grierson family of Quendale produced Sir Herbert Grierson, Professor emeritus of English Literature at Edinburgh University between 1915 and 1935. He was best known in later years for editing the works of Sir Walter Scott in twelve volumes, and in 1938 publishing his own book on the great author.

Shetland produced one famous surgeon in Sir Watson Cheyne of Fetlar, who was born at sea, the son of a captain. He became chief assistant to Lord Lister, and succeeded him as Professor of Clinical Surgery at King's College, London. He was also President of the Royal College of Surgeons.

There are several local poets and prose writers whose works are well loved in Shetland, but not one can compare with the best literary men of Orkney. Best remembered Shetland writer is James J. Haldane Burgess of Lerwick, who lost his sight while a student yet took his examinations orally to graduate. His writings fall into two groups—historical novels in English and poems and sketches in the Shetland dialect. The former group includes *The Viking Path*, which deals with the struggle between Christianity and Norse paganism. He died in 1927 at the age of sixty-five.

Most famous Shetlander of all was Arthur Anderson, born in 1792, co-founder of the P & O line. His early life of poverty and his success in London typified the ambitions of thousands of young Shetlanders of his own and succeeding generations. Seeing no opportunity of making a reasonable living in Shetland, they were compelled to leave the islands. Arthur Anderson's lasting interest in Shetland and his attempts to improve the situation have been described in Chapter 4. It is only fitting that his birthplace, the Böd of Gremista, north of Lerwick, is to be preserved. Of the £15,000 required to restore the building, £5,000 has been contributed by the directors of the P & O line.

10 LERWICK AND SCALLOWAY

ALTHOUGH the two largest settlements in Shetland are only 5 miles apart (7 by road) their origins are entirely different. While Lerwick is built on the North Sea, Scalloway faces the Atlantic. They were for long separated not only by a trackless moor cleft with deep gullies, but also by the memory of bitter rivalry and animosity. They developed independently, Scalloway growing very slowly and suffering periods of decay, while Lerwick expanded rapidly by trade to seize the position of power which its older rival once possessed.

SCALLOWAY

Historically Scalloway comes first. The name is Norse, originally *Skalavagr*, the bay of the skali or hall. We do not know who built the outstanding structure that gave the whole district its name. He may have been the chief justice for the islands, however, for we know that the great foude had his house in Scalloway in the later period of Norse rule.

Scalloway's importance was enhanced in 1600 when Earl Patrick Stewart built his castle on a promontory dividing the bay of Scalloway from East Voe, and made it the seat of the law court. This was only a temporary move, for some time after the execution of Earl Patrick and his son in 1615 the law court was moved again to the new town of Lerwick. In 1700 the Rev John Brand found the slates falling off the castle roof, and the timber starting to rot, but he could still see traces of elaborate paintings on the walls. The ruins of Earl Patrick's castle still dominate the village and harbour.

Scalloway stagnated throughout the eighteenth century. In 1700 there were fewer than 100 residents, but they included some quite important people, for several of the principal island lairds had houses there. In 1797 there were thirty-one inhabited houses, but the village was described as having 'fallen much into decay'.

In 1841 Scalloway was increasing in size—there was a school and a church being built—because of the development of the herring industry. Local fishermen had invested in larger boats, and in 1835 over 15,000 barrels of salt herring had been exported. One boat was recorded as having caught 297 crans for the season at an average price of 7s (35p) per cran.

But the fishing that first brought prosperity to Scalloway was the cod-fishing in fully decked sailing smacks. Pioneer of this fishery was Charles Nicolson, who, in 1820 as a lad of nineteen, founded the firm of Nicolson & Co. The firm is still thriving today, though its only link with the fishing industry is as ships' chandler. Its first vessels were small Shetland-built sloops of between 12 and 17 tons that mainly fished the home banks, with occasional trips to Orkney and the more prolific Faeroe banks. Larger vessels followed, such as the 40 ton ex-yacht *Alma*, which fished regularly at Faeroe, Iceland and Rockall, then spent the winter freighting cured fish to Southern Ireland.

The firm's last acquisition was the schooner *William Martin*, bought in 1894, which under an expert skipper prolonged the now dying cod-fishery until 1908. By this time Scalloway had become established as a centre for the new winter haddock-fishery, as well as an important herring port in the early part of the summer.

The increased trade of Scalloway in the mid-nineteenth century led to cargo vessels running in from Leith. Most famous was the clipper *Queen of the Isles* of 82 tons, built at Leith in 1845 for a Shetland syndicate. She was commanded for many years by Captain Robert Nisbet, who provided such a good service for passengers and traders that in 1881, when the 'North of Scotland' Company provided a Shetland west-side run from Leith and Aberdeen via Stromness, he was invited to take command of the SS *Queen*.

Blacksness pier at Scalloway, built in 1832 by Messrs Hay & Ogilvy, was just large enough to accommodate the steamship, but not until 1896 was a proper deep-water berth provided. In 1935 its administration was taken over by the newly formed Blacksness Pier Trust.

Communications between Scalloway and Lerwick remained

abysmal until the mid-nineteenth century. The lack of a road was a great hindrance to the growth of the herring industry, since curers' supplies had to be transported 50 miles by sea round the stormy headlands of Sumburgh and Fitful. During adverse weather conditions they were carried overland on ponies, and even on the backs of men and women.

Roadworks began in 1840 but were still not completed in 1847. Money for wooden bridges was raised by public subscription, the work being carried out by statute labour: every able-bodied man in the district was expected to give three days' unpaid work every year or pay the sum of 3s 4d instead. The road was completed under the 'meal roads' scheme of the late 1840s.

For some years transport was confined to pedestrians, with the occasional horse and cart. Then the Lerwick firm of Ganson Brothers provided a mail and passenger service with horse-drawn coach. Motor cars appeared in 1908, and motor lorries replaced carts, to transfer catches of line-caught haddock from Scalloway to Lerwick or vice versa, depending on which steamer was next to leave for Aberdeen and Leith. The ever-increasing numbers of motor lorries and the dwindling trade of the west side ports were factors in the withdrawal of the western steamer service in 1939.

Village improvements followed more slowly. As early as 1906 Scalloway had a water supply from springs. A drainage system was provided in 1910 but this did little to improve sanitary arrangements. In 1919 the local authority had powers to force householders to install water closets, but it was impracticable to do so until a satisfactory water supply was provided. In 1928, 111 out of 192 houses in the village had no conveniences. Scalloway was designated a special scavenging district, but it had no appointed scavenger, most families disposing of their refuse over the sea wall, whence it was washed up on the beaches to create a nuisance every summer.

In 1932 a new water scheme was completed at a cost of £4,690: it consisted of two filter beds and a clear water tank fed by gravity along a 5-in main from the loch of Njuggles Water. With an improved supply the old objection to improved sanitation was removed and the local authority began to use all its influence and legal powers to effect improvements. This was the beginning of the slow transformation into the attractive village of today.

About 1931 two firms of engineers installed generators and provided electricity for houses in the neighbourhood of each workshop. In 1936 electric lights replaced oil-burning street lamps and by 1939 a supply was available to the whole village. This service ended in 1948, when Scalloway was connected to the supply provided from Lerwick by the North of Scotland Hydro-Electric Board.

Scalloway's housing problem was not tackled until 1938, when a scheme for forty houses was begun by the County Council at a cost of £31,000. Fifteen of these were requisitioned to house military personnel during the early years of World War II.

The Shetland Bus

During World War II Scalloway became famous as the base for a group of Norwegian patriots taking its directives from British Intelligence. They sailed in wooden fishing vessels across the North Sea to their Nazi-occupied homeland, landing ammunition and saboteurs, and returning with refugees.

Their barracks was the old sail loft belonging to Nicolson & Co. For overhauling their vessels they built the Prince Olav Slipway, visited by the present king of Norway in 1942. Late in 1943 the US Navy lent three sub-chasers for this important work. Although much faster, their trips were even more dangerous, for they could not be disguised as harmless fishing vessels.

The effect on the morale of the Norwegian people of this base at Scalloway was immeasurable. When the situation became desperate 'to take the Shetland bus' became a synonym for escape. The story was told by David Howarth in *The Shetland Bus.*

Scalloway Today

Since 1938 the population of the village has almost doubled to stand at 1,160 in 1981. Its prosperity is based soundly on the fishing industry with around twenty seiners and trawlers based here at the peak of the season. Blacksness Pier was extended in 1959 and a covered fish market was added a year or two later. These developments soon proved inadequate for the expanding fleet and this problem was not solved until the early 1980s when a new breakwater and fish market were built at a cost of just under £4 million. Since the late 1970s the value of fish landed at Scalloway has exceeded £1 million a year.

The firm of William Moore & Sons, marine engineers, has expanded considerably and the largest of its three slipways can accommodate vessels up to 90ft long. Another two firms in the village specialise in installing and repairing electronic equipment. Since 1972 the port has been used occasionally as an oil-rig supply base.

Greater than either of these trades as a source of employment is the fish-processing industry. First factory to begin operating was that of Iceatlantic (Frozen Seafoods) Ltd in 1960, followed in 1964 by that of Thomas Fraser, trading under the name TTF. Since then the long established family business of L. Williamson has expanded to overtake the other two in both numbers employed and output. In 1970 the produce of these three factories was worth over £500,000, and 150 people were employed.

Transport costs and marketing problems in the UK long remained a problem until the firm of TTF developed a market in the USA and arranged a service with a Danish shipping company whereby the cartons of frozen white-fish fillets are shipped direct from Scalloway to Gloucester or Boston, Mass. All three local factories now use this service, and in 1970 the new processing-plants at Whalsay and Out Skerries also found it cheaper to send their product to Scalloway for shipment. In 1970 exports of fish products to the USA amounted to 2,150 tons, worth £626,000, and in 1971 to 4,500 tons, worth £1,500,000.

From Scalloway have come two inventions that have already proved their worth to the fishing industry. In 1966 James Smith, a sheep farmer, devised and patented a mechanical fish gutter, which has been installed on many British trawlers and seiners. It marks the first step in the mechanisation of an operation which has hitherto been done by hand. The Shetland gutting machine is being produced by a firm in Aberdeen and orders have come from as far afield as Canada and Russia. In 1971 Mr Smith patented a fish selector to be used in conjunction with his gutting machine, to grade fish according to size. For his contribution to the fishing industry he was awarded the MBE.

LERWICK

Lerwick is a comparatively new town, the oldest building being little more than 300 years old. It appears to be a small town, of only 7,000 inhabitants, but the size of its buildings and the quality of its shops demonstrate its importance. Lerwick is the only town in Shetland, and is the administrative and commercial centre for a population of over 23,000 people. At times the flags of a dozen nations fly from the mastheads of ships in the harbour, for Lerwick also dominates a wide area of the North Sea.

History

At the beginning of the seventeenth century Lerwick was merely a minor inlet of Bressay Sound. But the importance of this situation could not long be overlooked, for this was the most convenient harbour in Shetland for sailing ships and one of the best in Northern Europe. Bressay Sound had been known to seafarers for centuries; the Norsemen anchored their longships here in 1263 on their way to fight the army of King Alexander III of Scotland. First to make full use of the harbour, however, were Dutch fishermen from the sixteenth century onwards, and they indirectly caused the first settlement on the Mainland side of the sound. The large gathering of fishermen acted as a magnet to the country people, who flocked to the shores of Lerwick to sell their produce.

For this trade there sprang up a collection of huts that was reputedly the scene of much immorality and drunkenness. In 1625 the court of Scalloway ordered the huts to be 'utterlie dimolished and downe cassin to the ground'. Perhaps the ancient capital feared this threat to its hitherto unchallenged supremacy.

The building of the upstart village was only temporarily delayed. The tremendous potential of Bressay Sound both in peace and war had by this time been realised by the British government, and it was in a time of war that Lerwick had its real beginning. Again the Dutch were associated, this time as enemies. In 1653 ninety-four English ships commanded by Admirals Deans and Monk anchored in the Sound, troops were landed to garrison Scalloway Castle, and the building of a fort, the first permanent building, was begun at Lerwick.

Cromwell's troops stayed for only three years, but between 1665 and 1668 the fort was again garrisoned against a possible Dutch invasion. When peace was temporarily restored, the soldiers departed, taking with them the cannon. Then in 1673 Dutch sailors landed at Lerwick and burned the barracks and several of the best houses in the town.

The Dutch resumed their fishing after the wars and again visited Lerwick for trade and recreation. In 1700 the Rev John Brand found between 200 and 300 families in the prosperous new town. The people had built a church at their own expense, but it was visited only rarely by the minister of Tingwall parish, who had three other churches under his charge. It was on the recommendation of John Brand that Lerwick and the neighbouring district were disjoined from Tingwall in 1701 and made into a separate parish—a considerable rise in status for the town.

It grew very slowly during the eighteenth century. In 1767 the foundations of a town house or Tolbooth were laid with Masonic honours, Lodge Morton 89 having had its charter granted in 1762. In 1781, when Europe was again at war, the fort was repaired and named Fort Charlotte after the late Queen. In 1790 Lerwick had only 903 inhabitants, but a rapid rise took place thereafter, perhaps on account of increased trade with naval vessels, for by 1808 the population had increased to 1,600 and by 1821 to 2,224.

According to Dr Edmondston, Lerwick was extremely hierarchical at this time, with three distinctly defined groups. At the top were 'gentlemen of landed property, professional gentlemen, civil officers of the crown and the more opulent merchants', next came 'artizans and inferior shopkeepers', and lastly 'the labouring poor'.

It must have been a pleasant existence for the rich, whose numbers were then greatly increased by resident officers of both army and navy. Several officers wrote of the card clubs, the subscription balls and the lavish hospitality extended to them. Food was plentiful and cheap. In 1808 the average price of beef was 3½d a lb, a whole sheep could be bought for 6s, a hen cost 6d, a duck 8d or 10d and a goose at Christmas 1s 4d. Fish was described as very abundant. A large cod cost 3d or 4d, haddock were six a penny and oysters from Burra were seldom more than 8d or 10d per 100.

'The labouring poor' were the first of the many who were to forsake the country for the town. Disgruntled with poor seasons and high rents they preferred the chance of casual labour as a ferryman, or a berth in an Arctic whaler. Their living conditions were poor: they were crowded into houses in the lanes overlooking the shore, where the germs of typhoid and other fevers were seldom absent.

In 1862 Lerwick's first newspaper, *Shetland Advertiser*, appeared. From its advertisements it is interesting to note how many firms have been in business, in the same line and in the same building on Commercial Street, for over 100 years—R. Goudie & Sons, ironmongers; R. & C. Robertson, grocers; Laurenson & Co, drapers; and Malcolmson & Co, bakers.

A letter to the editor from Mr Ross Smith pointed out the drawbacks of the old part of the town and first put forward the idea of a new residential area in the parks north and west of Lerwick, with a proper feuing plan to provide for 'the further drainage and sewerage of a probable town to be built'. He envisaged 'proper frontage and wide streets and airy lanes', and at a meeting of the Feuars and Heritors of Lerwick on 7 May 1862 this plan was formally proposed.

The first building of any importance to be erected in the new town was the new parochial school, completed in 1865 and later to become the infant school. The county buildings, incorporating courtroom and prison, were opened in 1875. In 1878 a revised feuing plan was produced and the stage was set for a period of unprecedented growth.

Greatest impetus to the expansion of Lerwick was the development of the herring industry after 1878. Curing yards extended northwards, and prosperity was reflected in the new residential area. One of Lerwick's greatest assets was a talented architect and builder, John M. Aitken, famous also as designer and builder of lighthouses, including that of Sule Skerry, west of Orkney. His buildings in Lerwick include several churches and the Central Public School, opened in 1905, but most outstanding of all is the town hall.

The building of Lerwick's town hall reflects great credit on the leading inhabitants of the small community of those days. In 1880 Lerwick Town Hall Company Ltd was formed, with capital of £4,000, and in 1881 the directors accepted J. M. Aitken's offer to build it for £3,240. The designer was Alexander Ross, who had designed Inverness Cathedral.

The foundation stone was laid on 14 January 1882 by HRH

the Duke of Edinburgh. The result is the handsome building in baronial style, which dominates the skyline of Lerwick. A town clock and chime of bells were given later, and inaugurated on 21 June 1887, the occasion of the Jubilee of Queen Victoria.

In 1893 when the population stood around 4,000, Lerwick became a police burgh with the right to call its chief civic dignitary provost. It had been made a burgh of barony in 1818.

Innovations and improved facilities came slowly at first, then ever more rapidly. In 1817 there was only one cart in Lerwick; in 1828 the first wheeled carriage appeared; in 1908 the first motor cars arrived; and by 1911 there was sufficient trade for Mr Joseph Gray to open a motor and marine engineering business. In 1912 Ganson Brothers purchased a model T Ford, which marked the beginning of an association with the Ford Motor Company that still continues today.

In 1869 Sandy Loch was formed into a reservoir by building an embankment at the south-east corner. In 1871 Lerwick had a water supply to conveniently placed hydrants in the streets and to a few of the better houses. An improved supply was provided in 1898, filtration being provided inefficiently by the sand method; but in 1931 a satisfactory supply was finally provided by mechanical filtration capable of treating 30,000 gallons per hour.

Gas first lit the streets of Lerwick on 8 February 1856, and in November 1874 the price to consumers was reduced to 12s 6d per 1,000cu ft. In 1932 an electricity supply was provided by the town council, which offered to provide free connections for consumers up to the end of the year. The target was 300 connections but over 400 applied. By 1934 there were 720 consumers, and in 1936, when there were 968, the price of electricity was reduced to 7d a unit.

A picture palace, the North Star Cinema, opened on 24 September 1913. As can be imagined the crowd was so great that 200 people could not gain admittance. Seats varied in price from 3d and 1s (5p).

Lerwick's first successful weekly newspaper was *The Shetland Times* which appeared in 1872 and is still thriving. A second weekly newspaper, *The Shetland News,* an interesting much-loved publication, appeared in 1885 but closed down in 1963.

Youngest publication to be printed in Lerwick is the quarterly magazine *The New Shetlander.* Started in 1947 it includes articles of topical interest, short stories and poems in English and the Shetland dialect. No payment is made for contributions and few people expected the magazine to survive for long, but it is now far beyond its hundredth number.

Since 1918 Lerwick has grown at an astonishing rate. The first large municipal housing scheme began in 1921, and by 1923 120 houses had been completed at a total cost of £110,000, of which £42,000 had been paid in wages. The housing problem remained acute. In 1931 a study of a representative 10 per cent sample of 120 houses within the burgh showed that of 458 inhabitants 415 required rehousing. By 1934 two housing schemes were in progress, and they were completed early in 1936: 112 houses of three, four and five apartments rehoused 529 people, or 13 per cent of the population.

Outside the burgh of Lerwick but effectively part of the town, the region of Garthspool and the North Road area, occupied by working-class people, mainly fishermen, long remained an eyesore. A water supply had been provided here between 1902 and 1907, but it was hopelessly inadequate. In 1929, in an area occupied by 1,218 people, increased by 2,000 herring trade workers every summer, less than a dozen households enjoyed the luxury of a piped domestic water supply.

Sanitary arrangements there were primitive. Large quantities of shellfish were used in baiting lines and, in spite of repeated pleas by the authorities, piles of empty shells mixed with other refuse gathered round the houses, to cause a stench and attract vermin.

First step to improve matters was a scheme begun in 1931 to lay a larger water main and provide sewerage, which was completed in 1932 at a cost of £4,260. For the first time the local authority could exercise its right to enforce the installation of water closets, sinks and bathrooms, that is in houses not due for demolition, for the next step in improvement had already been taken with the start of a county council housing scheme at Garthspool. Finished in 1934 at a cost of £48,600, it rehoused 418 people, mainly fishermen and their families, in eighty houses.

Within the boundaries of the burgh the town expanded so rapidly that in 1938 the boundaries were extended, and with incorporation within the burgh the problem of the North Road area could be tackled effectively.

SHETLAND

The Harbour

In the eighteenth century Lerwick became the greatest centre in the islands for the export of dried fish, butter and knitted stockings to North Germany. By the beginning of the nineteenth century this trade was almost over, interrupted by the many wars of the period, and thereafter came increasing trade between Lerwick and the rest of Britain. In 1808, two sloops were making seven trips a year between Lerwick and Leith, and there was also a mail packet sailing between Lerwick and Aberdeen.

Smuggling played a great part in the early trade of the islands. The landowners reputedly gave it up about 1790, to be replaced by the merchants of Lerwick, each of whom had his own private jetty with storehouse or lodberry designed for the concealment of large quantities of contraband. When the cod fishery began at Faeroe, smuggling increased in spite of the efforts of revenue cutters to intercept the returning smacks. In addition, as they had done for centuries, the stolid friendly Dutchmen kept the islanders supplied with cheap tobacco and an incalculable supply of brandy and gin.

Throughout the nineteenth century Lerwick was increasingly busy as Greenland whalers called to complete their crews. Some merchants had financial interest in whaling companies based at Peterhead and Dundee. One such was Joseph Leask, shipowner, fish-curer, dock-owner and landowner; he was also an owner of sailing smacks, and his packets *Lady Alice* and *Rattlesnake* sailed weekly to the North Isles of Shetland.

The whalers arrived in March and stayed for ten or twelve days, causing a carnival atmosphere as the crews sought amusement ashore and local men thronged the agents' offices to seek a berth. On 9 March 1859 fifty whaling vessels were at anchor in the harbour. Each left for the Arctic with twenty or thirty Shetlanders on board.

Several merchants invested in cod smacks as the Faeroe fishing expanded. Joseph Leask's fleet included the schooners *Destiny* and *Anaconda*, and the fleet of G. L. Harrison & Co, drapers, included the 75 ton schooner *Cyclone* and the ketch *Cynthia*.

Most outstanding of the merchants were Hay & Co. In 1827 they built the *George Canning* as a cod-fisher. The largest vessel to be built at their Freefield yard was the schooner *Janet Hay*, and in 1842 and again in 1862 they sent her to fish in the distant

Davis Straits. She was commandeered for a time by the Admiralty and sent to the Mediterranean with a cargo of supplies for the British forces in the Crimea. The last cod-fisher bought by Hay & Co was the smack *Buttercup*, which fished from 1896 to 1905 at Faeroe, and acted for a few years longer as a herring buss in Shetland waters in an experiment to emulate the Dutch in curing her catch at sea. Today Hay & Co own only one vessel, the cargo vessel *Shetland Trader*, the only large ship to bear the name Lerwick on her stern, for the ships of the 'North of Scotland' Company are registered at Aberdeen.

Nearly every merchant participated in the herring boom of the 1880s : some owned only one vessel, and some had an interest in several, Hay & Co financing over a score. Their yard at Freefield was again active building sail drifters.

By the 1890s Lerwick was the major herring port in Britain. Boats came from Ireland, the Isle of Man, the Hebrides and from the whole east coast of Britain between Wick and Lowestoft; Dutchmen, Danes, Swedes and Finns made Lerwick their base at weekends. The number of boats and men was but one aspect of the scene of activity. The herring had to be gutted and packed in barrels, the boats had to be kept in repair, providing work for carpenters and sailmakers. Ships arrived daily, creating work for dockers and stevedores in discharging wood from the Baltic, salt from Cheshire, or coal from the Tyne. The ships were reloaded with cargoes of salt herring for Germany and the Baltic states.

The sailboats declined in numbers as the fleet of steam drifters increased. Although catches dwindled after 1905, Lerwick's relative importance increased as the Shetland herring industry became centralised there. In 1909 between 400 and 500 steam drifters fished at Lerwick, consuming in the season 50,000 tons of coal at £1 1s (£1·05) a ton. Besides coaling stations on shore there were twenty-three coal hulks at anchor in the harbour; these were disused sailing vessels and steamers of between 100 and 800 tons.

The growth of the herring industry highlighted the inadequacies of the shore facilities. Before 1886 freight had to be transferred to and from ships at anchor by small flit boats, though the smallest smacks could berth at Morrison's Pier. With commendable foresight local businessmen formed a committee, the forerunner of

Lerwick Harbour Trust and guaranteed a sum of £20,000 as security for government loans to erect a deep-water quay.

Victoria Pier was completed in 1886, the inter-island steamer *Earl of Zetland* being the first vessel to use it. From then on improvements and additions steadily obliterated the old seafront of sandy beaches and private jetties. In 1907 came the Alexandra Wharf scheme and fish market. By 1914 a breakwater had been built to form a small boat harbour and Victoria Pier had been extended.

The rise in revenue of Lerwick Harbour Trust illustrates the growth of shipping. In 1886 the income was £1,178, almost double that of the previous year. In 1905 it reached £2,584 and in 1914 £6,030. During two world wars the importance of Lerwick Harbour was clearly demonstrated, and it was defended by batteries at both entrances.

Between 1955 and 1960 £330,000 was spent in improvements to the harbour. These included the widening of Victoria Pier and extension of its arm. A spur jetty was built to ease the congestion caused by large numbers of Norwegian fishing vessels. In 1969 the revenue of the trust was just under £38,000, four times the income of 1954, and almost half of this sum was derived from the 'North of Scotland' company in dues on vessels and goods handled.

In 1971 work began on the first phase of yet another improvement scheme estimated to cost £250,000 to cater chiefly for the growing Shetland fleet. The following year, however, saw the arrival of the first oil service companies seeking space for quays, silos and warehouses and Lerwick Harbour Trust responded by embarking on the most remarkable building programme in their long history.

They were fortunate that in the North Harbour they had a long stretch of shoreline virtually unused since the days of the herring boom between the wars. They were fortunate, too, in being able to purchase Gremista estate, a large farm nearby, which enabled them to offer their customers a large amount of back-up land. First service base to be built was that of Norscot Services who leased a 30 acre site at the Green Head and they were followed by Shell and BP who co-operated in the building of their supply bases at Holmsgarth. In 1978 a fourth base became operational when Ocean Inchcape (Shetland) Ltd opened their premises at Holmsgarth. Yet another development of the mid-1970s was the construction of a roll on/roll off terminal at Holmsgarth built at a cost of £3·5 million to cater for the new ferries introduced by P & O Ferries (Orkney and Shetland Services). As a result of this increased activity Lerwick Harbour Trust's income rose to a record £1,153,000 in 1977.

Boat maintenance and repair are well catered for in Lerwick. Messrs Malakoff operate a slipway capable of handling vessels up to 90ft long and there are two other firms of marine engineers. At Garthspool the large ice factory run by Messrs J. & M. Shearer supplies flake and coarse ice for the entire Shetland fishing fleet and British and foreign callers.

Lerwick Today

Lerwick shows clearly the three main stages in its growth—the old town along the shore still the main commercial area, the 'new' town of the 1880s with its formal layout of streets and beautiful houses, and the postwar sprawl extending beyond Burgh Road, which was indeed the boundary of the burgh until the line was extended in 1938 to take in the North Road area, Gremista and the area round Clickhimin Loch. Even this extension was insufficient for the growth of Lerwick, and in 1966 the burgh was extended to include the old township of Sound.

Lerwick has grown considerably during the past decade with large new council estates to the north of the town and in the Sound area while private bungalows dominate the area to the west of Clickhimin Loch.

The old town has the greatest attraction for visitors. Here no two houses are alike, yet there is unity from the use of local sandstone. At the water's edge the lodberries or storehouses still reach out into the sea; subterranean passages discovered occasionally by workmen serve as a reminder of a more secretive but more colourful early trade. Commercial Street, paved from wall to wall with stone flags or concrete slabs, and as twisting as the old shoreline which it follows, is a paradise for pedestrians. Motor traffic, restricted by a 15mph speed limit, is further hampered by a one-way system and by the projecting corners of offices and shops. The quality of the shops is surprising: there is greater variety of merchandise than is found in most towns of comparable size, in spite of the absence of names like Boots and Woolworths.

At right-angles up the steep slope to the west of Commercial Street run the lanes, the old residential area, a particular feature of the town that is slowly changing. Some old buildings have been demolished to make way for car parks and a large indoor swimming pool.

At the south end of the town an attempt has been made to renovate some of the old houses and even recapture the atmosphere of the lanes in new erections—a scheme that gained for Lerwick a Saltire Society award. Recently attention was focused on the Widows' Homes, a gift to the town from Arthur Anderson a century ago. The trust fund left to finance upkeep had become insufficient and the town council petitioned the Court of Session to be allowed to take over the building. It has been converted into a block of nine flats.

Within the last decade several important new buildings have been erected in Lerwick. The new Gilbert Bain hospital, the new Anderson High School, the Mission to deep-sea fishermen, the county museum and library, and Lerwick Hotel are all of architectural interest.

A cosmopolitan atmosphere has long been a feature of Lerwick. For many years the Dutch, wearing clogs and baggy trousers, were part of Lerwick as they strolled along the street seeking their favourite peppermints, lozenges and china ornaments. A century ago even the children of Lerwick could converse in Dutch. Today the Norwegian influence is everywhere—the Norwegian mission, the Norwegian lifeboat, the shops in Commercial Street displaying signs in Norwegian as well as English. Soberly dressed Russians, crews of tugs and water tankers, have also become a familiar sight as they shop for more sophisticated presents than did the Dutch.

Up-Helly-Aa

The greatest communal effort in Lerwick, and the most outstanding spectacle of the year, takes place not in summer as a tourist attraction but in the heart of winter for the enjoyment of the Lerwegians themselves. On the last Tuesday in January is held the fire festival of Up-Helly-Aa.

In its present form it is a comparatively new festival, but it can be traced back to the celebration of Uphalliday, which was one of the pagan Norse festivals adopted by the pre-Reformation Church in Shetland, to mark the end of the long mid-winter celebration of Yule. Uphalliday was mentioned by George Low as still being celebrated in the late eighteenth century.

In the late nineteenth century, according to Dr Cowie, the young men of Lerwick celebrated Christmas (old style) on 5 January by dragging through the streets of the town wooden sledges each containing four to eight tubs filled with tar and wood chips and blazing furiously. The youths continued this pastime until first daylight, when they returned home; but instead of retiring to bed, they dressed in all manner of weird costumes and began a round of their friends' houses as guizers. These activities were usually repeated on a smaller scale on 12 and 29 January, that is at New Year (old style) and Up-Helly-Aa, as the latter festival was then known. All these associations—the ancient name, the blazing fire and the custom of guizing—come together in the modern festival. The burning of tar barrels was considered a nuisance by the more sedate townspeople and was finally prohibited in 1874.

Two years later permission was given for a torchlight procession, which soon became an accepted part of Christmas and New Year celebrations, followed by entertainment in houses 'open' to guizers. In 1881 for the first time the procession was held on the night of Up-Helly-Aa. In 1889 the burning of a model Norse longship was incorporated in the proceedings, the greatest step towards the modern festival; and 1896 saw the introduction of organised singing as the procession started, the song being 'The Hardy Norseman'. This was a period when interest in Shetland's Norse associations was high and the festival was adapting accordingly. In 1897 another song was specially written for Up-Helly-Aa, and is still sung at the festival as the 'Up-Helly-Aa Song'.

Preparations for the festival begin many months beforehand. A committee is elected and a guizer jarl or chief guizer is chosen. A lot of behind-the-scenes work is required in building the galley and making up to 800 torches from wood and sacking. The guizers themselves are divided into 'squads' of twelve or fourteen men who usually make their own fancy dress, which is based on a single theme and prepared in strict secrecy. The final task is the painting of the 'Bill', a 10ft high board, beautifully decorated, which pokes fun at local institutions and the year's events, and is eagerly examined by townspeople on the morning of Up-Helly-Aa.

The festival itself takes place at night, the flames from the torches illuminating the crowds lining the streets as the colourful Norse galley is dragged to its burning place. This is less than 1 mile from an Iron Age broch that was already ancient when the Norsemen arrived in Shetland. The burning of the galley marks the end of only the first half of the proceedings. Then begins the round of the halls, which each of the fifty or so squads must visit in strict order. Here the night's revelry is held, organised by hard-working hostesses. At each hall the squad provides entertainment in keeping with its theme, partakes of refreshment and joins in a dance.

Recently television has brought the spectacle of Up-Helly-Aa to millions of people on the mainland of Britain but not even colour TV can do justice to the scene.

11 SHETLAND TODAY

THE problems facing Shetland are different from those of any other part of Britain: the population is small and scattered over seventeen islands; the nearest industrial centre is 200 miles away in Aberdeen; and the natural resources are confined mainly to fish, wool and agricultural products yielded grudgingly by an unpredictable climate. In spite of all these difficulties, a transformation took place in the years following World War II leaving the islands more alive and more confident than at any time in their history. Then, as a result of the discovery of North Sea oil, came the massive developments of the 1970s bringing benefits as well as disadvantages and changing the whole fabric of island life.

LIVING CONDITIONS

The years following World War II saw a flurry of minor improvements in the traditional way of life. People began to improve their houses, installing kitchens and bathrooms with a private water supply piped from the nearest well, and in the more progressive areas scores of wind-driven electricity generating sets appeared. These examples of private initiative were but forerunners of large-scale improvements carried out all over the islands with grants from the Exchequer.

Most important were the improvements in housing. Between 1946 and 1969 324 council houses rehoused 1,184 people in rural areas and 391 houses were built by private enterprise. By 1970 more than a quarter of all occupied houses in Shetland had been built or substantially improved since 1946. In 1950 only Lerwick and Scalloway had a public water supply while by 1970 this had been provided in twenty-seven districts including the islands of Papa Stour, Out Skerries, Burra, Whalsay, Unst and Bressay. Between 1960 and 1970 Zetland

County Council provided fifteen water schemes at a total cost of £990,000.

Much of the credit for the improvement in living standards must go to the North of Scotland Hydro-Electric Board which was set up by an Act of Parliament in 1943 not only to harness the energy of rivers and lochs in the Highlands and Islands but also to promote social improvement and economic development within that area. In 1946 it took over an old diesel-driven power station in Market Street, Lerwick, where the regional office is now situated. The plant was too small for the schemes envisaged and a new station was built in 1953 at Gremista, just north of Lerwick, at a cost of £250,000. Additions to the power station became necessary every two or three years and by 1970 the maximum demand had increased to over 11,000kw and the total capacity of the power station was 17,000kw.

MEDICAL SERVICES

Improvements in the medical services in the immediate post-war period were no less spectacular. In 1948 with the inauguration of the National Health Service, Shetland's hospitals were brought under the control of the North Eastern Regional Hospital Board. The building of a new hospital at Lerwick was regarded as urgent but not until 1954 were funds set aside by the Board for this purpose. Work began in 1957 and the foundation stone was laid on 21 April 1959. The result was the new Gilbert Bain hospital with accommodation for forty-eight medical and surgical cases built at a cost of £410,000.

Care of the aged is regarded as the most important medico-social problem facing the islands as Shetland has a high proportion of elderly people. To assist people in their own homes the county council inaugurated a home-help service, meals-on-wheels and a free chiropody service. The home-help service increased its staff from three full-time and six part-time workers helping twenty-one people in 1955 to twenty-two full-time and ninety-one part-time workers attending 163 households in 1970.

Eventide homes are provided in Lerwick and Scalloway, the latter being run by the Church of Scotland. In order to help elderly people in their own communities flatlets have been erected in several districts. For geriatric patients there are forty-four beds in Brevik Hospital (formerly the County Homes) while Montfield Hospital (formerly the Isolation Hospital) and the old Gilbert Bain hospital are run in conjunction and together offer forty-three beds for elderly people.

The health of the islanders is generally good while infantile mortality is well below the average Scottish rate. The only disease of which there is an unusually high incidence is multiple sclerosis: with thirty cases in 1971, a rate of 170 per 100,000, Shetland has one of the highest incidences in the world. Several theories have been proposed to account for this, including a possible link between MS and sheep-rearing and the occurrence or absence of certain trace elements in the soil. Several groups of researchers have become interested in the islands in the belief that the answer to this crippling disease will be found in Shetland.

SCHOOLS

In 1945 there were seventy-two schools in Shetland, of which only the Anderson Educational Institute and Lerwick Central School provided secondary education. Between the ages of eleven and fourteen pupils sat an examination for admission to secondary school if they wished to do so and about thirty were selected for each school in Lerwick annually.

The Education (Scotland) Act of 1946 introduced a scheme making it compulsory for all pupils in class primary 7 (the elevens and twelves) to undergo a series of tests and each pupil was allocated to the secondary course that seemed most suited to his abilities. In addition to the secondary schools at Lerwick, junior secondary schools were established at Baltasound, Mid Yell, Whalsay, Urafirth, Brae, Aith, Happyhansel (Walls), Scalloway Hamnavoe and Sandwick to which pupils travelled daily from the surrounding area. Children of remote islands could if they wished remain at the local school but only those of Out Skerries did so.

The system was later reorganised, for rural depopulation in some areas had led to a reduction in the numbers of children attending school and junior secondary courses, and subsequent overstaffing. Thus, the secondary departments at Urafirth and

Happyhansel have been closed and the pupils transferred to secondary departments at Brae and Aith respectively. Following the construction of the bridges to Burra in 1972 the secondary department of Hamnavoe was also closed and the pupils transferred to Scalloway. These changes coincided with the trend towards comprehensive education which was being tried in Scotland for an initial period of ten years and is now an established part of the educational system. The promotion scheme of 1946 has been cancelled and tests are no longer necessary. Instead, every pupil is transferred from class primary 7 to the junior high school for his area.

A pupil now spends two years at a junior high school after which his parents can decide whether he (or she) should remain there or proceed to the new Anderson High School at Lerwick, formed in 1970 as a single six-year all-through comprehensive school by combining the AEI and the Central School. One of the advantages of the junior high school scheme is social, children being allowed to remain in their home area for the first two years of their secondary course.

As rural depopulation continued through the 1950s and early 1960s the closure of several primary schools became unavoidable. At the same time the benefits of educating children in larger numbers became obvious to the education committee and this policy no doubt played its part in the closure of one or two more. In Dunrossness, for example, four small schools were closed and a new primary school built with a roll of 110. After initial opposition from some of the parents it was soon agreed that the single school is a great success. As a result of these changes in the education system the number of schools in Shetland dropped to thirty-eight in 1972.

The mid-1970s saw a reappraisal of educational facilities in Shetland and the start of a massive building programme by the education committee. As many of the schools were built in the late nineteenth century, they were clearly unsuited to modern educational needs; further pressure was being brought about by a rising population. By 1978 new primary schools had been built at Whiteness and Cunningsburgh to replace existing schools while just outside Lerwick an entirely new primary school had been built in the growing suburb of Sound. The influx of workers for the oil and its allied industries has brought pressure to bear on several rural schools, notably that of Brae, where a new primary department was opened in 1977. The most spectacular building programme of all has been undertaken at the Anderson High School at Lerwick but even the large new wing opened in 1978 is proving too small to cope with the rise in the school's roll. Between 1975 and 1978 it rose from 736 to 902.

LIBRARIES

Ever since improvements in education began in the early nineteenth century, books have played a great part in the lives of the people of Shetland. The statistical account of 1841 lists several subscription libraries from Dunrossness in the south to Unst in the north.

Lerwick subscription library was formed in 1809 and continued until 1874. In 1828 a second library was founded there, the General Zetland Library, which existed for 35 years until it was absorbed by yet another library. In 1861 Shetland Literary and Scientific Society was instituted 'to promote general literary and scientific knowledge and the study of the antiquities and natural history of the Shetland Isles'. Its library opened in the Old Tolbooth on 8 December 1863 and consisted of 1,100 books including 700 transferred from the General Zetland Library.

At the beginning of the twentieth century James Coats of Paisley presented to towns and villages throughout the country not only collections of books but also the bookcases to hold them. Schools in Shetland benefited under the scheme. The present library service, however, had its origins in 1915 when Shetland was chosen, along with Orkney, Lewis and Staffordshire for one of the pilot schemes sponsored by the Carnegie United Kingdom Trust to test the feasibility of providing rural libraries. By the end of 1916 forty-seven rural libraries had been established.

Scottish county libraries were instituted by law in 1918, and in 1924 the education authority accepted responsibility for administering the library service in Shetland. The Carnegie UK Trust donated its entire local stock of books to the authority and reimbursed the authority for the cost of obtaining and equipping extra accommodation. The librarian of the Literary and Scientific Society became the first county librarian. Both libraries continued to operate as separate entities for the next twenty-four years but since the county library offered a free service and a better choice, membership of the Literary and Scientific Society declined. Finally, in 1948 its books were merged with those of the county library.

The inadequacies of the county library service became obvious during World War II, when Shetland's population was doubled by the influx of servicemen. The librarian was hard-working but untrained, classification and cataloguing of books were rudimentary and the building was too small. In 1947 Zetland Education Committee appointed a qualified librarian, George Longmuir, and purchased a redundant forces' canteen to house the library as a temporary measure. Like most temporary measures it lasted a long time, in this case eighteen years.

The present library and museum was opened in June 1966. One of the main features of the library is the Shetland room which houses the local collection of books, pamphlets, newspapers and manuscripts on local subjects. It is extensive since no community in Britain has a greater interest in its history and traditions. Two notable bequests housed here are the Reid Tait and the Goudie collections.

Book issues declined following the extension of television to Shetland in 1964, but, after a short 'honeymoon' period, the islanders once again became readers and in 1969 issues totalled just under 200,000 giving a ratio of 11.4 issues per head of population. In the same year a count of books showed a total of over 63,000. The number of readers in the county was estimated at 8,230 or 48 per cent of the population. Rural centres are operated in schools, public halls, post offices or lighthouses in all the smaller inhabited islands. Books are securely boxed and sent by inter-island ferry, by carrier or rural bus service. If necessary, books are sent to readers by post.

In 1964 a mobile library service was provided for the Mainland and this has now been extended to cover the islands of Unst, Yell Fetlar and Whalsay. Between 1964 and 1970 the number of books issued in the area served by the mobile library increased sevenfold, proving the value of this innovation.

Latest additions to the library at Lerwick are a record-lending library, started in 1967, which by 1978 had 1,032 discs, and a picture-lending library, started in 1968 and used mainly by schools and hostels, which now has 260 prints.

Mr George Longmuir retired in September 1976 and was succeeded by Mr John Hunter. Another valuable addition to the staff of the library is the archivist, Mr Brian Smith, who fills a new post set up in April 1976.

RURAL DEVELOPMENT

Improvements in the economic life of Shetland did not keep pace with social improvements and depopulation remained the most serious problem facing the islands in the years following World War II. There were certainly some rural bright spots: Whalsay, Burra and Out Skerries were struggling to maintain their fishing fleets; the parish of Dunrossness was developing its agriculture; and there were districts such as Sandwick and Voe where bakeries and knitwear units created employment and helped to stabilise the community.

The first formal attempt to improve the situation was the publication in 1955 of a development plan by Zetland County Council. It proposed improvements in basic industries, and the provision of piers, roads and amenities such as piped water and electricity in areas where they were still lacking. It recognised the need for a rise in population and the suggestion was made, quite seriously, that immigration should be encouraged from Scandinavia, implying that such immigrants were more likely to make a success of developing the islands than the current race of Shetlanders or the urban-minded Scots. The most constructive proposal was that a Shetland Development Council be established. This was implemented in 1957 and in the following year the body was renamed the Shetland Council of Social Service. The first county development officer was Mr R. Storey, appointed in 1961.

In 1962 a delegation from the county council went to Faeroe to study the miracle of the Faeroese economy. Between 1860 and 1960 the population of Faeroe had increased from 13,000 to 35,000 while that of Shetland had fallen from 31,000 to 18,000. The inescapable fact was that Faeroe had developed a thriving fishing and fish-processing industry, a lesson which had already been learned on a smaller scale in Shetland by the people of Whalsay, Burra and Out Skerries. Another lesson learned in Faeroe was the importance of larger communities in rural districts—villages large enough to stand on their own with all social and cultural amenities provided. Members of the Highland panel had discovered this on their visit to Norway and they advocated the establishment of 'growth points' in remote areas of Scotland. It is perhaps indicative of the more serious stage reached in Shetland that Zetland County Council adopted the name 'holding points' in their battle to stop depopulation. The selection of holding points caused a great deal of debate but finally Baltasound, Mid Yell, Symbister, Brae and Hillswick, Aith and Walls, Sandwick, Virkie and Toab were chosen. These districts were to be provided with such amenities as water and electricity, and investment wherever possible was to be steered into them.

The biggest boost to the economy of the islands was the establishment in 1965 of the Highlands and Islands Development Board which provided loans and grants for approved projects, taking shares in struggling business concerns and assisting others with accountancy. To the end of 1969 the board had invested almost £800,000 in 111 projects in Shetland and 425 jobs had been so created. The board helped in the purchase of new boats and in the building of knitwear units, fish factories, hotels and many more types of venture. But the board must not take all the credit for the transformation that took place in the 1960s. The initiative was here already and several projects had been started through private enterprise; the establishment of Iceatlantic (Frozen Seafoods) Ltd in 1960 was an example of the faith of a certain section of the community. What was lacking in Shetland was capital and this the HIDB supplied generously.

Apart from these developments in the basic industries a host of lesser ventures sprang up such as mink farming and stone polishing at Whiteness while Shetland Silvercraft at Weisdale began making brooches and ornaments based on ancient Celtic and Scandinavian designs. Sheepskin curing, long carried out by crofters to produce rugs, became a full-time occupation in several localities while the manufacture of articles from sealskin also became full-time work at Girlsta and in Unst. Crafts such as pottery, basketwork, and wrought-iron work began to be carried on as part-time pursuits under the active encouragement of Shetland Craft Guild. Even in the problem area of the North Mainland, Northmavine Development Council was set up and it helped to provide a jetty at Ronas Voe and a small fish factory.

The transformation from the decaying islands of the 1960s to the vigorous community that emerged during the late 1960s was astonishing and was seen clearly from the population statistics. By 1961 the population had dropped to 17,483 and it was to drop still further by 1966 but the census of 1971 produced a figure of 17,567, proving that the downward trend of more than 100 years had been reversed. The question now was how far the population could rise. It seemed that the development of Shetland's natural resources could go on indefinitely with a steady rise in population. Indeed, the need to attract more workers to live in Shetland to overcome an acute labour shortage became one of the main points of council policy and the problem was tackled by embarking on a building programme with sectional timber houses imported from Norway. These were set up in what was considered fairly large schemes of ten or a dozen at places like Scalloway and Whalsay where incoming workers were most urgently needed. Then in 1971 oil was discovered east of Shetland and plans for a modest growth in the islands' economy were swamped as Shetland became caught up in the North Sea oil boom.

NORTH SEA OIL

Had oil been discovered ten years earlier it would have been hailed as the economic salvation of Shetland but instead it came at a time of optimism and full employment, in marked contrast to the situation elsewhere in Britain at that time. It is not surprising, therefore, that while most people in the UK welcomed the discovery of oil many people in Shetland resented it as a threat to a prosperous and peaceful way of life and maintained that Shetland should have no truck with the oil industry. However, even if Shetland had wanted simply to opt out, it was not possible to do so. From their position as the land nearest the oilfields of the East Shetland basin it was clear that the islands would play a major role in the nation's race to get the oil ashore.

Zetland County Council was entirely unprepared for developments on the scale demanded by the new oil industry but acted with amazing speed to rectify this state of affairs. An Interim Development Plan was quickly devised, the most important of its proposals being the zoning of large tracts of land around the hamlet of Graven on Sullom Voe for major developments. At the same time the council was determined to prevent the proliferation of major installations and declared its intention to guide potential developers towards the establishment of one industrial complex in the Sullom Voe area.

The area around Graven was the obvious place for these developments. Sullom Voe itself is a large sea inlet off Yell Sound deep enough to accommodate the world's largest oil tankers and with a broad belt of reasonably flat back-up land, much of it lying derelict since World War II when it was used as a base by the RAF. No matter how obvious its merits might appear from a casual examination, the whole area had to be subjected to a rigorous examination and this was the remit given to the firm of Livesey and Henderson, appointed consulting engineers to the county council.

Developments at Sullom Voe were delayed by a bitter dispute that occupied much of 1973. An Edinburgh firm of financiers had foreseen the potential of Sullom Voe and had entered into agreements with landowners in the area. Having purchased or secured the option to purchase large tracts of land they produced their own plans for the area to provide the facilities required by the oil industry. They made it clear that they wished to work in conjunction with the local authority but the council by this time had begun to formulate its own ambitious plans and could see no need for the involvement of a third party between it and the oil companies. The outcome was protracted legislation at Westminster until the Zetland County Council Act of 1974 gave the council practically all the powers it had sought. It gave the council powers to exercise jurisdiction as port and harbour authority over the whole of Sullom Voe; to acquire land for the necessary developments within a designated area; to issue or refuse licences to dredge and licences to construct works within the three-mile limit; to take shares in commercial undertakings, and finally to establish a Reserve Fund. These were exceptional powers for a small local authority and their granting was a clear indication of Shetland's important role in the overall context of North Sea oil.

With legislation safely overcome the ZCC and its successor, the Shetland Islands Council, set up under the reorganisation of local government, could begin to put its plan into practice. The consultants' reports were now ready, covering every aspect of the proposed developments at Sullom Voe from constructional and navigational considerations to social and environmental implications. One of the most important recommendations was that the incoming workers should not be housed in a specially built new town but that existing hamlets in the parish of Delting should be enlarged to accommodate them.

It must be pointed out, however, that long before work commenced at Sullom Voe, Shetland was already deeply involved in the oil industry. From the earliest days of survey work in the East and West Shetland basins seismic survey vessels had paid frequent visits to Shetland harbours and specially designed supply bases were constructed at Lerwick and Sandwick. At the southern tip of Shetland, Sumburgh Airport found a new importance as the airport nearest the oilfields of the northern North Sea. The old terminal buildings and the runways themselves were no longer adequate and the entire airport had to be reconstructed. One of the most important developments here was the construction of a new east–west runway straddling the peninsula from the Atlantic to the North Sea which largely removed the problems formerly caused through cross-winds affecting the old single runway.

These developments, large as they were, have been completely dwarfed by the scale of developments at Sullom Voe where out of a once quiet inlet and a bare headland an entirely new port has been built, soon to become the largest oil terminal in Europe with a capacity for 70 million tons of oil a year at a cost of over £1,000 million. The building of the port has been carried out under a unique arrangement between the Shetland Islands Council and the oil companies. The SIC have built the tanker jetties at Calback Ness while the landward part of the complex is under the control of the Sullom Voe Association—a partnership of the SIC and the major oil companies. The council holds a 50 per cent interest in the SVA while the other 50 per cent is held by Shell and BP as operators of the Brent and Ninian pipelines.

One outcome of this co-operation between the SIC and the oil companies was the formation of the Sullom Voe Environmental Advisory Group, an independent body whose function was to ensure that the development of Sullom Voe should not materially harm the Shetland environment. This group included representatives of the oil companies and the SIC, and of such bodies as the Countryside Commission for Scotland, the Nature Conservancy Council and the Natural Environment Research Council. This group was replaced in 1977 by the Shetland Oil Terminal Environmental Advisory group with much the same representation as before.

Although the major contracts for the oil industrial developments went to firms from outside the islands, scores of local companies, including haulage contractors and plant-hire firms expanded to meet the growing demand for their services while new companies were formed to exploit market opportunities. Hoteliers, once restricted by the shortness of the summer season, found their rooms fully booked throughout the year. Merchants in every line of business benefited from increased trade while hundreds of Shetlanders earned high wages from their jobs at the supply bases or the construction sites.

While the benefits of the oil boom cannot be denied it must be pointed out that a large section of the business community not only received no advantage from oil but was positively harmed by it. Worst affected were the smaller firms employing only a handful of people to whom the loss of one key worker was an insurmountable obstacle. Several small firms had to close and the local bakery trade lost no fewer than eleven men between 1976 and 1978—all of them lured away by higher wages.

The indigenous industries were affected in different ways. Fishermen were severely hampered by pipe-laying activities east of Shetland and some of the best fishing grounds were destroyed while others were littered with discarded debris. Most processing plants were forced to work at reduced capacity so adding to the problems of the fishermen.

Worst affected was the knitwear industry which depends largely on women who work at home on a part-time basis. With oil came opportunities for girls, including well-paid office jobs, while at Sullom Voe and the construction camps nearby there was a keen demand for cleaners and canteen staff. As a result of these changes in the pattern of employment the knitwear industry was only a shadow of what it was before oil was discovered.

Crofting was not seriously affected by the construction boom. In most cases, even in normal times, it offers only part-time employment and many crofters were able to benefit from a well-paid job while working their land in their spare time. Inevitably there was less time to devote to tilling the land and many crofters sold their cattle replacing them with sheep which require much less attention.

In the early 1980s, as predicted, the pace of construction work slowed down as the giant oil terminal neared completion. (It was opened by Her Majesty the Queen on 9 May 1981). Many local people lost their jobs and were forced to seek employment outwith the oil industry. Far more disturbing, however, was the run-down in employment in the South of Shetland where the growth of Sumburgh Airport had created hundreds of new jobs. Unfortunately the demand for these services was less than expected while the introduction of long-range helicopters, capable of serving the rigs and platforms from Aberdeen, removed the main advantage that Sumburgh can offer—proximity to the oilfields of the northern North Sea.

This is a testing time for Shetland Islands Council with its declared intention of using money earned through its involvement with the oil industry to develop the traditional industries to provide prosperity and prevent widespread unemployment. Already nearly £30 million has accrued in the Charitable Trust from the proceeds of the Disturbance Agreement signed with the oil companies and from profit gained from the oil-related companies in which the council has an interest. Many people are quick to point out, however, that the council is deeply in debt, having borrowed heavily to provide its share of the facilities at Sullom Voe.

Already considerable sums have been paid to local industry and there are plans to spend much more. The most ambitious scheme so far is the Ten Year Plan for Agriculture which offers incentives for land improvement, the production of beef cattle, etc.

Already it is clear that while Shetland's involvement with the oil industry will last to the end of the century at least (and there may well be more surprises before then) the future of the islands will depend on the land and the sea and the traditional industries that sustained them for centuries before oil was discovered under the stormy waters of the North Sea.

POLITICAL CONSIDERATIONS

The year 1969 was important for Shetland, marking as it did the 500th anniversary of the mortgaging of the islands to Scotland. An important part of the celebrations was a series of lectures given in Lerwick by recognised experts in political, economic and social fields. They came from Norway, Germany, Holland and Scotland and outlined the contribution made by each of these countries to the unique amalgam which is Shetland today.

One of the most outstanding lectures was that given by Professor Robberstad of Oslo University on udal law in Shetland, which has never been abolished by Act of Parliament, although it has to a large extent in Norway. Although Shetland was largely feudalised, the process has never been formally acknowledged.

There are still survivals of udal law in Shetland. Any crofter can lift shingle from his foreshore without interference from or payment to his landlord, provided it is used for buildings on his croft. A landowner can sell shingle from his beaches, for an important aspect of udal law is that the Crown has no right to the foreshore. Crofters still claim the right to set nets off their own foreshore for salmon or sea trout in accordance with ancient usage in defiance of the laws of Scotland, which assert that these fish belong to the Crown. The quincentenary celebrations served to underline the need for an inquiry into the survival of Norse law, of which foreshore and fishing rights constitute only a small part.

In the late 1960s the proposed reorganisation of local government in Scotland and its effect on Shetland was by far the biggest single talking point in the islands. The shape of things planned was apparent when one by one the local fire, water and police services were amalgamated with those of Orkney and Caithness. When the report of the Royal Commission under the chairmanship of Lord Wheatley was published in 1969 it was proposed that Shetland be merged in a large Highland region extending southwards as far as the Mull of Kintyre. This caused a furore in Shetland, not from blind patriotism, but from the deeply held conviction that the suggestion was impracticable. The distance involved was colossal. It was pointed out that the southern extremity of the proposed region was as near the south coast of England as it was to Shetland. Again it was explained that Shetland's economic ties and links of communication were with Aberdeen and these could not be swept away overnight. Three members of the commission, however, disagreed with the views of the majority and proposed special first-tier status for Shetland as well as Orkney.

In 1971 a Government White Paper was published and with considerable relief it was noted that in the reorganisation Shetland and Orkney would each form a special all-purpose authority. There is little doubt that the success of this campaign strengthened the determination of Zetland County Council to seek special powers to control oil developments and to use them as far as possible for the benefit of Shetland. In this the council was again successful with the passing of the Zetland County Council Act of 1974.

The mid-1970s also saw a re-examination of the position held by Shetland within the UK and a reappraisal of the attitudes of Britain and Scandinavian countries to their remote communities. In particular, a comparison was made between Shetland and the Faeroe Islands. Faeroe remains part of the Danish state with two members in the Danish parliament but it has its own parliament for internal affairs, its own language and its own flag. Shetland, although a special island region, shares a member of parliament with Orkney and in spite of its historical and cultural differences does not even have the status of the Isle of Man.

This debate was instigated in part by the new wealth promised by oil, in part by the recent success of Zetland County

Council in winning greater control of Shetland's affairs and in part by events in other parts of the UK. The mid-1970s had also seen the rise of the Scottish National Party with its demands for an independent Scotland—a move which many Shetlanders viewed with alarm. While Shetland has long accepted its place in Scotland as part of the United Kingdom, its place in an independent Scotland cannot be accepted automatically. There was, however, no clear consensus of opinion as to the political status best suited for Shetland. While some advocated the retention of Shetland's links with Westminster others sought special island status similar to that enjoyed by Faeroe or the Isle of Man. At the same time the SNP also had its supporters in Shetland and its candidate did remarkably well in the 1973 election. In 1978 the SIC decided to test public opinion by holding a referendum in Shetland. The result was surprising, for in a 70 per cent poll Shetlanders voted by a majority of nine to one in support of the campaign by the islands' council for a commission to be set up to consider Shetland's position. In the same year a Shetland Movement was set up determined to press by all means possible for greater autonomy for Shetland.

The Common Market

Yet another talking point of the 1970s was Britain's membership of the European Economic Community. The greatest worry in Shetland was the effect on the islands' fish stocks if the twelve-mile limit or inner six-mile limit should be abolished and continental vessels were allowed to fish almost up to these shores. Alone of all European countries Britain has sought to preserve her fish stocks with strict controls to avoid over-fishing, with the result that the richest fishing grounds in the North Sea lie within British waters and around Shetland in particular. After protracted discussion a compromise was reached and incorporated in the 1972 Brussels Treaty of Accession whereby the inner six-mile belt would continue to be reserved for British fishermen as would certain parts of the outer belt, including the area around Orkney and Shetland. These concessions would run until 31 December 1982 when the situation would be reviewed by the EEC. In effect, this was not a solution but merely a shelving of the problem for ten years. These terms did not satisfy the electorate of Orkney and Shetland who voted in the national referendum by a large majority against Britain joining the Common Market. Fishermen elsewhere also campaigned to keep Britain out of the EEC but their voices were swamped by the overwhelming national support for membership.

The Fishing Limits Act of 1976 established a 200-mile zone around Britain on behalf of the EEC and gave Britain power to regulate fishing within this area. The allocation of the catch was, however, left in the hands of the EEC. Disagreement between Britain and other member countries over the share allocated to British fishermen led to constant wrangling and postponed the signing of a common fishing policy. By this time the herring stocks were nearing extinction and in the absence of international agreement on quotas Britain, acting unilaterally, imposed a total ban on herring fishing in the North Sea. The state of white-fish stocks was also causing concern being aggravated by the presence of large British trawlers displaced from their traditional grounds in the North Atlantic by conservatory measures there and now demanding a share of the hard-pressed stocks in waters around Shetland.

A Shetland Fishing Plan was drawn up with the aim of giving local vessels preference in a wide area around Shetland and with recommendations to limit the total catch to ensure conservation. Pressure was exerted on both the British government and the EEC to include such a scheme in the overall EEC Common Fisheries policy but no avail. The only concession to local opinion was the establishment of a 'box' around both Orkney and Shetland within which the largest trawlers will be limited by licenses. Fishermen in both groups of islands maintain that this does not go nearly far enough and they are determined to fight for the adoption of regional fisheries schemes. It is important that special consideration should be given to Shetland since this is one of the few areas in the UK where fishing is still the most important industry.

12 PLACES TO VISIT

It is impossible to include in a short chapter all the interesting sites that are to be seen. The archaeologist will find many more not listed here and the student of natural history will find much fascinating material outside the areas listed as nature reserves and sites of special scientific interest.

ANCIENT MONUMENTS

Many relics of the past have been destroyed through ignorance or indifference. Men of the Bronze Age and Iron Age, Vikings, Scots and crofters of the last century all plundered the buildings of preceding races to make their own houses, dry-stone dykes and sheep pens. Fortunately the attitude of the people has changed, and local interest is typified in the formation in 1966 of Shetland Archaeological and Natural History Society, which now has a membership of 200. One of its major projects was the excavation along scientific lines of a Neolithic and Bronze Age site at Sumburgh that has now been scheduled as an ancient monument.

Neolithic Sites

The sites of over sixty Neolithic houses have been located, but only three have been studied in detail—two at Gruting, the third at Staneydale. The houses were oval in plan, and built round a scooped-out floor to give greater headroom. The low walls varied in thickness from 6 to 15ft and average external dimensions were 54ft and 36ft along the axes. From the lower end of each building an entrance led into the main chamber, where a peat fire burned on a central hearth of flat stones.

More numerous than Neolithic houses are the heel-shaped burial cairns peculiar to Shetland, though most of them are now little more than large heaps of stones. Best preserved example is to be found on the island of Vementry near Aith. From the middle of the concave façade an entrance leads into a single chamber with a terminal and two lateral recesses forming the shape of a clover leaf. The scale is impressive, for the façade measures 36ft across. Largest Neolithic cairn in Shetland, and one of the best preserved, is at Mangaster, Northmavine; another is situated on the summit of Ronas Hill.

Of similar shape to the cairns but much larger are the temples that have been found at Staneydale and at Yoxie in Whalsay. The former measures 64ft by 47ft along its axes; and the walls, averaging 12ft in thickness, enclose an oval chamber measuring 39ft by 29ft. Two well constructed post-holes along the longer axes carried the wooden posts which supported the roof. The temple of Yoxie measures 50ft by 34ft with a fore-court 15ft long. The similarity between these buildings and those discovered on the islands of Malta and Gozo has been mentioned in Chapter 2.

Bronze Age Sites

Evidence in Shetland for the Beaker period that marks the opening of the Bronze Age in Britain rests on a few scraps of pottery. The earliest definite traces of Bronze Age people are again graves. They buried their dead, usually singly, in short cists or coffins of stone slabs. The graves were sometimes covered with cairns of stone smaller than those over Neolithic tombs.

The only example in Shetland of a two-storeyed cist was discovered accidentally beside the road through Tingwall valley near Asta. In the upper compartment were two steatite urns and fragments of human bone, while in the lower chamber were the remains of an adult and the cremated remains of an infant.

Most remarkable Bronze Age site in Shetland is at Jarlshof near Sumburgh airport. Some experts regard this as the most remarkable archaeological site in Britain, for Bronze Age, Iron Age, Viking and sixteenth-century buildings are superimposed one on top of the other to create a fascinating puzzle for those who excavated the site between 1931 and 1951. It is described fully in the Ministry of Works official guidebook. The site is maintained by the Ministry of Works and a guide is in attendance.

At the burn of Catpund, Cunningsburgh, are steatite quarries that were in use in Bronze Age times for the manufacture of cooking and storage pots. The manner in which they were fashioned can still be observed on the surface of the rock.

Also of Bronze Age date in all probability are the burnt mounds, almost 200 of which have been recognised in Shetland. They appear simply as grass-covered unnatural looking heaps, and they are composed entirely of fist-sized stones broken and discoloured by heat. Some mounds are small, but some are as large as 80ft in diameter. The largest is in Fair Isle, and measures 122ft and 88ft along its axes and is about 10ft high. None of these mounds has been scientifically examined.

The many standing stones of Shetland also puzzle the archaeologist. Even their age is not certain, though many are believed to date from Bronze Age times. One stands singly beside the road in Tingwall valley, and others stand in groups of two or more, like the Giants' Stones of Hamnavoe, Northmavine. Why they were erected is not known.

Iron Age relics

The brochs are the most outstanding feature of Iron Age times in Shetland. There are ninety-five known sites, but only four have been fully excavated—at Clickhimin, Jarlshof, Clumlie and Levenwick. Best known of the brochs is that on the island of Mousa. When built it was a very ordinary structure of modest dimensions, but it was destined to become famous, for here, in 1153 according to the *Orkneyinga Saga*, a couple eloping from Norway spent a prolonged honeymoon. It still stands today almost complete, the best example in Britain. It can be reached by hiring a boat from Sandwick.

The broch of Clickhimin within the burgh of Lerwick has been skilfully and scientifically cleared since World War II. Analysis of the results by the excavator, J. R. C. Hamilton, has produced revolutionary and far-reaching conclusions that are embodied in a new official guide entitled *The Brochs of Mousa and Clickhimin*, published by Her Majesty's Stationery Office in 1970.

Norse relics

Viking houses have been found at Underhoull and Sandwick in Unst, Breckin in Yell, Isbister in Whalsay and at a few places on the Mainland, including Jarlshof. The official guidebook to the latter site deals with the Norse period in detail. Of the many known and probable Norse burial mounds none has been fully examined. The finds described in Chapter 2 were all discovered by accident.

Evidence of prolonged Norse settlement is not derived solely from archaeological remains, but also in the continuation to the present day of Norse culture. Legacies of Norse times are the Shetland crofting townships, their ancient pattern of hill dykes still traceable in some places, though replaced by wire fences.

The Scottish Period

There is very little evidence of Scottish rule in Shetland before the time of the Stewarts. Robert Stewart built his mansion house at Sumburgh, later to be a source of inspiration to Sir Walter Scott. He invented the name Jarlshof and used it in his book *The Pirate*. The name Jarlshof was later applied to the whole complex of prehistoric remains covering 2,000 years of history.

Patrick Stewart completed his castle at Scalloway in 1600, and it still dominates the ancient capital of Shetland. The castle, four storeys and a garret high, is complete to the wall heads, and consists of an oblong block with a square wing attached to the south-west corner. The plan seems to have been based to some extent on Noltland castle in Orkney, and is believed to have influenced the design of the Earl's palace at Kirkwall. It can be visited upon application to the caretaker living in the cottage opposite.

Slightly older than Scalloway castle is the castle of Muness in Unst. It consists basically of an oblong block with two circular towers attached to opposite corners. It was originally three storeys high, but the upper storey was removed to build the wall which now encloses it.

Above the entrance is a panel with the following inscription in late Gothic letters.

> LIST ZE TO KNAW YIS BULDING QUHA BEGAN
> LAURENCE THE BRUCE HE WAS THAT WORTHY MAN
> QUHA ERNESTLY HIS AIRIS AND OFSPRING PRAYIS
> TO HELP AND NOT TO HURT THIS VARK ALUAYIS

It is followed by THE ZEIR OF GOD 1598 in Roman lettering.

Of the early trade of the islands not much evidence remains. Most outstanding relic of the trade with North Germany is the Pier house at Whalsay, built in the seventeenth century as the store of a trader. Some of the German traders spent a lifetime in Shetland, and two of them, Segebad Detken and Henrick Segelcken, were buried in the churchyard at Lunda Wick, Unst, in 1573 and 1585 respectively. Their tombstones can still be seen, though the inscriptions are difficult to decipher.

Oldest building in Lerwick apart from the broch of Clickhimin is Fort Charlotte, begun in 1665. It is built on top of a cliff overlooking the harbour, but is now rather obscured by buildings on three sides of it. It occupies over 2 acres of ground, and is roughly five-sided, with bastions projecting from each corner. The walls are high, with gunports facing the sea.

CHURCHES

None of the churches now in use are very old, though several are built on sites that have been hallowed by successive places of worship since the days of the Celtic missionaries of the sixth century AD. Of the known sites of Celtic churches, only that of St Ninian's Isle has been excavated, in 1958, when the excavators discovered the now famous hoard of Celtic silverware that can be seen in the National Museum of Antiquities in Edinburgh.

In this museum can also be seen the Bressay Stone found at Cullinsbrough, the site of another early Celtic church. It is a stone slab sculptured in relief on its two faces and inscribed on the narrow edges with Ogam writing. There, too, can be seen the famous Papil Stone, found at Papil in Burra—a rectangular slab of red sandstone almost 6ft high with unique Celtic designs incised or sculptured on one face. From this site came the Monks' Stone, which is one of the most prized exhibits of Zetland County Museum.

Fragments of twelfth-century churches can be seen at St Ninian's Isle, and at Lunda Wick in Unst. It is believed that they were built with an oblong nave opening through a rounded arch into a short chancel or sanctum. Part of a church dedicated to St Mary stands at Sand. There remains only a semicircular chancel arch, which tradition holds is part of a church erected by shipwrecked Spaniards in gratitude for their deliverance from the battle and storms that decimated the Spanish Armada. Other experts believe it to be in the typical Romanesque style of the eleventh and twelfth centuries in this area of Europe.

At Voe is a ruined church built in the late eighteenth century. Oblong in plan, it has a rectangular wing projecting from the middle of the north side. The wing is two-storeyed, the lower storey, entered through a gable, being the burial place of the Giffords of Busta.

The ruined church at Papil was built in the late nineteenth century, but it stands on the site of the twelfth-century church of St Lawrence, which was distinguished by a round tower. This in turn stood on the site of an early Celtic church.

Churches now in use are generally plain buildings in accordance with the mood of the reforming Presbyterians. One of the oldest is the church of Lunna, built in 1753. Incorporated in the porch are two inscribed slabs that evidently came from a pre-existing family mausoleum. The church of Tingwall stands on the site of another towered church, the most magnificent of three such buildings in Shetland. The churchyard contains many interesting tombstones, including that of the Master of Works who built Scalloway Castle.

RELICS OF TRADITIONAL LIFE

There are many relics of a way of life that lasted until the end of the nineteenth century. Ruins of watermills stand beside many streams, though several have been restored to working order, as at Huxter, Sandness and Vementry.

Old croft houses, some emptied of people during the clearances of the nineteenth century, stand roofless in many parts of Shetland, and in only one or two districts can a thatched house be seen. Most commendable of recent attempts at preservation is the restoration of the old croft house at South Voe, Dunrossness, complete with its steading and mill.

The ruins of several haaf stations can be seen round the shores. The drying beaches remain as they were, but the lodges of the fishermen are roofless. Best examples are at Fedeland and Stenness, both in Northmavine. Of the thousands of sixerns that once sailed from these beaches, one has been preserved and awaits a permanent home in Lerwick.

In the county museum at Lerwick is a marvellous collection of Shetland relics dating from Neolithic to recent times.

NATURE RESERVES

Most northerly nature reserve is that of Herma Ness, which comprises the whole peninsula of that name in Unst and the islands of Muckle Flugga and Out Stack. Greatest interest lies in its colonies of seabirds. In 1969 and 1970 a census on the numbers of breeding birds was carried out by the Seafarer Group and by the local officer of the Nature Conservancy. Their figures include about 5,000 pairs of kittiwakes, a similar number of gannets and about 15,000 individual common guillemots.

Just south of Unst lies Haaf Grunay, whose name means 'green island in the deep sea'. This island of serpentine rock became a national nature reserve in 1959, since it was worth conserving as an excellent example of a low fertile offshore holm. It is of interest to ornithologists, botanists and geologists, and is most easily reached from Uyeasound, where the part-time warden resides.

Best known of Shetland's nature reserves is Noss, which was created a national nature reserve in 1955 to preserve some of the most spectacular cliff-breeding colonies of seabirds in the British Isles. In 1970 the Nature Conservancy delegated to the RSPB responsibility for wardening, information services and arrangements for visitors, while retaining direct responsibility for general planning.

SITES OF SPECIAL SCIENTIFIC INTEREST

These include Ronas Hill, with its arctic-alpine flora; Mousa, where a colony of storm petrels nest in the ruins of the Iron Age broch; and Papa Stour, which has the best developed caves in Britain. At the south end of the Mainland lie the lochs of Spiggie and Brow. Spiggie Loch, the larger, is a favourite haunt of wintering wildfowl, including, usually, around 100 whooper swans. The marsh flora between the lochs is of outstanding interest. The main importance of the Keen of Hamar in Unst has been mentioned in Chapter 1.

Foula, which lies 27 miles west of Scalloway, is one of the most interesting islands in Shetland. Almost the entire coast consists of cliffs over 500ft high, while the Kame rises to 1,220ft. Much work has been done on the island's natural history by the Brathay exploration group.

GLOSSARY

anns—the 'beards' of bere.
ayre—a spit or bar of sand.
ben—the bedroom of a traditional croft house.
bere—a type of barley.
blaand—the final product of the churn, an acid tasting beverage.
blawn fish—fish dried unsalted in skeos, a practice abandoned in the early nineteenth century.
böd—a booth or store of a merchant of the eighteenth and nineteenth centuries.
bonxie—the great skua.
buckie—a large white whelk.
bught—a rather variable measurement applied to fishing lines (56–60 fathoms).
burn—a stream.
but—the living-room of a traditional croft house.
byre—a cow shed.
caa—to drive sheep for penning, or drive whales ashore.
caaing whale—the species *Globiocephala melaena.*
carding—the preparation of wool for spinning. This was frequently done on a communal basis and afforded an excuse for an informal dance.
claith—woollen cloth home produced until the late nineteenth century.
crook—a type of sheep mark cut on the ears to establish ownership.
dyke—a wall.
erne—white-tailed eagle.
Fifie—a Scottish type of sail fishing vessel of the nineteenth and early twentieth century.
first footing—the Scottish custom of visiting friends in the early hours of New Year's morning.
flaakie—a winnowing mat.
flay—to prepare moorland for peat cutting.
foude—a magistrate in the period of Norse rule.
geo—a minor inlet of the sea. Usually steep-sided.
glebe—the area of farmland attached to the manse of a Presbyterian minister.

gloup—a tunnel or sea cave, the roof of which has fallen in at the landward end.
grind—a gate.
guizing—the custom of attending a party disguised with a mask.
haaf—the deep sea.
hairst—harvest.
herring hog—the lesser rorqual.
hummel—to thresh bere (literally to chafe).
kirn milk—a soft cheese produced in the churn after the removal of the butter. Hot water is poured into the butter milk.
kishie—a large basket made from straw, willows or dock stems, and carried on one's back.
knocking stane—a hollowed-out stone, a simple device for bruising and husking oats.
knowe—a mound or hillock.
lawman—in Norse times the guardian of the book of laws.
lawrightman—an official appointed in Norse times to regulate weights and measures.
ley—fallow.
liri—the manx shearwater.
liver heads—a traditional recipe in which fish livers and oatmeal are stuffed inside fish heads and boiled.
liver muggies—a traditional recipe in which fish livers and oatmeal are stuffed into the stomachs of fish and boiled.
lodberry—a store house at the edge of the sea.
lum—the opening on the roof of an old croft house to let smoke escape.
merk—an indefinite Norse measure of land rarely used nowadays.
mert—a beast fatted for slaughter.
meshie—a net used for carrying hay, slung over a man's shoulder. It was used with a pony for transporting peats.
naust—a beach shelter for a small boat.
ness—a headland.
outset—a small farm reclaimed from the scattald during the nineteenth century.
pellack—a porpoise.
piltock—a young saithe between two and four years old.
pone—a slab of turf formerly used in roofing.
quern—a small hand mill.
ranselman—an officer appointed during the period of Norse rule and until the late nineteenth century for crime prevention.
rigga rendal—the ancient system of land use whereby each crofter had a share of the good and the poor land. The fields were narrow strips.

ripper—an implement used in preparing moor for peat cutting.
rit—a type of sheep mark cut on the ears to establish ownership.
rivlin—a shoe of sealskin or cow hide.
roo—to remove the fleece of the Shetland sheep by pulling as opposed to shearing.
röst—a dangerous tidal stream.
run-rig—the Scottish equivalent of rigga rendal.
Scaffie—a Scottish type of sail fishing vessel introduced in the mid nineteenth century.
scattald—the common grazing in the hills around a township.
shear—a type of sheep mark cut on the ears to establish ownership.
sid—a husk of grain.
sillock—a young saithe up to two years old.
skat—the Norse land tax.
skeo—a stone 'larder' in which meat or fish were preserved unsalted before the early nineteenth century.
skerry—a rocky islet.
sixern—the common inshore fishing vessel of the eighteenth and nineteenth centuries. Of Norwegian design it was propelled by six oars or a sail.
souming—the crofter's share of livestock on the scattald.
spilt—local name for a disease common until the end of the eighteenth century, loosely termed 'leprosy'.
stack—a detached steep-sided rock in the sea.
tangle—seaweed of the species *Laminaria digitata.*
teinds—tithes payable to the church during the period of Scottish rule.
ting—the law court in Norse times.
trow—a malevolent supernatural being once believed to inhabit the hills.
tushkar—the Shetland peat spade.
udal law—the Norse legal system, fragments of which still remain.
udaller—a landowner under udal law.
voe—a long narrow sea inlet.
visecks—songs sung to accompany dances until late eighteenth century.
vivda—hard dried meat produced in skeos.
wattle—a tax imposed under Scottish rule.
wick—a bay.
yoal—a small open boat of Norwegian design still in use in the parish of Dunrossness.
Zulu—a Scottish type of sail fishing vessel introduced in the late nineteenth century. One or two are still afloat.

BIBLIOGRAPHY

Agriculture and Fisheries for Scotland, Department of. *Scottish Peat Surveys*, Vol 4 (Edinburgh, 1968)
AITKEN, W. R. *A History of the Public Library Movement in Scotland to 1955* (Glasgow, 1971)
ANDERSON, J. (Editor). *The Orkneyinga Saga* (Edinburgh, 1873)
BALL, R. G. 'The Shetland Garrison, 1665–1668', *Journal of the Society for Army Historical Research* (March, 1965)
BRAND, REV J. *A Brief Description of Orkney, Zetland, Pightland Firth and Caithness* (Edinburgh, 1701)
BRÖGGER, A. W. *Ancient Emigrants* (Oxford, 1929)
BRUCE, R. S. 'Some Old-time Shetlandic Wrecks', *Viking Club Old Lore Miscellany*, Vols 1–5 (1907–12)
BURGESS, J. J. H. *The Viking Path* (Edinburgh, 1894)
CAIRD, J. B. and COULL, J. R. *Report of the Survey of the Island of Yell* (1964)
CARSON, R. L. *The Sea Around Us* (London, 1951)
CHAPELHOW, R. 'On Glaciation in North Roe, Shetland', *The Geographical Journal*, Vol 131, Part 1 (1965)
CLARK, W. F. *The Story of Shetland* (Edinburgh, 1906)
CLUNESS, A. T. *The Shetland Isles* (London, 1951)
CLUNESS, A. T. (Editor). *The Shetland Book* (Lerwick, 1967)
COWIE, R. *Shetland, Descriptive and Historical* (Aberdeen, 1879)
CRUDEN, S. *The Early Christian and Pictish Monuments of Scotland*, Ministry of Works illustrated guidebook (Edinburgh, 1957)
DASENT, SIR G. W. *The Story of Burnt Njal* (Edinburgh, 1861)
DONALDSON, G. (Editor). *The Court Book of Shetland, 1602–1604* (Edinburgh, 1954)
DONALDSON, G. *Northwards By Sea* (Edinburgh, 1966)
DONALDSON, G. *Shetland Life Under Earl Patrick* (Edinburgh and London, 1958)
DREVER, W. P. *Udal Law in the Orkneys and Zetland* (Edinburgh, 1914)
EDMONDSTON, A. *View of the Ancient and Present State of the Zetland Islands*, Vols 1 and 2 (Edinburgh, 1809)

EDMONDSTON, REV B. and SAXBY, J. M. E. *The Home of a Naturalist* (London, 1888)

EDMONDSTON, T. A. *Flora of Shetland* (Aberdeen, 1845)

EDMONDSTON, T. 'On the Native Dyes of the Shetland Islands', *Trans Bot Soc Edinburgh*, Vol 1 (1841)

EVANS, A. H. and BUCKLEY, T. E. *A Vertebrate Fauna of the Shetland Islands* (Edinburgh, 1899)

EVERSHED, H. 'On the Agriculture of the Islands of Shetland', *Trans of the Highland and Agricultural Society of Scotland*, Vol 6 (1874)

FENTON, A. 'Early and Traditional Cultivating Implements in Scotland.' *Proc of the Society of Antiquaries of Scotland*, Vol 94 (1962–3)

FLINN, D. 'Coastal and Submarine Features Around the Shetland Islands', *Proc of the Geologists' Association*, Vol 75, Part 3 (1964)

FLINN, D. 'Continuation of the Great Glen Fault beyond the Moray Firth.' *Nature*, Vol 191, No 4788 (August 1961)

GAILEY, A. and FENTON, A. (Editors). *The Spade in Northern and Atlantic Europe*, published by the Ulster Field Museum and the Institute of Irish Studies, Queen's University, Belfast (1969)

Geological Sciences, Institute of. *A Summary of the Mineral Resources of the 'Crofter Counties' of Scotland*, HMSO (1969)

GIFFORD, T. *Historical Description of the Zetland Islands* (1786, reprinted Edinburgh 1879)

GOODLAD, C. A. *Shetland Fishing Saga* (Lerwick, 1971)

GOUDIE, G. (Editor). *Diary of the Reverend John Mill* (Edinburgh, 1889)

GOUDIE, G. *The Celtic and Scandinavian Antiquities of Shetland* (Edinburgh and London, 1904)

HALCROW, CAPT A. *The Sail Fishermen of Shetland* (Lerwick, 1950)

HAMILTON, J. R. C. *Excavations at Jarlshof, Shetland*, Ministry of Works, Archaeological Report No 1 (Edinburgh, 1956)

HAMILTON, J. R. C. *The Brochs of Mousa and Clickhimin*, HMSO (1970)

HEINEBERG, H. *Wirtschaftsgeographische Strukturwandlungen auf den Shetland-Inseln*, University thesis (Bochum, 1969)

HENDERSON, I. *The Picts* (London, 1967)

HIBBERT, S. *Description of the Shetland Islands* (Edinburgh, 1822, reprinted Lerwick, 1891)

Highlands and Islands Development Board. *Fishing in Shetland*, Special Report No 3 (Inverness, 1970)

Highlands and Islands Development Board. *Shetland Woollen Industry*, Special Report No 4 (Inverness, 1970)

HOPPE, G., FRIES, M. and QUENNERSTEDT, N. 'Submarine Peat in the Shetland Islands', *Geografiska Annaler*, Vol 47, Ser A (1965)

HOWARTH, D. *The Shetland Bus* (London, 1951)

IRVINE, S. G. 'An Outline of the Climate of Shetland', *Weather* (October 1968)

JAKOBSEN, J. *An Etymological Dictionary of the Norn Language in Shetland* (London and Copenhagen, 1928–32)

JAKOBSEN, J. *The Dialect and Place-Names of Shetland* (Lerwick, 1897)

JAKOBSEN, J. *The Place Names of Shetland* (London and Copenhagen, 1936)

LINKLATER, E. *Orkney and Shetland* (London, 1965)

LOW, G. *A Tour Through Orkney and Schetland in 1774* (Kirkwall, 1879)

MACWHIRTER, A. 'The Early Days of Independentism and Congregationalism in the Northern Isles of Scotland', *Records of the Scottish Church History Society* (1966)

MANSON, T. *Lerwick During the Last Half Century* (Lerwick, 1923)

MANSON, T. and J. *Shetland's Roll of Honour and Roll of Service* (Lerwick, 1920)

MANSON, T. and J. *The Amazing Adventure of Betty Mouat* (Lerwick, 1936)

MANSON, T. M. Y. *Guide to Shetland* (Wartime reprint, Lerwick, 1942)

Mansons' Shetland Almanac and Directory (Lerwick)

MARTIN, M. *A Description of the Western Islands of Scotland* (London, 1703)

MILLER, J. A. and FLINN, D. 'A Survey of the Age Relations of Shetland Rocks', *Geological Journal*, Vol 5, Part 1 (1966)

MITCHELL, C. E. *Up-Helly-Aa* (Lerwick, 1948)

MOAR, J. P. 'Roads in the Shetlands', *Journal of the Institution of Highway Engineers* (1962)

MOFFAT, W. *Shetland: The Isles of Nightless Summer* (London, 1934)

Napier Commission. *Evidence taken by HM Commissioners of inquiry into the conditions of the crofters and cottars in the Highlands and Islands of Scotland*, Vol 2 (Edinburgh, 1884)

NELSON, G. M. *The Story of Tingwall Kirk* (Lerwick, 1965)

NEUSTEIN, S. A. 'A Review of Pilot and Trial Plantations Established by the Forestry Commission in Shetland', *Scottish Forestry*, Vol 18, No 3 (1964)

New Statistical Account of Scotland. *Shetland Islands* (Edinburgh, 1841)

NICOLSON, JOHN. *Arthur Anderson* (Lerwick, 1932)

ODDIE, B. C. V. 'The Composition of Precipitation at Lerwick, Shetland', *Quarterly Journal of the Royal Meteorological Society*, Vol 85 (April, 1959)

O'DELL, A. C. *The Historical Geography of the Shetland Islands* (Lerwick, 1939)

O'DELL, A. C. and WALTON, K. *The Highlands and Islands of Scotland* (Edinburgh, 1962)

PALMER, R. C. and SCOTT, W. *A Check-list of the Flowering Plants and Ferns of the Shetland Islands* (Scalloway and Oxford, 1969)

PLOYEN, C. *Reminiscences of a Voyage to Shetland, Orkney and Scotland* (Lerwick, 1894)

RAMPINI, C. *Shetland and the Shetlanders* (Kirkwall, 1884)

READ, H. H. 'The Metamorphic Geology of Unst in the Shetland Isles', *Quarterly Journal of the Geological Society of London*, Vol 90 (1934)

REID TAIT, E. S. (Editor). *The Hjaltland Miscellany*, Vols 1–5 (Lerwick, 1934–57)

REID, J. T. *Art Rambles in Shetland* (Edinburgh, 1869)

ROLLO, D. *History of the Orkney and Shetland Volunteers 1793–1958* (Lerwick, 1958)

ROUSSELL, A. *Norse Building Customs in the Scottish Isles* (London and Copenhagen, 1934)

RUSSEL, REV J. *Three Years in Shetland* (Paisley, 1887)

SANDERSON, I. *Follow the Whale* (London, 1958)

SANDISON, C. *The Sixareen and her Racing Descendants* (Lerwick, 1954)

SAVILLE, A. and PARRISH, B. B. 'The Growth of Purse-seine Fishing in the Northern North Sea', *Scottish Fisheries Bulletin*, No 25 (1966)

SAXBY, H. L. *The Birds of Shetland* (Edinburgh, 1874)

Shetland Development Council. *Report on the Fisheries of Shetland* (1958)

SHIRREFF, J. *General View of the Agriculture of the Shetland Islands* (Edinburgh, 1814)

SHULDHAM-SHAW, P. 'Folk Music and Dance in Shetland', *Journal of the English Dance and Song Society*, Vol 5, No 2 (1947)

SIBBALD, SIR R. *Description of the Islands of Orkney and Shetland* (Edinburgh, 1711)

SIMPSON, W. D. *The Viking Congress, 1950* (Edinburgh and London, 1954)

SINCLAIR, SIR J. *The (Old) Statistical Account of Scotland* (Edinburgh, 1791–99)

SINCLAIR, C. *Shetland and the Shetlanders* (Edinburgh, 1840)

SKODVIN, M. 'Shetland and Norway in the Second World War', *Norwegian Yearbook of Maritime History* (1969)

SMALL, A. 'The Distribution of Settlement in Shetland and Faroe in Viking Times', *Saga Book*, Vol XVII, Parts 2–3. *Viking Society for Northern Research* (University College, London, 1967–8)

SMITH, J. 'A Description of the island of Shetland and the fishing thereabout' (1633), MacFarlane's geographical collections, Vol 3

STEWART, J. 'An outline of Shetland archaeology', *The Shetland Times* (August-September 1956)

SVENSSON, R. *Lonely Islands* (Stockholm, 1954)

SWAN, DR M. A. 'The Girlsta Char', *The New Shetlander*, No 69 (1964)

THOWSEN, A. 'The Norwegian Export of Boats to Shetland and its Influence upon Shetland Boat-building and Usage.' *Norwegian Yearbook of Maritime History* (1969)

Truck Commission. *Report of the Commissioners appointed to enquire into the Truck System Together with Minutes of Evidence*, Vol 11, Minutes of Evidence (Edinburgh, 1872)

TUDOR, J. R. *The Orkneys and Shetland* (London, 1883)

TULLOCH, B. and HUNTER, F. *A Guide to Shetland Birds* (Lerwick, 1970)

VENABLES, L. S. V. and U. M. *Birds and Mammals of Shetland* (Edinburgh, 1955)

Viking Society Publications

WAINWRIGHT, F. T. (Editor). *The Problem of the Picts* (Edinburgh, 1955)

WAINWRIGHT, F. T. (Editor). *The Northern Isles* (London, 1962)

WILLIAMSON, K. *Fair Isle and its Birds* (Edinburgh and London, 1965)

WILLS, J. W. G. *Bressay*, Unpublished thesis (University of Edinburgh, 1968)

SUPPLEMENTARY BOOKLIST

Anderson, P. D. *Robert Stewart, Earl of Orkney and Lord of Shetland* (Edinburgh, 1982)

Balneaves, E. *The Windswept Isles* (London, 1977)

Beenhakker, A. *Hollanders in Shetland* (Lerwick, 1973)

Berry, R. J. and Johnston, J. L. *Natural History of Shetland* (London, 1980)

Button, J. (Editor) *The Shetland Way of Oil* (Sandwick, 1976)

Cant, R. G. *The Medieval Churches and Chapels of Shetland* (Lerwick, 1975)

Coleman, V. and Wheeler, R. *Living on an Island* (Findhorn, 1980)

Fojut, N. *Prehistoric Shetland* (Lerwick, 1981)

Gronneberg, R. *Island Futures* (Sandwick, 1978)

Gronneberg, R. *Island Governments* (Sandwick, 1976)

Gronneberg, R. *Jakobsen and Shetland* (Lerwick, 1981)

Irvine, J. W. *Footprints* (Lerwick, 1982)

Irvine, J. W. *Up-Helly-Aa* (Lerwick, 1981)

Laing, L. *Orkney and Shetland: an Archaeological Guide* (Newton Abbot, 1974)

McNicoll, I. H. *The Shetland Economy* (Glasgow, 1976)

Martin, S. *The Other Titanic* (Newton Abbot, 1980)

Marwick, E. *The Folklore of Orkney and Shetland* (London, 1975)

Nicolson, J. R. *Lerwick Harbour* (Lerwick, 1977)

Nicolson, J. R. *Shetland and Oil* (London, 1975)

Nicolson, J. R. *Shetland Folklore* (London, 1981)

Nicolson, J. R. *Traditional Life in Shetland* (London, 1978)

Robson, A. *The Saga of a Ship* (Lerwick, 1982)

Shetland Islands Council. *Shetland's Oil Era* (Lerwick, 1979)

INDEX

Italic page numbers indicate illustrations

Aberdeen, 12, 93, 97, 113, 126, 141, 149, 166; University, 42
Aberdeen Airways, 109
Aberdeen, Leith, Clyde & Tay Shipping Co, 78, 98
Aberdeen Milk Marketing Board, 125
Actinolite, 17
Adie, T. M., 145
Agricola, 31
Agriculture: deterioration in, 58, 73–6; early, 31–3, 41,; improvement in, 74, 75, 80, 81, 118–25; modern, 115, 116, 123–7, *176*; traditional, 64, 65, 116–18
Agricultural shows, 183
Airfields, 108, 109
Air services, *see* Communications
Aith, 108; lifeboat, 174, 177, 178
Aithsting, 12, 61, 62
Aitken, John M., 193
Alexander III, King of Scotland, 44, 191
Alginate Industries (Scotland) Ltd, 161
Allied Airways, 109
Alma, 187
Althing Social Group, 182
Alting 12, 40, 48
Amalgamation, 216–17
America, *see* USA
Anaconda, 196
Ancre, River, Battle of, 94
Anderson, Arthur, 77, 78, 82–3, 144, 185
Anderson Educational Institute, 78, 82, 83, 206
Anderson, Isabella, 88
Annexation by Scotland, 45, 56
Anthophyllite, 17
Anticyclones, 17
Asquith, H. H., 170
Asta, 220
Atlantic Ocean, 20, 21, 94, 99, 163, 186
Aurora borealis, 17
Australia, 90, 92
Ayres, 21

Bailie, 48
Bain, Inga, 88
Balta Isle, 173
Baltasound, 14, 135, 148, 152
Baltic trade, 197
Baptist church, 60
Barclay, Rev P., 61
Bard Head, 21, 153
Barilla, 161
Basta Voe, 14
BEA, 109
Beaches, 21
Beaker people, 220
Beeby, W. H., 23
Ben Doran, ST, 174, 177
Bere, 64, 117, 127
Berry, R. J., 25
Bigton, 161
Bird Observatory, 15, 27, 159
Birds, 26–9, *67*; as food, 42, 46; preservation, 28, 226
Bishopric, 43, 52
Blaand, 69
Blacksness Pier, 187, 189, *157*
Bloodletting, 71
Bluemull Sound, 105
Board for the Relief of Highland Destitution, 106
Board of Agriculture, 81
Board of Trade, 147, 174
Boatbuilding, 151–3
Boats, *see* Fishing vessels

Boddam, 112
Böd of Gremista, 185
Botany, 22–4
Bothwell, Bishop Adam, 52
Bothwell, Earl of, 162
Boulder clay, 20
Brae, 30, 214, 215
Brand, Rev J., 53, 54, 70, 81, 87, 164, 186, 192
Brathay Exploration Group, 226
Bressay, 13, 18, 94, 105, 150, 153, 173, 224
Bressay Bank, 165
Bressay Sound, 44, 54, 162, 165, 191
Bridges, 107, 108
Brindister, 156
Brochs, 33–5, 221, *85*
Brögger, A. W., 38
Bronze Age, 33, 221
Brora, 145
Brow, 22; loch, 226
Bruce Hostel, 84
Bruce, Laurence, 51, 223
Bruce, Robert, 84
Bryden, Rev J., 63, 118
Buckley, T. E., 25
Burgess, J. J. Haldane, 185
Burra, 13, 14, 105, 108, 138, 213
Burrafirth, 20
Burravoe, 14
Bus services, 108, 111
Busta Voe, 101
Butter, 54, 69
Butterflies, 25, 28

Cabbages, 28, 117
Cairns, 32, 220, 221
Caledonian orogony, 17
Caledonian rocks, 17, 18
Caledonians, 34
Canada, 90, 92
Captains, 82, 172, 173
Cardings, 182
Carl Constantin, 174
Carysfort, HMS, 172
Catfirth, 94
Cattle: beef, 119, 120, 125; dairy, 121, 125, 126; Shetland breed, 23, 117, 125
Caves, 21
Celts, 34–7, 42
Chapels, 43
Char, 26
Charles I, 72
Charles II, 56
Charles VI, King of France, 44
Cheyne, Sir Watson, 185
Chieftain's Bride, SS, 102
Christian I, King of Denmark, 44
Christianity, introduction of, 35, 42, 43
Christmas, 183, 201
Chromite, 154–5
Churches, 43, 53, 165, 180, 223, 224; *see also* Lund, Papil, St Ninian's Isle
Church of Scotland, 53, 59–60, 63; *see also* individual ministers
City and Guilds of London certificates, 209
Clarke, Eagle, 25
Claude Cecil Staniforth, 174
Clearances, 75, 76, 90, 119, 123
Clibberswick, 38
Clickhimin, Broch of, 34, 35, 221
Cliff (Unst), 81
Cliffs, 20, 21, 29, 226, *50*, *67*
Climate, 15–17; climatic changes, 18
Clothing, *see* Dress
Clousta, 159
Clunies-Ross, J., 184
Coastguard service, 177; *see also* US Coastguard
Coats, James, 207
Cocos Islands, 184
Collafirth, 170
Columbine, 102
Commercial St, 193, 199
Commissioners of Supply, 79
Commons, *see* Scattalds
Communications: air, 108, 109; overland, 60, 62, 106–8; sea, 12, 60, 62, 78, 97–106, 187, 188, 196, 217
Community life, 72, 73, 181, 182, 203–11
Congregational Church, 60
Conservation: birds, 28; fish stocks, 166–8, 218
Copper, 154
Council houses, 189, 195, 199, 203
Country Acts, 56, 101, 166
County buildings, 193
Court of Session, 75, 169, 200
Cowie, Dr Robert, 72, 73, 75

Crabs, 66, 142
Craft industries, 210, 211
Crime, 179, 180
Crofter-fishermen, 57–76, 115, 120, 136
Crofters' Commission, 80, 81, 84, 127
Crofters Holdings (Scotland) Acts, 80, 90, 116, 127
Crofting, *see* Agriculture
Crofts, 29, 115, 117, 127, *65*, *68*, *86*, *176*
Cromwell, Oliver, 56, 191
Cullivoe, 14
Cunningsburgh, 24, 154, 173
Curle, Dr, 33
Cyclone, 196
Cynthia, 196

Dale, 119
Dancing, 181, 182
Dart Herald, 109
Davis Straits, 132
Day length, 17
Deans, Admiral, 191
Decca Navigator stations, 173
De Liefde, 163
Delting, 12, 118, 151, 171
Denmark, 44, 45, 112, 190; Danish fishing industry, 167
Department of Agriculture, 81
Depopulation, 11, 13, 90–2, 211
Depressions, 116
Destiny, 196
Development, 12, 209–11; *see also* individual industries
Dialect, 11, 46, 48, 182, 195
Diana, 169
Diet (traditional), 64–9
Disasters, 73, 131, 134
Dishington, Rev. A., 71
Dissenters, 60, 63
Dogs, 23
Dolphin, TS, 173
Donaldson, Prof Gordon, 51
Dragon, De Havilland, 108
Drainage, 87, 188, 203
Drama, 182
Dress, 61
Drifter, *see* Fishing vessels
Druce, Dr G. C., 23
Drunkenness, 61
Duncan, Walter, 152
Dundas, Sir Laurence, 56
Dundas, Sir Thomas, 59, 62
Dunrossness, 12, 65, 80, 125, 127, 128, 154, 208, *68*, *103*, *176*
Dyes, 145

Earldom: Norse earls, 38, 43; Scottish earls, 44, 45, 48, 51, 56
Earl of Zetland, MV, 100, 105
Earl of Zetland, SS, 102, 105, 198, *104*
Edinburgh, 48, 70, 89, 185
Edinburgh, HRH the Duke of, 193, 194
Edmondston, Dr A., 43, 57, 71, 129, 133, 171, 172, 184, 192
Edmondston, Dr L., 184
Edmondston, T., 23, 24, 25, 145, 184
Education, 81–4, 205–7, *176*
Egg production, 120, 126
Electricity, 189, 194, 203, 204
El Gran Grifon, 162
Emigration, 76, 84, 89–92, 131, 136
Enclosure of farmland, 74, 119
Engineering (marine), 189, 199
English language, 11, 48
Episcopacy, 52, 53
Erosion, 18, 20–2, *50*
Esha Ness, 18, *50*
European Economic Community, 218
Evans, A. H., 25
Eventide homes, 204
Evershed, H., 120, 123
Evictions, *see* Clearances
Exnaboe, 18
Exports, *see* individual items

Fair Isle, 15, 18, 90, 105, 128, 159, 162, 163, 167, 174; knitwear, 15, 144–6; lifeboat, 174
Fallow, 117
Famine, 69
Fanshawe, Capt, 172
Faeroe Islands, 11, 112, 132, 133, 169, 181, 187, 217
Fares, 101
Fedeland, 131, 224
Ferries, 15, 101–6
Fetlar, 14, 17, 29, 62, 70, 81, 92, 154, 156, 159, 163, 166

Fishing grounds, 128, 131, 132, 133, 164, 187
Fishing industry: early commercial, 54; haaf fishing, 57, 128–31; herring industry, 90, 95, 133–7, 148, 187, 197; illegal fishing, 138, 167; industrial fishing, 150, 167; modern industry, 14, 15, 137–42; shellfishing, 141–2, 150; smack fishery, 131–3, 187, 196; subsistence, 30, 66, 128
Fishing limits, 167, 218
Fishing vessels: buss, 131, 133, 165, 197; drifter, 90, 134–7, 152, 197, *122*, *135*; motor line boat, 138, 177; purse-seiner, 137, 141, 167; *122*; seiner, 138, 167; sixern, 128–31, 134, 151, 224, *129*; smack, 131–3, 187, 196; trawler, 166, 167; yoal, 128, *103*
Fish-processing: canning, 150; curing, 54, 77, 129–36, 148, 149; freezing, 14, 15, 149, 150, 190; kippering, 148, 149; meal and oil, 13, 150–1; shellfish, 150
Fitful Head, 22, 154, 188
Fladdabister, 24, 153
Flagstones, 18, 153, 199
Florevag, Battle of, 43
Food, *see* Diet (traditional)
Folklore, 183–4
Ford Motor Co, 194
Foreshore ownership, 160, 216
Forestry, 23
Fort Charlotte, 56, 106, 172, 191, 224
Football, 182
Fossils, 18
Foudes, 40, 48
Foula, 15, 18, 21, 26, 70, 105, 112, 152, 226
France, trade with, 145, 146
Franchise, 77
Fraser, Thomas (TTF), 190
Freight charges, 100, 101, 112, 138, 149
Frogs, 25
Fuel, 30, 63, 64, 155–6; *see also* Peat

Ganson Brothers, 111, 188, 194
Garrison theatre, 182
Garth, 90
Gas, 194
General Assembly of Church of Scotland, 53, 60, 82, 97
Geology, 17–20; sketch map, 19
George Canning, 196
Geos, 21
Germany: seamen, 93, 163, 174; trade, 53, 54, 97, 128, 134, 144, 148
Gifford, Thomas, 51, 81, 180
Gilbert Bain Hospital, 88–9, 204
Girlsta, 26, 153, 211
Glasgow, 12, 149, 184
Gneiss, 17
Gondola, 132
Good Shepherd, MV, 105
Gordon Highlanders, 93
Goudie, Gilbert, 47, 208
Gozo, 32
Granite, 18, 20, 153
Grassland, natural, 22; *see also* Reseeding
Gray, Capt J., 172
Gray, Joseph, 194
Graven, 96, 150, 212
Great Britain, SS, 172
Gremista, 77, 185, 204
Grierson, Rev J. 97
Grierson, Sir H., 185
Grutness, 105, 162
Gruting, 32, 220
Guizing, 181, 201
Gulf Stream, 16

Haaf Grunay, 154, 226
Haakon, King of Norway, 44
Hagdale, 155
Halcrow, Capt A., 134
Haldane, James, 60
Hamnavoe, 30, 87, 152
Harald, Earl of Orkney, 43
Harald Fairhair, King of Norway, 37
Haroldswick, 38
Harriet Louisa, 132
Harvie-Brown, J. A., 25
Hay & Co, 113, 132–3, 152, 197
Hay & Ogilvy, 134, 151, 187
Hay, George, 73
Hay, William, 119
Health, 70–2, 84–8, 204; *see also* Hospitals

Hemelingk, Geert, 162
Herma Ness, 20, 29, 226
Herring, *see* Fishing industry
Herring Industry Board, 138, 141, 149
Hertigen, 174
Hibbert, Dr S., 69, 71, 131, 154, 155
Highland Airways, 108
Highlander, SS, 99
Highlands and Islands Development Board, 116, 138, 148, 150, 210
Hildasay, 92, 153
Hillswick, 17, 159, 168
Hillwell, 125
Holding points, 210
Holiday accommodation, 156, 159, 200
Holland: Dutch fishermen, 54, 97, 131, 133, 165, 191, 196, 200; Dutch seamen, 163, 164, 191; trade, 54, 120, 144
Hollanders' Knowe, 54
Horses, *see* Ponies
Hospitals, 88–9, 204–5
Hoswick, 169
Hotels, 156, 159
Housing, 63, 64, 84–7, 188, 189, 195, 199, 203, 204, *65*, *86*
Howarth, David, 152, 189
Hunter, Fred, 25, 27

Ice Age, 18, 26
Iceatlantic (Frozen Seafoods) Ltd, 150, 190, 210
Iceland, 132; sagas, 37, 162
Ice factory, 138, 199
Immigration: Norse, 36–8; Scottish, 47; recent, 179
Imports, 54, 100, 198
Independents, *see* Congregational Church
Ingram, Rev J., 63
Innes, Rev W., 60
Inoculation, 71
Inverness, 125, 145
Ireland, trade with, 130
Ireland (Dunrossness), 43
Iron Age, 33–5, 222
Iron ore, 154
Isabella, 110
Islander (aircraft), 109

Jacobite rebellion, 59
Jakobsen, Dr J., 45
James III, King of Scotland, 44
James V, King of Scotland, 48
Janet, 102
Janet Courtney Hostel, 84
Janet Hay, 196
Jarlshof, 31, 33, 35, 39, 221, 223, *85*
John and Frances MacFarlane, 177
Johnton, J. L., 25
JU 52s, 109
Juniper, MT, 178

Kames, the, 22, 156
Kelp, 160–1
Kemp, Rev J., 82
Kennemerlandt, 163
Kent, HRH the Duchess of, 144
Kergord, 23
Kippering, *see* Fish-processing
Kirkcaldy, Sir W., of Grange, 162
Kirstan Hole, 21
Kishies, 117
Knitwear: handknit, 54, 61, 112, 143–6, *139*; machine-knit, 145–7; factories, 14, 146
Kollies, 64
K.T.J.S., 174

Lady Alice, 196
Lady Ambrosine, SS, 102
Lady Jane and Martha Ryland, 174
Lairds, 56–9, 62, 73–6, 118, 119, 134, 159, 169, 184, 185
Land Court, 116, 125
Land tenure, 41, 57, 58, 62, 73–6, 80, 116, 118
Laurenson, Robert, 111
Law, Bishop, 51, 52
Lawman, 40, 48
Lawrightman, 40, 48
Laxfirth, 119
Leask, Joseph, 196
Leith, 97, 100; nautical college, 173
Leprosy, 70
Lerwick, 30, 54, 84, 90, 94, 113, 134–6, 148, 153, 159, 172, 190–202, *158*; harbour, 196–9, *see also* Bressay Sound; lifeboat, 166, 174; town hall, 193
Lerwick Central School, 83, 193, 206
Lerwick Harbour Trust, 198

Lerwick Instruction Society, 82
Lerwick Life-saving Company, 177
Lerwick (Parish), 13, 192
Lessing, 163, 174
Library services, 209–11
Lighthouses, 14, 15, 95, 173
Limestone, 17, 20, 153
Living conditions, *see* Housing
Lobsters, 141, 150, 168
Local government, reorganisation of, 79, 216–18
Loganair, 109, 112
Longevity, 72, 206
Low, George, 24, 46, 89, 120, 165, 166, 181, 200
Lund, Lunda Wick, 54, 224
Lunna, 95, 225
Lunnasting, 12, 36

mac Alpin, Kenneth, 35
MacKenzie, Sheriff, 169
Magnetite, 154
Mail-order, 112
Mail services, 62, 78, 98, 110–12
Malakoff slipway, 199
Malta, 32
Margaret, Princess of Denmark, 44
Mary, Queen of Scots, 48
Matchless, 98
Mavis Grind, 20, 45, 96, 106
'Meal roads', 69, 106
Medical services, 87–9, 204, 205
Menzies, Rev J., 61
Merchant Navy, 82, 94, 131, 136, 171–3
Merchants, 53, 54, 57, 77, 128–31, 134, 144, 145, 150, 190, 192, 196, 197
Meteorological observatory, 15, 17, 23, 112
Methodist Church, 60, 110
Midland Red, 159
Mid Yell, 14, 210
Mill, Rev. J., 59, 97, 164
Mills, 47, 224
Mining, 153–6
Moar, Peter, 39
Monk, Admiral, 191
Moore, Wm & Sons, 189
Moraines, 20
Mortgaging of Orkney and Shetland, 45; commemoration, 216
Morton, Earls of, 56, 164, 168
Morton, Lodge, 192
Mossbank, 111
Motor cars, 14, 107, 108, 111, 188, 194
Mousa, 18, 153, 225; broch, 34, 221, *85*
Muckle Flugga, 14, 25, 173, 226
Muckle Roe, 13, 18, 108
Multiple sclerosis, 205
Muness, 51, 223
Music, 181

Napier Commission, 80
National Museum of Antiquities, Edinburgh, 33, 224
National Trust for Scotland, 27
Natural Environment Research Council, 29
Natural history, 23–9, 226
Naust, 30, *103*
Naval bases, 94
Neolithic Age, 31, 32, 220, 221
Nesting, 12,
New Brunswick, 90
New Statistical Account, 62, 63
New Shetlander, The, 194
New Zealand, 90, 92, 169
Nicolson & Co, 132, 133, 187
Nicolson, Charles, 187
Nicolson, John, 178
Nisbet, Capt R., 187
Norseman, SS, 101
Norsemen, 36–44; influence, 11, 26, 45–7, 142, 151, 152, 179, 201; language (Norn), 11, 26, 46, 48; remains, 38–9, 221; legal system, 40–2, 45, 216–7
North Isles, 14, 20, 113, 154; air service, 109; shipping service, 102, 105
Northmavine, 12, 21, 53, 128, 143, 221
North of Scotland & Orkney & Shetland Shipping Co, 98–105, 187, 198
North of Scotland College of Agriculture, 127
North of Scotland Hydro-Electric Board, 189, 204
North Star Cinema, 194
Norway, 11, 43, 47, 216; bases,

95–6, 189; fishermen, 165, 168, 174, 198, 200; trade, 151; whaling stations, 170; *see also* Norsemen
Noss, 18, 21, 27, 29, 226, *67*

Oats, 64, 117, 119
Oceanic, SS, 94
Oddie, B. C. V., 23
Oil, 190, 199, 211–216; impact of, 109, 114, 211-16
Olaf Trygvesson, King of Norway, 40, 42
Old Red Sandstone, 18, 21
Old Statistical Account, 58–62, 72, 169, 171
Olnafirth, 170
Ord Head, 21, 153
Orkney, 11, 23, 29, 54, 77, 90, 113, 125, 126, 160, 185, 217
Orkney and Shetland Fencibles, 93
Orkney and Shetland Telegraph Co Ltd, 112
Orkney and Shetland Journal, The, 78
Orkneyinga Saga, 37, 42
Outsets, 74
Out Skerries, 15, 56, 82, 95, 102, 108, 113, 138, 163, 181, 210
Out Stack, 14, 226
Oxna, 92

Palmer, R. C., 24
P & O Company, 78, 185
Papae, 35–7
Papa Stour, 13, 18, 21, 37, 70, 92, 112, 178; sword dance, 181
Papil, 36, 37, 223
Pardoun, Marion, 52
Patronymics, 46
Peat: content, 22, 156; cutting, 155–6, *140*; formation, 20, 22; reclamation, 22, 123, 125; submerged, 18, 20
Pelikaan, 162
Picts, 35–7
Piers, 187, 197, 211, 212
Pigs, 117, 124
Pionair, 109
Pitcairn, James, 51
Planking of farmland, 74
Plant life, 22–4
Ploughs, 74, 75, 117
Ployen, C., 119, 120, 134
Police, 180
Ponies, 23, 106, 117, 120, 124, 126, 156, *121*
Poor Law Amendment Act, 73
Population, rising, 11, 57, 211; *see also* Depopulation
Postal services, *see* Mail services
Potatoes, 64, 69, 117, 127
Poultry, 117, 124, 126
Power station, 156, 204
Presbyterianism, 51; *see also* Church of Scotland
'Press Gang', 60, 171
Prince Olav Slipway, 189
Public Health Act, 84
Purse-seines, 137, 141, 167

Quarff, Hill of, 113
Queen, SS, 99, 187
Queen of the Isles, 187
Quendale, 119, 168
Querns, 46, 66

Radio-carbon dating, 21
RAF, 14, 95, 109
Rainfall, 16
Rangor, MT, 177
Rankine, The, 174
Ranselmen, 40, 48, 56, 180
Rapide, De Havilland, 109
Rattlesnake, 196
Reawick, 21, 151
Recreations, 181–3
Reformation, the, 52
Reform Bill, 77
Regattas, 183
Reid, Nicol, 40
Religion, 35–7, 42, 43, 52, 53, 59, 60, 180
Representation in Parliament, 77, 217
Reseeding, 115, 125
Rigga rendal, 41
Rivlins, 46, 61
Roads, 69, 106–8, 153
Rockall, 132
Roman Catholic Church, 53
Romans, 31, 34
Ronas Hill, 16, 18, 20, 24, 221, 226
Ronas Voe, 102, 142, 169, 170, 211

Rose-Innes, Mr, 89
Ross, Alex, 193
Rotation of crops, 119, 123
Roussel, Aage, 47
Royal Highland Show, 141
Royal Humane Society, 173
Royal National Lifeboat Institution, 174, 178
Royal Naval Reserve, 93, 94, 172
Royal Navy, 77, 89, 93, 171–3; *see also* 'Press gang'
Royal Society for the Protection of Birds, 25, 29, 226
Royal touch, 72
Royal visit, 194
Run-rig, 118
Russia: fishing fleets, 165, 166, 200; trade, 134

Sabbath observance, 52, 56, 180
St Catherine, SS, 100
St Clair, SS, 99
St Clair, MV, 100
St Clair, Wm, Earl of Orkney, 45
St Clement, SS, 99
St Fergus, SS, 99
St Giles, SS, 99
St Magnus, SS, 99, *104*
St Magnus Bay, 13, 94, 165
St Nicholas, SS, 99
St Ninian, MV, 100
St Ninian's Isle, 21, 36, 53; treasure, 42, 216, 223
St Ola, MV, 100
St Rognvald, SS, 99
St Rognvald, MV, 100
St Sunniva, SS (1), 99, *104*
St Sunniva, SS (2), 99
Sales, John, 174
Salinity of air, 23
Salmon, 26
Salt Tax, 57
Salvesen, Christian, & Co, 171
Sand, 223
Sandison, A & Sons, 148, 152
Sandlodge, 154
Sandness, 13, 18, 24, 108, 161, 177
Sandsting, 12, 61, 62
Sandstone, 18, 153
Sandwick, 30, 112, 113, 136, 147, 164
Sandy Loch, 194
Sanitary inspectors, 84, 85
Satan, 59, 183
Saunders, H., 25
Saxavord, 17, 20
Saxby, H. L., 25
Scallops, 141
Scalloway, 13, 30, 93, 95, 113, 125, 135, 186–90, *157*; castle, 48, 56, 186, 222, *157*
Scatsta, 174
Scattalds, 29, 30, 41, 75, 80, 117, 124; apportionment, 125
Scenery, 20–2, *49*, *50*
Schools, 81–4, 193, 200, 206–9, *176*
Scotia Tours, 159
Scots: influence, 47, 48, 179; language, 11, 48; legal system, 48–52; settlers, 47–52
Scottish Airways, 109
Scottish Mainland, contact with, 12, 47–52, 71, 78, 97–101, 108, 109, 111–13, 187, 196
Scottish Motor Traction Co, 108
Scottish Tourist Board, 159
Scottish Women's Rural Institute, 182
Scousburgh, 113
Sea angling, 160
Seamen, 60, 61, 82, 93, 94, 136, 171–3
Seaweed, 117, 160–1
Seine net, 138, 141, 167
Serpentine, 17, 24, 154
Shearer, J. & M., 199
Sheep: ear-mark, 41; heavy breeds, 120, 123, 125; Shetland breed, 23, 41, 117, 120, 123, 124, *103*, *121*
Sheepdog trials, 183
Shetland, origin of name, 12
Shetland Advertiser, 193
Shetland Angling Association, 26
Shetland Archives, 209
Shetland Bank, 134
'Shetland bus', 95, 189
Shetland Council of Social Service, 209
Shetland Craft Guild, 211
Shetland gutting machine, 190
Shetland Invincibles, 93
Shetland Islands Steam Navigation Co, 102
Shetland Islands Trading Co, 101
Shetland Journal, The, 78

Shetland Knitwear Trades Assoc, 147
Shetland Marine, 152
Shetland News, The, 80, 194
Shetland Times, The, 194
Shetland Tourist Organisation, 160
Shetland Trader, MV, 197
Shetland Woollen Industries Assoc, 147
Shynd Bill, 41, 51
Sieves, 65
Sinclair, Hercules, 53
Sinclair, Sir John, 58
Sites of Special Scientific Interest, 24, 226
Sixerns, *see* Fishing vessels
Skat, 41
Skaw, Holm of, 166, 174
Skeld, 151
Skeos, 66, 69, 180
Smallpox, 70–1, 88
Smiling Morn, MV, 177
Smith, Capt J., 128
Smith, James, 190
Smith, L. J., 145
Smith, Peter, 123
Smith, Ross, 193
Smuggling, 61, 62, 97, 196
Sobriety, 62, 70
Social life, 181–3, 200
Society of the Free British Fishery, 133
Society of Friends, 69
Soils, 22
Sound, 87, 199
South Georgia, 171
Sovereign, SS, 78, 98
Spain: Armada, 15, 144, 162; trade, 130
Spades, 47, 74, 117
Spiggie, 27, 226
Sport, 182–3
SSPCK, 81, 82
Standen, Edward, 144
Standing stones, 222
Staneydale, 32, 221
Stenness, 131, 225
Stewart, earls, 48–52, 163, 186
Stone Age, *see* Neolithic
Storey, R., 209
Stout, Sir R., 184
Strathair, 109
Sullom, 110, 154
Sullom Voe, 95, 212–15, *175*
Sumburgh, 38, 48; airport, 108, 109
Sumburgh Head, 12, 163
Sumburgh Mining Co, 154
Sumburgh Röst, 11, 12
Superstitions, 183, 184
Surnames, 46, 179
Sutherland, J. B. A., 152
Sverre, King of Norway, 43
Swan, MV, 152
Swarbacks Minn, 94
Swedish fishermen, 165
Symbister, 210

Tacitus, 31
Tacksmen, 47, 56
Tait, Grace, 173
Talc, 17, 154–5
Taxes, 62; *see also* Skat, Tithes
Tea, 61
Telegraph, 112–14
Telegraph, 132
Telephone, 112–14
Temperatures, 15, 16
Temples, 32, 220
Territorial Army, 93
Tings, 12, 40
Thomson, Sinclair, 60
Tingwall, 12, 40, 60, 62, 126; church, 43, 224
Tithes, 42, 59, 62
Tombolos, 21
Tourism, 12, 156–60
Townships, 29, 222, *68*
Trade, origins of, 53–5; *see also* individual countries
Transport, *see* Communications
Trees, 23; submerged, 18, 20
Trondra, 13, 105, 108
Trout, 26
Trows, 183
Tweed, 146–7

U-boats, 94
Udal law, *see* Norsemen, legal system
Udallers, 41, 52
Unemployment, 149
Up-Helly-Aa, 160, 181, 183, 200–2
Unicorn, 162
Unst, 14, 17, 20, 72, 123, 128, 141, 144, 154

INDEX

Urafirth, 215
USA, 90, 92, 153; trade, 147, 190
US Coastguard, 173
Uyeasound, 14

Vaccination, 88
Vaila, 13, 77
Vandela, 163
Veensgarth, 75, 81, 123
Vegetation, 22–4
Vc Skerries, 25, 177
Vementry, 94, 96, 220
Venables, L. S. V. and U. M., 25
Victoria, Queen, 144, 194
Vikings, 37–8, 42; *see also* Norsemen
Viscount (aircraft), 109, 112
Visecks, 181
Voe, 225
Voes, 12, 20, *49*

Wages, 58, 61, 63, 116, 117, 130, 134, 146, 169
Wales, HRH the Prince of, 144
Wallace Arnold Co, 159
Walls, 13, 18, 24, 105, 151
Wars, 77, 93–6, 99, 100, 111–12, 161, 173, 189, 192
Water supplies, 84, 87, 188, 194, 204
Weaving, *see* Tweed
Welfare, 69, 72–3, 204
West Burrafirth, 142
Westing, 123
Westwing, 109
Whales, 25–6, 168, 170
Whaling, 58, 168–71, 196
Whalsay, 13, 21, 138, 181, 205, 208, 210
White Fish Authority, 138
Whiteness, 38
Widows' homes, 78, 200
William Hogarth, 99
William Martin, 133, 187
Wind speed, 16–17
Witches, 52, 183
Williamson, Kenneth, 27
Williamson, L., 190
Williamson, John, 71
Wool, 42, 120, 143, 148, *103*
Woollen industry, 143–8; mill, 148; trade mark, 147–8; *see also* Knitting, Fair Isle, Tweed
Wrecks, 94, 98–9, 162–4

Yachting, 183
Yell, 14, 22, 43, 62, 120, 156, 210
Yell Sound, 14, 102, 105, 161
Youth hostel, 159
Yoxie, 32, 221

Zetland County Council, 79, 111, 204, 212
Zetland County Museum, 36, 38, 47, 224
Zetland New Shipping Co, 98
Zetland Rifles, 1st, 93
Zetland Roads Act, 106
Zetland Roads Dept, 107